This book offers the first thoroughgoing literary analysis of William Cobbett as a writer. Leonora Nattrass explores the nature and effect of Cobbett's rhetorical strategies, showing through close examination of a broad selection of his polemical writings (from his early American journalism onwards) the complexity, self-consciousness and skill of his stylistic procedures. Her close readings examine the political implications of Cobbett's style within the broader context of eighteenth- and early nineteenth-century political prose, and argue that his perceived ideological and stylistic flaws – inconsistency, bigotry, egoism and political nostalgia – are in fact rhetorical strategies designed to appeal to a range of usually polarized reading audiences. Cobbett's ability to imagine and address socially divided readers within a single text, the book argues, constitutes a politically disruptive challenge to prevailing political and social assumptions about their respective rights, duties, needs and abilities. This rereading revises a prevailing critical consensus that Cobbett is an unselfconscious populist whose writings reflect rather than challenge the ideological paradoxes and problems of his time.

CAMBRIDGE STUDIES IN ROMANTICISM 11

WILLIAM COBBETT

CAMBRIDGE STUDIES IN ROMANTICISM

General editors
Professor Marilyn Butler   Professor James Chandler
University of Oxford   *University of Chicago*

Editorial board
John Barrell, *University of York*   Paul Hamilton, *University of Southampton*
Mary Jacobus, *Cornell University*   Kenneth Johnston, *Indiana University*
Alan Liu, *University of California, Santa Barbara*   Jerome McGann
University of Virginia   David Simpson, *University of Colorado*

Cambridge Studies in Romanticism is a series of original critical studies devoted to literature in English from the period 1780–1830, written against the background of the French Revolution, the Napoleonic and American wars, urbanisation, industrialisation, religious revival, an expanded empire abroad, and the reform movement at home. Books in the series will have an interdisciplinary bias, examining for example the relations between literature and politics, science, philosophy and religion; or looking at gender relations, notions of literature and literary history, as revealed in Romantic writing and the critical and theoretical traditions which the literature of this period has helped to shape.

TITLES PUBLISHED

1 *Romantic Correspondence: Women, Politics and the Fiction of Letters*
by Mary A. Favret
2 *British Romantic Writers and the East: Anxieties of Empire*
by Nigel Leask
3 *Edmund Burke's Aesthetic Ideology*
Language, Gender and Political Economy in Revolution
by Tom Furniss
4 *Poetry as an Occupation and an Art in Britain, 1760–1830*
by Peter Murphy
5 *In the Theatre of Romanticism: Coleridge, Nationalism, Women*
by Julie A. Carlson
6 *Keats, Narrative and Audience*
by Andrew Bennett
7 *Romance and Revolution: Shelley and the Politics of a Genre*
by David Duff
8 *Literature, Education, and Romanticism: Reading as Social Practice, 1780–1832*
by Alan Richardson
9 *Women Writing about Money: Women's Fiction in England, 1790–1820*
by Edward Copeland
10 *Shelley and the Revolution in Taste: The Body and the Natural World*
by Timothy Morton
11 *William Cobbett: The Politics of Style*
by Leonora Nattrass
12 *The Rise of Supernatural Fiction 1762–1800*
by E. J. Clery

WILLIAM COBBETT
The Politics of Style

LEONORA NATTRASS
Nottingham Trent University

CAMBRIDGE UNIVERSITY PRESS

Published by the Press Syndicate of the University of Cambridge
The Pitt Building, Trumpington Street, Cambridge, CB2 1RP
40 West 20th Street, New York, NY 10011-4211, USA
10 Stamford Road, Oakleigh, Melbourne 3166, Australia

© Cambridge University Press 1995

First published 1995

Printed in Great Britain at the University Press, Cambridge

A catalogue record for this book is available from the British Library

Library of Congress cataloging in publication data

Nattrass, Leonora.
William Cobbett: the politics of style / Leonora Nattrass.
p. cm. – (Cambridge studies in Romanticism)
Includes bibliographical references and index.
ISBN 0 521 46036 0 (hardback)
1. Cobbett, William, 1763–1835 – Literary art. 2. Great Britain – Politics and government – 1789–1820 – Historiography. 3. Rhetoric – Political aspects – Great Britain – History – 19th century. 4. Journalism – Great Britain – History – 19th century. 5. Style, Literary. 6. Polemics. I. Title. II. Series.
DA522.C5N38 1995
941.07′3′092 – dc20 94-14479 CIP

ISBN 0 521 46036 0 hardback

For Mark

Contents

Acknowledgements	*page* x
A chronology of Cobbett's life	xi
Introduction: change and continuity	1

PART I: THE CREATION OF COBBETT

1	Early writings 1792–1800	33
2	A version of reaction	62
3	Oppositional styles 1804–1816	89
4	Representing Old England	119

PART II: COBBETT AND HIS AUDIENCE

5	Dialogue and debate	135
6	A radical history	157
7	Tracts and teaching	183
8	Constituting the nation	205
Notes		217
Bibliography		238
Index		247

Acknowledgements

Many people have helped in the writing of this study. Tim Webb and Hugh Haughton introduced me to Cobbett in 1987, on their MA course in English Romantic Literature at the University of York. Tim Webb supervised the resulting MA dissertation which reappears somewhat altered in this study. Helen Braithwaite and Robert Miles both read portions of the manuscript and made valuable suggestions. The fact that my husband Mark can recite certain passages verbatim is indicative of the level of help and support he has given. I have received advice, support and encouragement from Dr John Stevenson, Brian Burns, Marilyn Butler, James Chandler and Josie Dixon. I would also like to acknowledge the assistance of the William Cobbett Society, which published a short extract of the book in its journal, and whose members responded with courtesy to my requests for help.

My most enduring debt of gratitude is to my doctoral supervisor, Derek Roper, who showed unfailing interest and patience during the course of my studies, and provided me with an example of scholarship which I am only too well aware of not living up to. I hope that this rewritten version meets with his approval. The University of Sheffield awarded me a research studentship with which to support my doctoral studies. Any errors of judgement or of fact are my own.

A chronology of Cobbett's life

1763 — Born at the Jolly Farmer pub in Farnham, Surrey.
1783–4 — Runs away to London to become a lawyer's clerk. Hating the work, he enlists as a private soldier.
1785–90 — Posted to Canada, Cobbett learns grammar and is promoted to Regimental Sergeant-Major. Meets his future wife, Ann Reid.
1790–1 — Regiment returns to England. Cobbett leaves the army and marries. Conducts an abortive attempt to court-martial his superiors for fraud against the common soldier. Writes *The Soldier's Friend* (published 1792). Escapes to France in fear of retaliatory prosecution. Remains in France for six months.
1792–3 — Amid revolutionary chaos Cobbett and Ann leave France for the United States. They arrive at Philadelphia and Cobbett unsuccessfully approaches Thomas Jefferson for employment. Cobbett begins a career as an English teacher. First child born.
1794 — Second child stillborn. First child dies. Cobbett publishes *Observations on the Emigration of Dr Priestley*.
1795–8 — Third child born 1795. Cobbett publishes a spate of pamphlets. Jay's Anglo-American treaty negotiated and ratified 1796. Cobbett sets up as bookseller and continues to publish his own writings. Prosecuted for libel over his comments on the treatment of yellow fever practised by Dr Benjamin Rush. Fourth child born 1798.
1799–1800 — Moves to New York due to accumulating libel cases, and then returns to England in 1800. Offered ownership of government paper, but refuses. Starts *The Porcupine* which fails. Fifth child born.

1802	Starts *Weekly Political Register* which coincides with the Peace of Amiens.
1803	Cobbett (anonymously) publishes *Important Considerations for the People of this Kingdom*. Sixth child born.
1804–9	Seventh, eighth and ninth children born. Cobbett's political views swing slowly towards Reform, aided by a formative trip to Horton Heath in 1804. Series of open letters addressed to Pitt trace this disaffection from his previous position. Tories elected in General Election of 1807. Ely Mutiny 1809 rouses Cobbett to the attack.
1810–12	Prosecuted for the Ely article and sentenced to two years' imprisonment despite ignominious (and later denied) attempts to negotiate with the Government. Writes continually and voluminously from jail. Is released to public acclaim.
1813–15	Tenth child born. Waterloo 1815. Worsening conditions lead to increased demands for Reform.
1816–17	Luddite riots spur Cobbett to launch the cheap *Register*. He briefly wields immense popular influence. Habeas corpus suspended, and Cobbett flees to the United States. Cobbett's reputation among Radicals is much weakened by this desertion.
1818–19	Cobbett remains in America. Publishes *A Journal of a Year's Residence in the United States of America* and his *Grammar of the English Language*. 16 August 1819 Peterloo massacre in Manchester. With the passage of the repressive Six Acts, this effectively ends agitation. Habeas corpus is restored. Cobbett returns to England with Paine's bones.
1820	Publishes *Cottage Economy* and *Cobbett's Sermons* in parts, 1821–2. Coronation of George IV. Cobbett is deeply involved in the Queen Caroline affair. Cobbett stands at Coventry in the General Election of this year and is defeated. Goes bankrupt.
1821–7	Cobbett undertakes his Rural Rides. *A History of the Protestant Reformation* published in parts, 1824–6. *The Poor Man's Friend* is published in parts, 1826–7 as a part of his general election campaign in Preston. He is defeated. Ann Cobbett attempts suicide.

1828–32	Catholic Emancipation 1829. Growing agitation for Reform. Whigs take power in 1830. George IV dies. Cobbett publishes *Advice to Young Men*, and *Rural Rides*, and takes an increasingly active part in agitation for Reform. Captain Swing riots 1830. Cobbett is implicated and unsuccessfully prosecuted in 1831. Great Reform Bill passed after much political trauma in 1832. Cobbett is elected Member for Oldham in ensuing General Election.
1833–5	Cobbett, estranged from his family and increasingly paranoid, devotes his time to Parliament and to farming. Dies aged 72 in 1835.

Introduction: *change and continuity*

ISSUES

To communicate to others the knowledge that I possess has always been my taste and my delight; and few, who know anything of my progress through life, will be disposed to question my fitness for the task. Talk of rocks and breakers and quagmires and quicksands, who has ever escaped from amidst so many as I have! Thrown (by my own will, indeed) on the wide world at a very early age, not more than eleven or twelve years, without money to support, without friends to advise, and without book-learning to assist me; passing a few years dependent solely on my own labour for my subsistence; then becoming a common soldier, and leading a military life, chiefly in foreign parts, for eight years; quitting that life after really, for me, high promotion, and with, for me, a large sum of money; marrying at an early age; going at once to France to acquire the French language, thence to America; passing eight years there, becoming bookseller and author, and taking a prominent part in all the important discussions of the interesting period from 1793 to 1799, during which there was in that country a continued struggle carried on between the English and the French parties; conducting myself, in the ever-active part which I took in that struggle, in such a way as to call forth marks of unequivocal approbation from the Government at home; returning to England in 1800, resuming my labours here; suffering, during these twenty-nine years, two years of imprisonment, heavy fine, three years' self-banishment to the other side of the Atlantic, and a total breaking of fortune, so as to be left without a bed to lie on; and, during these twenty-nine years of troubles and punishments, writing and publishing every week of my life, whether in exile or not, eleven weeks only excepted, a periodical paper, containing more or less of matter worthy of public attention; writing and publishing, during *the same twenty-nine years*, a Grammar of the French and another of the English language, a work on the Economy of the Cottage, a work on Forest Trees and Woodlands, a work on Gardening, An Account of America, a book of Sermons, a work on the Corn-plant, a History of the Protestant Reformation; all books of great and continued sale, and the *last* unquestionably the book of greatest circulation in the whole world, the Bible only excepted; having, during *these same twenty-nine years* of troubles and embarrassments without number, introduced into England the manufacture of straw-plat; also several valuable trees; having introduced, during *the same twenty-nine years*, the cultivation of the corn plant, so manifestly valuable as a source of food; having, during the same period, always (whether in exile or not) sustained a shop of some size in London; having, during the whole of the same period, never employed less, on an average, than ten persons, in some capacity or other, exclusive of printers, bookbinders, and others connected with papers and books; and having, during these twenty-nine years of troubles, embarrassments, prisons, fines, and banishments, bred up a family of seven children to man's and woman's state.[1]

This is William Cobbett, five years before his death, describing his eventful life. The self-satisfied tone is a characteristic of his writings familiar to his contemporaries and to subsequent critics, biographers and historians. Yet, as Hazlitt noted, Cobbett's egoism was often well-founded.[2] His life-story is one of extraordinary social elevation from his birth as the son of a country innkeeper and small farmer in 1763 to his death as a famous Radical journalist and MP in 1835.[3] Having acquired only the most rudimentary literacy during a childhood otherwise given to agricultural labour, Cobbett taught himself the rules of English grammar during his army career. At the turn of the nineteenth century such inauspicious beginnings made fame and financial success unlikely. Yet Cobbett's life was characterized by periods of relative affluence and by a widespread and persisting fame.

He began his literary career in the 1790s, during one of the greatest political debates in British history. The French Revolution, which had exploded in 1789, had been by turns welcomed, feared and exploited by the British Establishment. Seen initially as an emulation of the English Revolution of 1688, and then as a levelling Utopia likely to be emulated in turn by British Radicals, the French experiment ultimately fulfilled Burke's early predictions of anarchy and bloodshed, and confirmed prevailing assumptions about the dangers of democracy. Cobbett's contribution to this debate took place in America and through the focus of American politics, between 1794 and 1800. Strangely, given his plebeian origins, he entered the debate on the conservative side, writing virulently against the French influence in the United States and defending the British political system. During the course of this crusade he found himself in violent opposition to Thomas Paine, then achieving an extraordinary influence in Britain with his radically vernacular *Rights of Man*. Yet in the years that followed, Cobbett's political position was transformed partly by reading Paine's economic writings[4] and by 1810, at which time he was imprisoned for two years on charges of seditious libel, he was developing a 'democratic' literary style which also owed much to Paine. Reviling the financial markets of nascent capitalism, patronage, sinecures, taxation and corruption, by 1816 Cobbett would be as influential in working-class Radical circles as Paine had ever been.

Cobbett is best remembered by biographers, historians and political theorists as a colourful character, a player in the agitation for Reform in the period leading up to the Great Reform Act of 1832, and as a less than satisfactory political thinker. But he achieved his social advancement and considerable contemporary fame first and foremost as a writer, and that is the focus of this book. For thirty-three years, at home, in prison, or in self-imposed exile he unfailingly produced a weekly newspaper, for which he wrote the editorial, while in addition he produced the stream of extremely varied publications, some of which he describes above. It has been calculated that during his literary career he wrote more than twenty million words.[5] From 1800 until 1835 he was also one of the most successful writers in England. In a period when the total population of the United Kingdom was twenty millon, newspaper circulations were small. The popular *Sunday Observer*, for example, achieved a weekly circulation of only 7,000 copies. Cobbett's most influential period, in 1816 and 1817, saw his weekly paper achieving an unprecedented national circulation of between 40,000 and 70,000 copies. Seven years later the combined Sunday press sold only 100,000 copies per week.[6]

Nor was his readership drawn from any one social class. Cobbett began as a conservative writing, in both England and America, in broad support of the Tory administrations of the late eighteenth and early nineteenth centuries. As a mainstream, respectable journalist he gained a solid readership for his *Weekly Political Register* among the refined classes. Gradually, over a period of ten years, his views swung leftwards, but this swing did not mean that he lost his existing audience. In 1816 and 1817, when he achieved his largest circulations, he did so by distributing twopenny off-prints of the *Register*'s leading article to a working-class audience. At this time, in other words, Cobbett was read by everyone from government ministers to ploughboys. Hazlitt summed up this influence by suggesting that he was a 'fourth estate' in the politics of the country.[7]

The success of his conversational writings, addressed to the poor in a period of unrest, was one factor leading to the Gagging Acts against the press and the suspension of habeas corpus in 1817. Cobbett, still bound over to keep the peace from his previous term of imprisonment in 1810 to 1812, hastily departed for America to avoid a second conviction. Returning home in 1820, he acknowledged his ideological and literary debts and aimed for a grand symbolic gesture by bringing with him Paine's bones, dug up from their obscure and unconsecrated American grave.[8] The 1820s and 1830s saw the publication of the most famous of Cobbett's works – among them *Rural Rides*, *Cottage Economy*, *A History of the Protestant Reformation in England and Ireland* and *Advice to Young Men*.

Despite this fame and publishing success Cobbett has been, at best, a marginal figure in critical accounts of the literature of the Romantic period. We can postulate two principal reasons for this, of varying weight. First, his ephemeral political concerns and many 'Augustan' attitudes seemed incompatible with the traditional literary-critical construction of Romanticism which dominated discussion of this period for many years. The recent rethinking of Romantic categories, however, involving an increasingly complicated understanding of the relationship between the 'literary' and 'historical' makes it no longer necessary to argue this case. The second more serious reason for this neglect is that Cobbett's bluster, bigotry and self-publicity have been read by most historians and biographers as unselfconscious quirks which betray an artlessness suggestive of intellectual superficiality and unworthy of serious literary consideration. I question this assessment, arguing that Cobbett's writings have been too readily dismissed as the unmediated output of a thoughtless if talented journalist. On the contrary this book argues that there is self-conscious artifice at work in Cobbett's prose and suggests that those aspects of his writing commonly seen as 'problems' can be reread as transgressive and politically enabling rhetorical tools which are often the real interest and practical strength of his work.

In order to situate this literary and rhetorical reading within previous Cobbett criticism, it is useful to note that there have been two recurring but conflicting critical approaches to his work, one admiring and the other hostile. Historians like J. R. Dinwiddy,

J. C. Belchem and W. H. Wickwar, as well as E. P. Thompson, dwell on the extraordinary influence of Cobbett's journalism, and on his involvement in practical attempts at parliamentary reform and social amelioration. Thus, for instance, Wickwar quotes Leigh Hunt's contemporary eulogy on Cobbett's virtual invention of the popular press: 'the invention of printing itself scarcely did more for the diffusion of knowledge and the enlightening of the mind than has been effected by the Cheap Press of this country. Thanks to Cobbett! The commencement of his twopenny register was an era in the annals of knowledge and politics which deserves eternal commemoration'.[9] Similarly Belchem dwells on Cobbett's relations with other popular writers and politicians of the time, and on his political common sense, citing Cobbett's journalism as one spur to 'Orator' Hunt's entry into the Reform movement, depicting him as sharply aware of political expediency, and as a steadying influence upon his Radical contemporaries.[10] Again, Dinwiddy portrays Cobbett at the vanguard of the movement for Reform, providing a practical sense of direction for others: 'in the face of... [ideological] diversity it made quite good sense for the reformers to follow the advice given by Cobbett... that since many evils existed, and they could all – in so far as they were curable – be cured by a parliamentary reform, attention should be concentrated on this "great and single object" rather than on its hoped-for consequences'.[11]

These images of Cobbett are forceful, positive and dynamic. E. P. Thompson similarly values Cobbett's 'democratic' stylistic clarity as he argues that 'in tone will be found at least one half of Cobbett's political meaning'.[12] This is an easy point to substantiate and is, perhaps, the least contentious aspect of Cobbett's work. Even *The Times*, which had been the object of Cobbett's hatred for more than twenty-five years, acknowledged in its obituary these stylistic strengths:

The first general characteristic of his style is, perspicuity unequalled and inimitable. The second is homely, muscular vigour. The third is purity, always simple, and raciness often elegant. His argument is an example of acute, yet apparently natural, nay involuntary, logic, smoothed in its progress and cemented in its parts by a mingled stream of torturing sarcasm, contemptuous jocularity, and fierce and slaughtering invective.[13]

Cobbett's colloquial and energetic writings cut self-consciously through the refined circumlocutions of eighteenth-century political discourse – in 1810 he declared that his aim and achievement was to offer his readers '*truth* in *clear language*'.[14] An example is provided by a series of articles in the *Register* of 1810 to 1812, published under the collective title *Paper Against Gold*. Written in prison, these articles took the form of open letters, addressed 'To the Tradesmen and Farmers In and Near Salisbury'. The first article is characteristic as it makes clear its clarifying aims:

Gentlemen,
During the last session of parliament, a Committee, that is to say, ten or twelve members, of the House of Commons were appointed to inquire into the cause of the high price of Gold *Bullion*, that is, Gold *not coined*; and to take into consideration the state of the circulating medium, or money, of this country. This Committee have made a *Report*, as they call it; but, it is a great book that they have written, and have had printed; a book much larger than the whole of the New Testament. Of this Report I intend to enter into an Examination; and, as you have recently felt, and are still feeling, some of the effects of Paper-Money, I think it may not be amiss, if, upon this occasion, I address myself to you.[15]

Two pages later Cobbett considers the change from gold to paper money in bluntly experiential terms which again are characteristic:

There are few of you, who cannot remember the time, when there was scarcely ever seen a bank note among Tradesmen and Farmers. I can remember, when this was the case; and, when the farmers in my country hardly ever saw a bank-note, except when they sold their hops at Weyhill fair. People, in those days, used to carry little bags to put their money in, instead of the paste-board or leather cases that they now carry. If you look back, and take a little time to think, you will trace the gradual increase of paper-money, and the like decrease of gold and silver money ... It is the *cause* of this that is interesting to us; the cause of this change in our money, and, in the *prices* of goods of all sorts and of labour.[16]

By the twenty-fourth letter of the series, Cobbett and his reader are confident enough to take on the experts who warn of dire but vague consequences of a return to the Gold standard:

But, Gentlemen, is there any *ground* for these apprehensions? Are such apprehensions to be entertained by *rational* men? No: the corn and the grass and the trees will grow without paper-money; the Banks may all break in a day, and the sun will rise the next day, and the lambs will gambol and the birds will sing and the carters and country girls will grin at each other and all will go on just as if nothing had happened.

'Yes,' says some besotted Pittite, 'we do not suppose, that the destruction of the paper-system would put out the light of the sun, prevent vegetation, or disable men and women to propagate their species: we are not fools enough to suppose that.' Pray, then, *what* are you fools enough to suppose? *What* are you fools enough to be *afraid of*? For, if the destruction of the paper produces, and is calculated to produce, none of these effects, how can it be a thing to excite any very *general* apprehension? *Who* would it *hurt*? 'Oh! It would create universal *uproar* and *confusion*: it would destroy all property; it would introduce anarchy and bloodshed, and would annihilate, *regular government, social order*, and our *holy religion*.' These are the words that JOHN BOWLES, the Dutch Commissioner, used to make use of. This is the declamatory cant, by the means of which the people of this country have been deceived and deluded along from one stage of ruin to another, till, at last, they have arrived at what they now taste of. If, when JOHNNY BOWLES, or any of his tribe, had been writing in this way, a plain tradesman, who gets his living by fair dealing and who has no desire to share in the plunder of the public, had gone to the writer, and, taking him fast by the button, had said to him: 'Come, come! tell me, in definite terms, what you mean, and show me *how I should be a loser* by this thing that *you* appear so much to dread. None of your *rant*; none of your *horrifying descriptions*; but, come, JOHN, tell me HOW I should be made worse off in this world, and HOW I should be more exposed to go to hell, if that which you appear to dread were actually to take place:' if any such man had so addressed this Treasury scribe, the scribe would have been puzzled much more than he was by his per cents about the Dutch Commission.[17]

This is typical Cobbett, with its rude name-calling, its downright language, and its dramatic structure based on an imagined dialogue between opposing views. Here the political effect of such tactics is plain, as the stylistic choice of making his arguments in colloquial language, and placing them in the mouth of the 'plain tradesman' he is addressing, emphasizes that plain tradesmen have a right to engage in political debate and asserts that they are likely to have a sounder grasp of practical realities than their obfuscating superiors.

This preoccupation with the political rights and abilities of the ordinary citizen takes us back to Leigh Hunt's euphoric vision of Cobbett's invention of the popular press in 1816. We will see later that the radicalism of Cobbett's decision to address the poor in that year is particularly apparent in the context of widespread press hostility to the working classes. This hostility, and Cobbett's radical willingness to oppose it, can be initially sketched by the following extract from the *Register* of 1812. Here Cobbett is reporting on food riots occurring nationwide, in which a woman was killed:

The TIMES, in speaking of the extent of the danger from the riots, coolly observes: 'we would not wish the public to apprehend more from them, or in them, than there really is. They are mere Mob Riots, which, resulting from *disorderly force*, are to be suppressed by *a force that is ordered and organized.*' With what perfect coolness; with what sang-froid; with what a disregard of the lives of the people this must have been written! The man who wrote this must look upon the mass of the people as little better than brutes, and must regard the soldiers as raised and kept in pay for the purpose of making war upon them. You hear from him no expression of sorrow at the death of this poor woman, who has, perhaps, left a family of children. All is defiance on his part; all hostility towards the people. Is this the sort of feeling that an Englishman ought to have upon the perusal of news like this? He, alas! knows not what it is to feel hunger, and to hear children crying for bread.[18]

One approach to Cobbett, then, stresses his practical achievements and his radically democratic style and readership. The second common approach stresses weaknesses of content – particularly his nostalgia and bigotry which, hostile critics argue, make his work both offensive and irrelevant to subsequent developments in political thought. Noel O'Sullivan in his book *Conservatism* dismisses Cobbett as no more than a warning to conservatives: a sad tale of a thinker unable to cope with the new and pointlessly clinging to outmoded values. Practically Cobbett's only contribution to the history of ideas, he tells us ironically, is his obsessive and irrational loathing of tea.[19] Crane Brinton similarly chooses Cobbett's preoccupation with food and drink as a metaphor for his political 'tastes' in order to suggest that he does not think political positions, but rather feels them: 'he disliked paper money exactly as he disliked tea.'[20]

Cobbett's political nostalgia has seemed increasingly irrelevant to the concerns and values of the Left which has preferred to identify with Paine's more philosophical radicalism as the intellectual forerunner of current political thought. As a result, his supporters on the Left, like E. P. Thompson, G. D. H. Cole and Raymond Williams, have felt obliged to excuse his nostalgia and populism by representing them as lapses unfortunately common in the work of an otherwise well-meaning but thoughtless writer. Raymond Williams's *Cobbett*, for example, is framed as an exercise in the rereading and rehabilitation of Cobbett's political analysis;[21] J. L. Hammond, in the introduction to his edition of Cobbett's *The Last Hundred Days of English Freedom* declares that 'when it came to constructive measures Cobbett was often wrong; he thought government a simpler matter than it was; his likes and dislikes were apt to disturb his judgement;

but he stands out among the great forces of his time because he used a talent unrivalled in his age, in the effort... to destroy the fatal superstition of the day that the rich could be trusted to act for the poor';[22] while E. P. Thompson acknowledges that 'it is not difficult to show that Cobbett had some very stupid and contradictory ideas, and sometimes bludgeoned his readers with specious arguments'.[23]

Unlike these reluctant critics, Joel Wiener puts the case against Cobbett comprehensively:

> What was wrong with William Cobbett is that in place of considered thought he too often blurred the distinction between personal bigotry and political idealism. His anti-semitism – crude and shocking – pervades all of his writings. His violent opposition to birth-control propaganda transcends by far the level of prudery; it was a prejudice, albeit not one peculiar to him, which did much to retard working-class enlightenment in this important area. Cobbett's assaults upon urban life were little more than reflections of a self-moulded cultural primitivism. Nor did his cantankerous use of invective recognize perceptible boundaries; in an age in which journalistic inhibitions were almost non-existent, Cobbett often sank to new depths of personal interchange.[24]

These varying responses to Cobbett indicate that his writings are open to differing interpretations depending upon the aspect of his work under discussion and upon the ideological standpoint of his critic. For historians interested in the practical upshot of his writings, Cobbett can be a positive figure. For those who approach his writings as a part of the theoretical debate over the future of Britain, Cobbett seems at best irrelevant. But either way, as Martin Wiener has argued,[25] and as we can see from the uneasy judgements just quoted, Cobbett's critics seem drawn to evaluate his writings ultimately through the filter of their own political views.

This study prefers to re-evaluate Cobbett's political prose primarily through the focus of rhetorical strategy, presenting an account of what his texts are attempting to achieve and constructing a set of meanings for their formal practices which may explain their significant contemporary success with the audiences they address. In certain key respects this re-evaluation is a positive one. But arguing that Cobbett is a more skilful and self-conscious writer than has usually been allowed is not necessarily to defend the substantive political content of his writings – on the contrary it may cast Cobbett in a darker light if we say that he is self-conscious in writing what is indefensible:

To confine myself, at present, to the Negroes, (with a promise, however, not to forget the Jews another time) who, that has any sense or decency, can help being shocked at the familiar intercourse, which has gradually been gaining ground, and which has, at last, got a complete footing between the Negroes and the women of England? No black swain need, in this loving country, hang himself in despair. No inquiry is made whether he be a Pagan or a Christian; if he be not a downright cripple, he will, if he be so disposed, always find a woman, not merely to yield to his filthy embraces, that, amongst the notoriously polluted and abandoned part of the sex, would be less shocking, but to accompany him *to the altar*, to become his wife, to breed English mulattoes, to stamp the mark of Cain upon her family and her country! Amongst white women, this disregard of decency, this defiance of the dictates of nature, this foul, this beastly propensity, is, I say it with sorrow and with shame, *peculiar to the English*.[26]

A rhetorical analysis of this passage argues that this is not unconscious bigotry absorbed from the cultural biosphere and thoughtlessly disgorged onto the page by a writer who does not know his own mind. Rather this extract comes from a conservative article of 1804 which supports colonial interests and opposes the campaign to abolish the slave trade. In this context the reasons for employing crude racism are clear, as the text seems aimed to activate the prejudices of its readers in order to undermine any more rational sympathy they may feel towards Wilberforce and his campaign.

To recognize the aims and rhetorical management of racism in this way is not an easy route out of hard political questions. Rather, a stylistic evaluation often obliges us to recognize, if not to resolve, the complex relationship between rhetoric and ideology which an approach too narrowly concerned with content might elide. This can be seen most clearly if we compare the passage just quoted with another example of Cobbett's problematic bigotry from later in his Radical career:

VIRGIL was one of the basest scoundrels that ever lived; one of the most crawling and disgusting parasites, and a pander even to unnatural passions into the bargain. The books of this man, which are put by parsons into the hands of our youth, are a complete course of villainy. They teach flattery, gross, fulsome, nauseous flattery of an execrable tyrant, who gained his power by deliberate perfidy and murder. They teach every species of vice, and not very equivocally give countenance to that horrid vice which has grown up in England with the introduction of foreigners and foreign manners and foreign effeminacy. – ... Why, this miscreant, if he were living in England, would, if the Attorney General ordered him to do it, come with his tongue and lick all the dirt off his feet and off his carcass too; and, one of the reasons why we see so much want of public-spirit, and such a proneness to abject submission, amongst so many of those who have had what is called (as it were ironically) a liberal education, is, that they are, when young, taught to admire the works of VIRGIL and HORACE, two of the basest, most abject, most self-degraded wretches, that ever existed ...[27]

While at first sight this passage looks as irrational and bigoted as the first, a rhetorical analysis begins to encounter complexities which make it not only more difficult to assess but also more interesting than the first. We may be relieved to recognize that in the first passage stylistic evaluation does nothing to qualify our sense that it is abhorrent. While, as I have indicated, there may be polemical reasons for its deployment of racist discourse, that deployment merely parrots irrational bigotry in a way which is as familiar as it is banal. But the second passage is far more difficult and complex to assess. Written in 1811, during Cobbett's conversion to Radicalism, this passage deploys populist prejudices against 'foreigners' and against 'effeminacy' not to reinforce conservative prejudices but instead to invite its readers to despise and deride the Classical education seen as the basis for upper-class power. Working self-consciously within the nostalgic tradition of the ancient constitution which rejects Britain's Roman and Norman heritage in favour of a Saxon one[28] it nevertheless argues for Radical political and constitutional change. Paradoxically, in other words, it aims itself at ingrained prejudices in order to undermine the authority of cultural practices and values which perpetuate the status quo. From a rhetorical perspective this seems a polemical master stroke, as Cobbett appropriates and subverts the very same aspects of popular ideology with which, as we shall see, entrenched power attempts to maintain itself in the period.

APPROACHES

The contemporary influence and stylistic strengths of Cobbett's prose provided the occasion for this book, which was conceived as an attempt to fill the gap in Romantic studies noted by Marilyn Butler in *Burke, Paine, Godwin and the Revolution Controversy*. Butler there observed that 'Cobbett awaits the literary treatment his style deserves'.[29] But while I demonstrate and explore the uncontested strengths of Cobbett's prose style, my central points are made in relation to the 'problems of Cobbett' I have been outlining.

In his essay 'Rethinking Chartism', Gareth Steadman Jones asserts that the common perception of Chartism as confused and intellectually inadequate is the inevitable result of reading it retrospectively through a Marxist focus. He stresses the need to attend instead to the language within which Chartist ideas are purveyed, as an expression of an ideology which may not necessarily be a failed socialism, but merely a *different* one.[30] These observations about Chartism seem equally relevant to the anxieties I have been tracing in the criticism of Cobbett; anxieties which are created largely by his failure to conform to subsequent intellectual trends and particularly, as we shall see, by his failure to anticipate the progressive Marxist attitude towards the industrial revolution and the capitalist economy.[31]

My study relies on a converse willingness to attend to and acknowledge the contemporary rhetorical benefits of now obsolete discursive formations (such as the debate on the ancient constitution) and even, as we have seen, of populist bigotry. I view Cobbett not as a failed philosopher or unselfconscious bigot, but as a rhetorician, whose writings are, rather, a field where shared contemporary discourses are played out and exploited for political effect.[32] In this chapter I will place Cobbett's political nostalgia, for example, amid the various discursive formations of constitutionalism and will argue that his deployment of constitutional rhetoric may be individual, but that it is certainly not unrepresentative of or irrelevant to his period. The following four chapters will argue for the pragmatic nature of his exploitation of available discourse, and for an understanding of his famously egoistic persona as a rhetorically-driven literary creation. Part 2 addresses the vexed question of his populism, which often involves superstition, racism and anti-Semitism, in the context of his manipulation of varying readerships. In this context, as I have already shown, my interest is to analyse the rhetorical effect and ideological implications of these usages, rather than to debate the rightness and wrongness of those attitudes in partisan ways. I argue that at the very least Cobbett's bigoted writings can be fruitfully analysed as exhibiting tensions and anxieties within and between the ideological positions he inhabits, while in his best writings populism can even be an enabling and subversive argumentative strategy.

My task in this study, then, is to reorientate attention onto literary practice and away from any approach which confounds the biological Cobbett with his fictional persona and which under-estimates his rhetorical self-consciousness. Historical and biographical criticism has tended to collude in the representation of Cobbett as a hasty and thoughtless egotist who spills onto the page spontaneous humanity and constructive rage along with unmediated bigotry and useless hatreds. I argue that, neglecting the literary strategies in play in Cobbett's writings, biographers have in this way confused literary persona with self-revelation, while political theorists have treated polemical comment as political philosophy. I examine Cobbett's writings as artefacts constrained by what it is possible to say in the period, and bound by the often conflicting needs to reach certain target audiences, to make a living, and to avoid prosecution. The readings which follow try to get away from the idea that Cobbett is unselfconscious either personally or politically. On the contrary, they stress the highly-wrought self-consciousness of his writings which are always striving for a calculated effect. And to return to the ideological lapses within Cobbett's radical prose, which the Left has found so troubling, we have already seen that it is, in fact, Cobbett's ability to mimic and to confound usually separate ways of thinking and writing that often constitutes his most significant polemical achievement.

CONTEXTS

Having identified the contingency of many hostile critical responses to Cobbett, in so far as they are determined by the critic's own historical and ideological location, it would be folly to insist that the vision of Cobbett which follows is somehow the 'true' one, or that the contexts within which I place him are the only ones of value. Meanings and contexts, as we have seen, are constructed by the critical consciousness which assembles them, and critical consciousness is in turn constructed by the contexts and meanings within which it functions. How convincing or otherwise the reader finds this version of Cobbett will in the end depend upon its relevance to the critical practices and cultural concerns of the present, rather than by any appeal to an objective historical past.

The remainder of this chapter will place Cobbett within discursive and rhetorical contexts which have become of increasing interest to historians and to critics of political rhetoric over the last decade. It will argue, first, that the 'democratic' nature of Cobbett's best prose is apparent if we examine the political significances of linguistic practice in the period, both within explicitly political writing and within aesthetics. It will go on to argue that our understanding of a number of Cobbett's apparent weaknesses is crucially revised by an examination of the historical narratives dominant within the period's political discourse. And it will conclude by placing Cobbett among the various political alignments available to him, in order to suggest further reasons for his contentious critical reputation.

Cobbett's 'democratic' methods and preoccupations, as he aims at the representation of '*truth* in *plain language*', are loaded with political significance in the period between the French Revolution and the Great Reform Act of 1832. The British debate on the French Revolution established lines of argument for and against democratic reform which were preoccupied with class. Such arguments were particularly powerful in a period of transition, which we might sketch as characterized by population explosion, dramatically increasing literacy, industrial and political revolutions at home and abroad, and burgeoning Radical agitation for democratic reform. All these characterized a moment midway between the stable agrarian economy of the early eighteenth century in which a tiny fraction of the population had a say in Parliament, and the industrial economy of the later nineteenth century with its increasingly powerful middle class and politicized proletariat. The anxieties and repressions of the 1790s are often presented as characteristic of a period of economic and social transformation: the conventional years associated with the nascent industrial revolution are 1780 to 1830,[33] while English Romanticism spans the same period and has often been seen as a literature in response to its vertiginous social context. The period, viewed from any of these angles, is seen as a time of extraordinary and accelerating change. Conservative writers of the Revolution debate seem keenly aware of the social realignments demanded by the rising middle class, and attempt to stave off more radical changes by playing on certain assumptions about the relative rights and abilities of the different classes. These assumptions are encoded in the fabric of the language in which political issues are discussed, and give political meaning to literary style.

This, at any rate, is the persuasive conclusion of Olivia Smith's important study, *The Politics of Language 1791–1819*. The eighteenth and nineteenth centuries, according to Smith, saw a growing sense of class consciousness about language. The breakdown of traditional hierarchical social structures and the rapid increase in working-class literacy and authorship in this period altered the political significance of linguistic usage. While early in the eighteenth century Swift had tested his clarity of expression by reading his books to his servants,[34] the political and cultural elite of our period (according to Smith) anxiously defended its position by denigrating such levelling linguistic practices. Increasingly from 1750 onwards language was seen as falling into one of two categories: the 'refined' or the 'vulgar'.[35]

The refined is the discourse of authority: its sophistication indicates the sophistication of thought required for participation in decision-making, and is characterized by complex syntax and an avoidance of the concrete in favour of the abstract. Vulgar language, in contrast, is characterized by simple syntax and a concern with the concrete, the particular and, therefore, the passions. The lack of restraint and considered thought implied by this characterization of vulgarity means that such usage indicates an unfitness to participate in the political life of the country.[36]

This distinction obviously followed broad social lines and assumed certain things about the classes – for instance that people who lacked a classical education were incapable of abstract, sophisticated thought. This assumption was illustrated in the pages of Cobbett's *Register*, when in 1807 he launched an attack on the 'learned languages' which evoked strong responses from his readers. The classics were central to the eighteenth century's literature; to the education of a gentleman; and to the developing codifications of English grammar described by Smith, which attempted to fit English usage to classical models. The correspondence between Cobbett and his readers confirms the class assumptions underlying the high value placed on a classical education in the period. Cobbett's first statement on the subject asserted that '*as a part of a general education*, those languages are worse than useless.' Responding to the subsequent reaction from his readers, Cobbett indirectly acknowledges that he is initiating a power struggle based on class prejudice, where his own self-educated, working-class status will be an issue:

Here I should have stopped, had not the 'late member of Queen's College, Oxford,' who, as the reader will see, dates from *the Temple*, thought proper to question my *seriousness*, in challenging his brethren to the discussion. His contempt of me, as an antagonist, was to be looked for, as a matter of course; but his snips and snaps at wit and point are, also, perfectly in character; but, I must forewarn him not to think me in jest; for, he will find, that, unless my proposition can be over-set, I shall question the justice and the policy of leaving so large a portion of those means, which are so much wanted for the creditable maintenance of our starving parish priests, to be wasted at Oxford, Cambridge, and elsewhere; and this, I take it, is *no jesting* – [37]

This debate, initiated in January, rumbled on for months. In June of 1807 one correspondent defended a classical education in terms which make the class issue explicit, and which exactly correspond to the observations made by Olivia Smith:

Sir; – I mean, omitting the consideration of all other advantages of the Learned Languages, to confine myself to one which none of your correspondents seem hitherto to have thought of. We have divine authority for preserving the different gradations in society; high and low, rich and poor, are of God's holy appointment, and are therefore not to be levelled. In the University it used to be held that, not comparative merit alone, but a different kind of knowledge was requisite to entitle a person to the respective ranks of honours conferred at the taking of the bachelor's degree; and it is surely no very unsound opinion, that the higher orders of society should possess an extension and expansion of mind, a better way of thinking on all subjects and in all circumstances, than the lower orders. It is generally true, that neither time nor chance will alter the cast of an early disposition to virtue, virtue in its most unlimited sense, whether moral, religious, military, or civil; it is proverbially true, that evil communications corrupt good manners. In opposition, therefore, to your sentiment, that 'the time given to the learned languages is lost,' I conclude, that it keeps those together who are to fill the several posts of the higher orders of society, and that it keeps them separate from those of the lower orders; that it so tends to preserve the best distinctions of high and low, and that it is therefore a positive and important good.[38]

If a classical education is a means to instil and to maintain the intellectual and moral superiority necessary for political power, as this correspondent seems to suggest, then plebeian Radical writers like Cobbett and the class he represents are handicapped. Smith portrays Radicals like Thomas Spence, Thomas Paine, William Hone and Cobbett as defying the vulgar/refined opposition by speaking at all, but at the same time as faced with enormous problems of credibility which can only be overcome by attempting to overturn this binary paradigm. There are several tactics available. One method is that pursued by many writers, most successfully by Thomas Spence, who wrote in a belligerently vulgar style, expressing his ideas through existing working-class language and literary forms. This tactic asserts the possibility of discussing politics in vulgar language, but its hostility to the refined and its self-limitation to an unauthorized language is often in danger of merely confirming upper-class prejudices and contributing to its own rejection and marginalization.[39] William Hone by contrast takes over authoritative religious discourse, which cuts across the refined/vulgar divide, for Radical ends. Biblical discourse achieved this ambivalent status as it was subject to refined criticism – due to its vulgarly concrete diction, images and stories – yet could hardly be rejected by the upper classes. This ideologically ambivalent style along with its equal authority with, and availability to, all classes disrupts linguistic categories and furnishes Dissent and working-class Radicalism with an unassailable language resonant across the social boundaries. Hone exploits this to good effect in funny and seditious rewritings of prayers and forms of service.[40] Paine's achievement is more innovative as he develops a new 'intellectual vernacular' which is neutral, neither refined nor vulgar, and thus conducts political debate in a way which *avoids* the issue of class.[41] Cobbett's *Grammar of the English Language*, addressed especially to 'Soldiers, Sailors, Apprentices, and Ploughboys', conversely acknowledges the authority of refined usage and offers the politically voiceless access to this language of power.[42]

However, this political linguistic battle is not one simply conducted between the vast ranks of the 'vulgar' on the one hand, and the 'refined' minority on the other. It is an endemic conflict also evident within 'refined' poetics – and here it becomes clear that having access to refined language may not in itself be the answer to political and social marginalization as evidenced by the experience of the Cockney school. Blackwood's articles on The Cockney School first appeared in 1817, and the ground for their attacks was a crude class-consciousness. Lockhart's original insults, which set a benchmark for Hunt's reputation, were prefaced by the observation that 'Mr Hunt cannot utter a dedication, or even a note, without betraying the *Shibboleth* of low birth and low habits'.[43] In *The Spirit of the Age* Hazlitt makes this point about the critical reception of Leigh Hunt's poetry:

> Mr Hunt ought to have been a gentleman born, and to have patronised men of letters. He might then have played, and sung, and laughed, and talked his life away; have written manly prose, elegant verse; and his *Story of Rimini* would have been praised by Mr Blackwood ... His crime is, to have been Editor of the Examiner ten years ago, when some allusion was made to the age of the present King, and though his Majesty has grown older, our luckless politician is no wiser than he was then![44]

Here Hazlitt asserts the political motivation of aesthetic judgements in the Romantic period. His phrasing of this point is ambiguous, however. When he asserts that had Hunt been a gentleman he would have written 'manly prose' and 'elegant verse', does he mean that Hunt's output would have been *judged* in this positive way had his social origins been gentlemanly, or that his writing *itself* would have been different? The latter is an assumption in line with the attitudes identified by Olivia Smith and Hazlitt's phrasing raises the possibility that such assumptions are correct. With his subsequent reference to *The Story of Rimini*, however, (which makes it clear that he is talking about Hunt's existing output) it seems that Hazlitt is making a more difficult but more convincing suggestion: first, and obviously, that prevailing critical snobbery defines aesthetic value on non-literary criteria; second, his ambiguous phrasing seems to suggest, criticism *constructs* and *realizes* the material with which it engages in this politically motivated way. We might compare to this Olivia Smith's extract from a parliamentary petition of 1793 described by members of parliament as 'highly indecent and disrespectful':

Your petitioners are lovers of peace, of liberty, and justice. They are in general tradesmen and artificers, unpossessed of freehold land, and consequently have no voice in choosing members to sit in parliament; – but though they may not be freeholders, they are men, and do not think themselves fairly used in being excluded the rights of citizens.[45]

It is clear that the perception of this passage as indecent and disrespectful is a construction created by refined assumptions, not a function of the text's own practices except in so far as it dares to use the language and claim the rights of its superiors.

What is most interesting about this historical episode, then, is the way in which aesthetics are politicized by the preoccupation with the class languages described by Smith. As Daniel Cottom notes, 'the critical consciousness of that age is a defensive consciousness directed less to arguing what art is or should be than to arguing that it is not and must not be popular – a property of the common people'.[46] 'Taste' becomes at once a category threatened by plebeian self-assertion which might posit different aesthetic criteria, and at the same time a weapon to be wielded against such plebeian rivalry as it seeks to make its partial standards universal. Cottom argues that 'taste is thus a massive metaphorical tool presented as aesthetic truth, devoted to aristocratic values, overtly justified by appeals to the conditions necessary to rational communication, and covertly appealing to fears about the social disorder that would result if the lower classes were to emerge from their ideological imprisonment and "communicate with" their superiors'.[47] As Olivia Smith has shown, this communicative task is one shouldered by Radicals throughout this uneasy period of change.

Moreover, if the assumptions about 'refinement' and 'vulgarity' identified by Olivia Smith clarify the Cockney School episode as I have suggested, then the relations between Cobbett's sphere of 'vulgar' Radicalism and that of 'refined' poetics begins to become more complex and more relative. For aristocratic Radicals like Byron and Shelley, the potentially problematic relationship between refinement and vulgarity is particularly vexed. While Shelley famously used Cobbett's *Register* as a major point of contact with English politics during his sojourn in Italy, his Radicalism is one troubled by class anxieties. Shelley's declaration that 'Cobbet [sic] still more & more delights me, with all my horror of the sanguinary commonplaces of his creed'[48] betrays more than a hint of patronage. For Byron, Cobbett represented the popular Reform movement as a whole, and focussed his own anxieties. Malcolm Kelsall identifies Byron's anomalous position as a Whig 'friend of the people' in a period when the Whigs were almost continually in opposition, and notes the paradox that while speaking a rhetoric of opposition in this period, the Whig opposition is nevertheless a refined one, and that the 'Whig, in office, is indistinguishable from a Tory'.[49] The ambivalence of Byron's Radicalism is clear when he writes to Hobhouse: 'I have always been a well-wisher to and voter for reform in Parliament – but ... such infamous scoundrels as Hunt and Cobbett – in short the whole gang ... disgust and make one doubt of the virtue of any principle or politics which can be embraced by similar ragamuffins'. The class basis for his dislike is made clear as he adds 'I know that revolutions are not to be made with rose water ...'[50] By contrast, those writers who inhabit the nebulous region between refinement and vulgarity, such as Leigh Hunt and John Keats, clearly identify themselves with Cobbett. We have already seen Hunt's enthusiasm for the twopenny *Register*; Keats was similarly unequivocal. As a writer himself in dialogue with high literary culture,[51] it is perhaps unsurprising that he wrote of the Coventry election in 1820: 'Cobbet [sic] is expected to come in. O that I had two double plumpers for him'.[52]

Hazlitt's recognition that criticism constructs and realizes its subject by means of the assumptions brought to it returns us to the often hostile critical reception of Cobbett's writing. In what follows, I will seek to provide an alternative and redemptive context for his now unpopular political nostalgia by invoking the discourse of the ancient constitution.

As we have already seen, Cobbett's failure to follow Paine's Enlightenment stress on progress is seen as a serious intellectual flaw by critics. Cobbett champions agricultural concerns and organic social systems characterized by complex hierarchies, and writes firmly in the then more widespread tradition of the 'ancient constitution' which looked backwards for political models to some mythic age of universal manhood suffrage and annual parliaments. By contrast, Paine's Radical rhetoric brilliantly anticipates the effects of the industrial revolution and key concerns of the twentieth century and is now seen as the dominant Radical voice from the turn of the nineteenth century.

But as I have already indicated, it is possible to recognize the historicity of this judgement, which is made by political theorists who inhabit an ideological world dominated by progressive forms of capitalism and socialism. Marx identified Cobbett as a nostalgist,[53] and nostalgic socialism as 'half lamentation, half lampoon; half echo of the past, half menace of the future; at times, by its bitter, witty and incisive criticism, striking the bourgeoisie to the very heart's core; but always ludicrous in its effect, through total incapacity to comprehend the march of modern history.'[54] Paine's discourse, in this context, seems more appropriate to the enduring concerns of the Left.

But this does not mean that Paine's influence was necessarily so overwhelming in his own day. Indeed, much work has recently been done to rehabilitate the 'ancient constitution' and to point out its contemporary success. Even Marx, in the passage quoted above, acknowledges the frequent successes of the rhetoric of nostalgia. Similarly, social historians point out that by 1800 Paine's influence had been neutralized, his character assassinated, and his ideas vilified. Conversely, Cobbett's ability to avoid a similar fate, and his practical influence over a large audience drawn from all social classes, identifies him for historians as a major figure in the movement for democratic reform. It may be that this success is (at least partly) the result of *not* following Paine, and of appealing to the unregenerate emotions of his target audiences, who exist in a web of discourse – of possible ways of thinking and writing – in which Paine's Enlightenment rationalism might be only a minor strand.

If we remember at all times in approaching Cobbett's polemical works that they are polemic and not philosophy then our standards for evaluation shift. If the primary aim of Cobbett's text is to mobilize its reader's emotions and ideas in certain directions, we should not be looking for intellectual purity, argumentative rigour or ideological novelty, but instead should reorientate the focus of discussion and replace theoretical consistency with other standards for evaluation which emphasize the text's relationship with its reader, its negotiation of external constraints, and the ideological implications of its own language use.

In the late eighteenth and early nineteenth centuries the ideas of the ancient constitution and the Norman Yoke were common currency among reformers, who saw the latter as having suppressed the former. As a radical concept the ancient constitution has a noble pedigree, stretching back virtually into prehistory. That is, as both Christopher Hill and Raymond Williams have noted, people seem always to have looked back to some mythical prior state of social harmony: ultimately to the garden of Eden.[55] Raymond Williams, in *The Country and the City*, goes on from this general point to trace the idea back at least as far as Magna Charta and the Domesday-book.[56] This is significant, as many eighteenth- and nineteenth-century Radicals followed their forebears in identifying the Norman Conquest as the political Fall, when power relationships first went hopelessly askew.

Concern over 'boroughmongering' and the 'monied interest', images of corruption and decadence, and appeals to the superior virtue and wisdom of the past are typical and recurring parts of the constitutional discourse of opposition. Thus, when Cobbett moves towards a Radical position in the early years of the nineteenth century, he signals this shift by stressing the degeneracy of the present. He chastises

that Italian-like effeminacy, which has, at last, descended to the yeomanry of the country, who are now found turning up their silly eyes in ecstasy at a music meeting, while they should be cheering the hounds, or measuring their strength at the ring; the discouragement of all the athletic sports and modes of strife amongst the common people, and the consequent and fearful increase of those cuttings and stabbings, those assassin like ways of taking vengeance, formerly heard of in England only as the vices of the most base and cowardly foreigners ... the almost entire extinction of the ancient country gentry, whose estates are swallowed up by loan-jobbers, contractors, and nabobs ... [57]

This catalogue of decline and effeminacy seems typical Cobbett of the worst kind. But it is also a version of typical Bolingbroke, from the oppositional (Tory) *Craftsman* of 1729. There Bolingbroke identified the following as signs of corruption and social decay in the prevailing Whig order: '*Luxury* and *Extravagance* ... *Necessity* and *Prostitution* ... *Prodigality* and *Excess* ... *Distress, Bankruptcy, Dependence* ... *Perjury* and *Forgery*' all resulting from '*Venality of Offices*' and '*Corruption* in Office.'[58] In another article Bolingbroke depicted the contrasting virtues of the earlier age, with an interesting mixture of the capitalistic and the constitutional:

Our illustrious Ancestors were equally jealous of their *Trade* and of their *Liberties*; they justly esteemed them *dependent* on each other, and therefore were always upon the watch, and ready to oppose any *Innovations* or *Encroachments* upon either of them; they considered that their *Religious* and *Civil Rights* could not be safe without *Strength*; that *Power* was to be procured and preserved by *Wealth*, and that no Nation can become rich, but by a *well managed* and *extensive Commerce* ... [59]

The Whig *Morning Chronicle* similarly invoked ancestral authority on 9 August 1804, in its reaction to the election of Radical Sir Francis Burdett to Westminster:

A contested Election for a great and populous district is one of the happy occasions which renovate the spirit of Britons – recal [*sic*] to them the energy of their fathers – and make them feel the importance of the privilege which they enjoy in delegating their voice to a Representative in Parliament as a check on Executive power. It is in this moment that an Englishman truly glories in the distinction between the subject of a limited Monarch and the slave of a Despot.

Two years later Cobbett appealed to the same electors in similar terms: 'my hope is ... you will look back to the days of your forefathers, and revive in your minds the arduous and successful efforts, which at various times, they made for the preservation of the privilege, which you will soon have an opportunity of exercising ... '[60]

But a view of the political state which sees antiquity as conferring authority and dignity to social and electoral arrangements is not simply restricted to Radicals. Like progress, nostalgia is a value claimed by more than one side, and from the seventeenth to the nineteenth centuries the idea of the political mandate lying in the past was expedient and important for all sides.

J. G. A. Pocock depicts the conservative version of the ancient constitution as growing out of the writings of Sir Edward Coke, of around 1600.[61] As formulated by Coke, the idea was allied closely to the contemporary conception of the Common Law of England as both native to the British Isles and immemorial. Pocock documents the way in which the Norman origins of the feudal law had at this time been forgotten, thus allowing Coke to deny outside influence on the shape of English law, and also, more importantly, allowing him – unlike the Radicals – to deny the influence of William the Conqueror. This is crucial, as for Coke and his contemporaries the value of the ancient constitution theory of English politics was that, being immemorial, it could deny any 'first mover'. No sovereign, it declared, shaped the constitution, but rather it grew out of the common custom of the people, and drew its authority from that source. In the period leading up to the Civil War this denial of monarchical sanction was clearly a political as much as a philosophical manoeuvre, and as such, still an essentially Radical one. As we shall see in Chapter 3, however, Coke's refusal to recognize any individual *creator* of the Common Law also lends itself to conservative arguments against attempts individually to *alter* it.

After 1689 the concept changed to accommodate the Glorious Revolution and the Bill of Rights, which incorporated the monarchy into the constitution for all time. This new element in constitutional rhetoric is equally open to appropriation by Radicals and conservatives. Pocock traces the conservative reading of 1689 which asserts that the Revolution in fact reaffirmed the constitution as articulated in Magna Charta, establishing the 'mixed' or 'balanced' constitution, and representing the apotheosis of English political wisdom. In this way a more or less oppositional view of constitutional law is accommodated to a conservative viewpoint. By 4 July 1810, for example, the *Courier* could oppose Sir Francis Burdett's Radical constitutionalism with one of its own: 'No Sir! however some parts of it may seem to need repair, *the thinking portion of the community* are not yet quite so dazzled with the lustre of your talents as to permit your unhallowed hands to new model their ancient Constitution'. The concept is clearly related here to Burke's legalistic discussion of the

Declaration of Rights in his *Reflections on the Revolution in France*,[62] as well as articulating the position of the Whig oligarchy that ruled throughout the eighteenth century.

But the long domination of Whig rule in the eighteenth century itself led to the re-emergence of the radical version of the concept, as frustration led 'Radical' Tories and 'country gentlemen' to deny that 1689 had re-established the ancient constitution at all, in the absence of annual parliaments, the persistence of standing armies, and the perceived corruption of the executive. At the same time, Dissenting Radicals of the Revolution Society, like Richard Price, continued to see the Glorious Revolution as an enduringly Radical expression of the rights of the populace to choose and – if necessary – to depose their rulers.

The persistence of this (itself contested) constitutional language of opposition into the nineteenth century is also assessed by Pocock.[63] And while he recognizes the Jacobinical discourse of the 1790s as a new and transforming rhetoric, he argues that it failed to imbue oppositional discourse as the nineteenth century progressed. Pocock acknowledges the accession of 'new artisan, lower-middle-class and worker groups' to political expression but concludes that they – Cobbett among them – ultimately reverted to the established nostalgic, agrarian and hierarchic constitutional discourse of opposition.[64]

Pocock is not alone in recognizing such continuity between the eighteenth and nineteenth centuries. Janice Lee has described the constitutional nature of much Radical rhetoric of the 1790s, and described the attempts made to discredit it by the Establishment,[65] while James Epstein has identified a continuing use of constitutional discourse as late as the Chartist movement of the 1840s. Epstein attempts to account for this persistence, recognized by Lee and Pocock, by arguing that the older imagery holds an emotional resonance that Jacobin rhetoric failed to provide.[66] Jacobinism, associated with the failed French democracy and vilified by the Establishment, is in danger of positively alienating its target audience. Ian Dyck has used similar arguments to defend Cobbett's use of constitutional rhetoric. He asserts – I think rightly – that Cobbett politicized the working class more effectively by remaining culturally close to them. Evincing confused but very English values and moderate political aims, Cobbett did not scare his audience as Paine had done. Not less important, he argues, is that Cobbett also wooed a refined audience by stressing the ways in which he differed from the devil Paine.[67] In other words, if the rhetoric of the ancient constitution and the historical landmark of 1689 are contested political values, read differently and claimed by opposing sides, this may mean that they are more pervasive and therefore more *powerful* than the one-dimensional and novel rhetoric of Jacobinism and of Paine.

This picture of a simultaneously conservative and radical culture, which seeks ways of discussing change through familiar language, tallies with other aspects of the period. Earlier in this chapter, I briefly delineated the period as one of rapid and accelerating change, as traditional hierarchies were challenged by the rise of the middle class and the increasing urbanization and literacy of the poor. But this is a simplistic picture of an unregenerate age. Radical demands for social and parliamentary Reform were to some extent granted in the mid-thirties in the form of Factory Legislation and the Great Reform Act, but while the Factory Act reduced child workers' hours to ten per day, conditions for adults remained grim. A year later the Poor Law Amendment Act set up the workhouses which were effectively to punish poverty. Similarly, the Reform Act of 1832, which represented the culmination of Radical pressure for Reform in the period, actually changed little, and virtually nothing for the working class as the Chartists would realize in the period immediately following Cobbett's death. Such ambiguous change and amelioration also characterizes the economy itself. Though the period is commonly associated with the birth of industry, the vast majority of labourers were still employed in agricultural work. E. A. Wrigley has recently questioned prevailing views of the industrial revolution as a 'cumulative, progressive, unitary phenomenon', instead stressing among other things this continuing dominance of the prevailing agricultural order well into the period commonly designated industrial. Adam Smith and others, he argues, failed to foresee the increased productive capacity later to be provided by fossil fuels, while the greatest technological advances between the Tudor and Victorian ages were in fact agricultural.[68] This complex picture of sporadic and fortuitous economic development seems in line with earlier arguments made by David Miller and Eric Hobsbawm who both suggest that a full contemporary appreciation of the real economic and social changes to come was – perhaps inevitably – impossible. Both have described the failure of philosophers, legislators and monarchs alike to foresee the massive changes that would eventually attend industrial advances.[69] Such arguments put Cobbett's non-progressive, agricultural preoccupations in perspective, and tally with the picture of circuitous social, political and ideological change which is evident from other political and literary writings of the period.

The French Revolution debate itself, where Enlightenment visions of reason and perfectibility received perhaps their greatest public hearing in Britain, was won by the forces of reaction. By the end of the eighteenth century France had betrayed her British champions and Napoleon had begun his programme of conquest. By 1804 France would be headed by an Emperor and the democratic experiment would be at an end. In the same period the Gothic literary mode achieved its greatest popularity in England with the writings of Ann Radcliffe, where fear of the past jostles with apparent nostalgia for the medieval.[70] Lois Whitney has traced the general confusion within ideas of progress and primitivism in the eighteenth century, and the transition of the 'noble savage' in popular literature and thought of the period from being a representative of natural Enlightenment reason to a creature of sentiment.[71] And despite the best efforts of Enlightenment philosophy, reactionary ways of thinking can be traced, as we have already seen, even in the writings of 'Radical' Shelley, disciple of Godwin. Despite his democratic writings and agitation, Shelley reacted as follows to meeting an educated but working-class Radical activist: 'vile beast...it is disgusting to see such a person talk of philosophy. Let refinement and benevolence convey these ideas.'[72] Here we find ourselves disconcertingly returned to the unregenerate ideological landscape depicted by Olivia Smith.

The material conditions of political discourse in the period present a similarly confused picture. The number of political voices increased as did the range of audiences available to them. Many historians have charted the growth in literacy and the increasing struggle for free expression of democratic ideas in the period. Radical societies both patrician and plebeian flourished during the 1790s and distributed Jacobin literature to the briefly politicized working class. Later, in the next burst of Radical activity after Waterloo, Cobbett, Wooler, Hone and Carlile again addressed a labouring-class Radical public; titles like Cobbett's *Weekly Political Pamphlet* and Wooler's *Black Dwarf* evading politically-motivated tax regulations on printed matter in order to provide their readership with newspapers they could afford. Later again, in the early 1830s, Hetherington's *Poor Man's Guardian* led the war of the unstamped press against government taxation in a crusade to make cheap, Radical reading matter available to the poor. More respectable conservative and oppositional political writing flourished in the daily and periodical London press, the literary Reviews, and in one-off publications like Burke's *Reflections on the Revolution in France*.

The most vulgar strain of political writing in the period has been described by Ian McCalman, whose central figure is Thomas Spence. Olivia Smith, we remember, was troubled by Spence's extremely plebeian Radicalism which effectively restricted his influence to the margins of society. McCalman does not deny this, indeed he establishes a new polarity: where Smith draws the line between the 'refined' and the 'vulgar', McCalman draws his between 'respectable' if vulgar Radicals like Cobbett, Henry Hunt and Francis Place, and the 'rough' Radicalism of the unregenerate underworld populated by Spence, Robert Wedderburn, Thomas Evans and others. Again, this reminds us that there are tensions and differences within the broad linguistic categories identified by Smith. If, with Leigh Hunt, we saw an example of divisions within the ranks of the 'refined', with McCalman we encounter polarizations within the 'vulgar'. Operating in ale and coffee houses and blasphemous chapels, in the discourses of songs and toasts, and through the confounding of the obscene, the atheistic, and the millennial, the Radical underworld is revolutionary, separatist, and populist. McCalman sees 'respectable' Radicalism disowning this vulgarity and moving with the Victorian times to come, while populist Radicals resist such change and development. The Radicals described by McCalman subvert authority by refusing to conform to the expectations of refinement, or to join in the Victorianization of morals. McCalman sees this as a problematic activity, and as one likely to fail, but he nevertheless values 'a tradition of plebeian unrespectability and irreverence in the face of powerful countervailing forces' which he suggests exists into the present day.[73]

McCalman's categorization of Cobbett as a 'respectable' Radical draws our attention to the instability of Cobbett's position within these fluid categories. While Cobbett celebrates his own vulgarity through a preoccupation with his own social origins and a use of downright language, and is reviled by Bentham as well as by Byron, it is nevertheless true, as I noted at the beginning of this chapter, that he attracted an astonishing cross-section of society to his writings and achieved a huge social advancement to end his life as an MP. When McCalman characterizes Cobbett as a respectable Radical he does so by contrasting him to Thomas Spence, yet in fact their social backgrounds and the philosophical thrust of their political programmes are very similar. Both are born into unskilled labouring families; both are self-taught. Both espouse an essentially agricultural Utopia; both argue for natural rights based in the land. Yet one is 'unrespectable' and marginalized, though seldom attacked for his views; the other 'respectable', credited with a good deal of national political influence, and the subject of much acrimonious comment. How does Cobbett escape his apparently inevitable 'vulgar' destiny of marginalization to achieve his major influence, and why does this attract such hostility?

Cobbett's ideological career was an unstable one. His first published writing was an anonymous Radical pamphlet, published in London shortly after his discharge from the army in 1791. Cobbett had left the army in order to mount a prosecution against his officers for fraud against the private soldier. The prosecution failed and Cobbett was obliged to leave the country for fear of retaliatory action. Before he left, however, he published *The Soldier's Friend* which described, in terms recognizably Radical, the system of fraud practised by the officers. This early Radicalism rapidly evaporated in America and Cobbett entered the American debate on the French Revolution on the conservative side. Back in England in 1800, however, Cobbett was soon shifting back towards Radicalism. The period 1804 to 1810 saw a gradual change, while two years' imprisonment for seditious libel in 1810 consolidated his oppositional attitudes.

Despite the hostility which this inconsistency has attracted from critics who point to this as yet more evidence of his flawed intellect, Cobbett's political inconsistency actually gained him an important victory over the forces of reaction and helped to create his successful rhetorical space. Writing as a conservative in America, supporting Britain and her monarchy, 'Peter Porcupine' was widely assumed to be a member of the refined elite. As he himself gleefully put it, when discussing the discovery of his real identity and of his impoverished background, it 'is therefore too late to decry my performances as tasteless and illiterate, now it is discovered that the author was brought up at the plough tail, and was a few years ago a private soldier in the British army'.[74] On his return to England, as a staunch and famous supporter of British interests in America, he was personally welcomed as a government ally by Pitt and his cabinet. In this context his later political change presented the Establishment with an insoluble problem. A belated rejection of Cobbett's character and style as vulgar and irrelevant would be as unconvincing for them as it would have been for his American opponents, and as a consequence Cobbett gained a unique status which set him apart from Spence and other plebeian Radicals like Carlile, Wooler or Hetherington. Cobbett became a genuinely working-class Radical writer in possession of an impeccable social and literary pedigree.[75]

This biographical series of social and political transgressions sets in motion the chain of events which leads to Cobbett's mainstream influence, including his acquisition of a weekly newspaper and of a refined audience for the early conservative years of the *Political Register* which he never entirely lost. But if, in this sense, Cobbett is indeed a 'respectable' Radical, as McCalman claims, it is also true that there is a clear link between the blasphemy, pornography and populism of the underworld that McCalman describes and the worst examples of Cobbett's bigoted writings; and that, as we shall see, Cobbett often exploits the same plebeian literary methods which McCalman ascribes to Spence: 'the language and literary forms of the vulgar, poor and semi-literate (including chapbooks, ballads, posters and almanacs)'.[76] This apparent paradox provides us with a clue to the similarly transgressive nature of Cobbett's rhetorical achievement. If he is indeed both refined *and* vulgar, rhetorically a part of both the political mainstream *and* the underworld, then this might explain not only his particular success, but also his curious ability to annoy so many people.[77] This book suggests that Cobbett's self-conscious and polemical solution to increasing class polarization is indeed different to that tried by Paine – perhaps not an attempt at solution at all, but an exploitation of the polarity. Cobbett, I will show, can pragmatically exploit populist motifs and methods – of bigotry, superstition, and combativeness – and reproduce conservative images and values, in a highly self-conscious way, for Radical ends. His potentially uneasy location between a series of oppositions – progressive and regressive Radicalism, respectability and roughness, refinement and vulgarity, influence and marginality – opens up a transgressive rhetorical space in which his particular polemical skills can operate.

Writing of Cobbett's groundbreaking letter 'To the Journeymen and Labourers' of 1816, Olivia Smith makes a similar point, arguing that within it Cobbett 'writes the swinish multitude into a dignified and traditional, particularly Burkean, social fabric' by mimicking and reconciling opposing voices and ideas.[78] But while Smith's stress on the 'healing' nature of this project identifies an aspect of Cobbett's writings to which we will return, I prefer to see this mimicry as challenging and combative, as Cobbett pits one discourse against another, brings oppositions into unexpected congruities, and addresses normally polarized audiences within a single text, in order to *subvert* as well as to resist encroaching social polarization and to oppose the devaluing of the working class. Cobbett's method is to exploit conventional literary polarization in order to undermine his opponents' views, exploring their relationship to the discourses, values and individuals they despise by incorporating opposing voices and playing them off against each other rather than by attempting to develop an alternative, untainted discourse. Cobbett's Radical persona, in other words, resembles the state of his society as I have presented it: combining the familiar and the innovative, the progressive and the unregenerate, combining images of continuity *and* change.

PART I

The creation of Cobbett

CHAPTER I

Early writings 1792–1800

In the previous chapter I suggested that the transgression of class boundaries is central to Cobbett's rhetorical authority, and that his early American writings precipitate this state of affairs as his conservative loyalties and literary success as Peter Porcupine briefly ally him with the English ruling class. How this happens will be the subject of this chapter.

Before we can begin to examine these writings, however, we need to address the problematic issue of Cobbett's ideological inconsistency in the period covered by Part 1 of this study. Turning from apparent Radical in *The Soldier's Friend* of 1792 to apparent conservative in his American writings from 1794, and then back to an increasingly democratic version of Radicalism by 1810, Cobbett was accused by critics and betrayed allies of being inconstant or even mercenary, changing his opinions merely to activate new publishing markets. He defended himself (and has been defended by sympathetic critics since) as fundamentally consistent. The most recent version of this defence has been made by Ian Dyck. He argues that Cobbett's consistently developing interest is in the welfare of the agricultural labourer. Realizing more and more his own self-identification with this rural class, only Cobbett's perception of how their interests are to be safeguarded changes. Between 1794 and 1804, the argument goes, Cobbett believed the Tory Country Party to be the natural guardians of the labourer's interests. In 1804, Dyck argues, empirical evidence to the contrary changes Cobbett's mind back to its previous Radicalism.[1]

While this is probably the most convincing explanation for Cobbett's later ideological change, it does not really explain the earlier shift from Radicalism to conservatism which is the subject of this chapter. The issue is particularly vexed since Cobbett did not claim authorship of the Radical *Soldier's Friend* until very late in life,[2] and never explained its ideological context. In many ways it seems like a false start, lacking particularly the elaborate self-projection of the writings produced from 1794 in America, under the pseudonym 'Peter Porcupine', which seem to mark the real beginning of Cobbett's literary career.

Critical accounts of the transition from the belligerent Radicalism of this piece to the monarchist patriotism of Peter Porcupine tend to follow one of two paths. Either they echo Cobbett's own account of 1804 which declares that his natural chauvinism was irritated into print by the anti-British rhetoric of American Republicans at this time; or they follow Hazlitt in ascribing Cobbett's changes to natural combativeness. Many contemporaries accused him of wilful opposition, identifying in the energetic combativeness which underlies much of his writing the mainspring of his talent – as Hazlitt put it: 'In short, wherever power is, there is he against it: he naturally butts at all obstacles, as unicorns are attracted to oak-trees, and feels his own strength only by resistance to the opinions and wishes of the rest of the world'.[3] Both of these explanations have their attractions, but both leave much unexplained. The former conceals his previous foray into literature with *The Soldier's Friend*, it also omits to mention the letter he wrote to Thomas Jefferson upon his arrival in America, in which he offered Jefferson his literary services and claimed a Radical ambition to become a citizen of a free state.[4] The latter, while it will be of enduring rhetorical relevance to this study, neglects the undeniable continuities traced by critics like Ian Dyck. This chapter does not claim to offer answers to this ideological puzzle, but rather aims to trace the interesting problems, anxieties and at times rhetorical brilliance of the writings of this enigmatic period.

If we accept Cobbett's claim to authorship of *The Soldier's Friend* there are immediate and interesting consequences for our understanding of Cobbett's rhetorical and literary methods. This is the case since in *The Soldier's Friend* many of Cobbett's characteristic stylistic practices and rhetorical tactics are already plain, some of which disappear during his conservative phase only to re-emerge in his Radical maturity, while others form a consistent part of his style regardless of his ideological position. This being so, it seems that while the Radical writings of 1816 to 1835 constitute Cobbett's largest achievement historically, they are not necessarily the culminating point of a smooth stylistic growth. Rather, the achievements of *The Soldier's*

Friend suggest that Cobbett's changing practices are dictated more by his changing contexts than by the state of his talents which seem well-developed at the very start of his career. We will see throughout Part 1, moreover, that many of his practices remain constant, only their meaning changing in different discursive contexts. The following passage from *The Soldier's Friend*, for example, is characterized by the same clarity of expression, preoccupation with truth, direct address to a plebeian audience and indignation at upper-class attitudes towards the poor which we saw in *Paper Against Gold* of 1810–11:

> It particularly becomes you, the British Soldier, to look upon this matter in its proper light... I would have you observe here, and observe it well too, how partially the military law is made to operate. If you should have the fortune to become a non-commissioned Officer, and were to deduct but a penny from a man unlawfully, you know, the consequence would be breaking and flogging, and refunding the money so deducted; but here you see your Officers have been guilty of the practice for years, and now it is found out, not a hair of one of their heads is touched; they are even permitted to remain in the practice, and a sum of money is taken from the public to coax you with, now it seems likely that you may be wanted.[5]

The Soldier's Friend also shares the 'contempuous jocularity' identified by *The Times* as a feature of Cobbett's mature style, as it takes 'the Secretary at War' to task for his equivocal explanation of the recent decrease in soldiers' pay: 'notwithstanding this law, which so positively declares that the Foot Soldier shall receive three shillings *per* week subsistence, it has "so happened of late years that he has had only eighteen pence or two shillings!" It has "*so happened!*" and for years too! astonishing!'[6]

Cobbett's observations concerning the nature and constitution of the nation in *The Soldier's Friend* also anticipate later preoccupations. What does the 'Britishness' of the soldier symbolize in the first passage quoted above? The following extract will show us that Cobbett is already engaged in an attempt to define and redefine patriotism and nationality in ways which, we will see later in this study, are crucial to the formal practices of his later radical discourse. In a way which we will see is characteristic, the following extract from *The Soldier's Friend* resists the appropriation of patriotism as only a conservative value. We have already seen Cobbett asserting that the restitution of monies to the soldiery is a bribe from the ruling class 'now it seems likely that you may be wanted'. A page later he continues:

Soldiers are taught to believe everything they receive, *a gift from the Crown*; – cast this notion from you immediately, and know, that there is not a farthing that you receive but comes out of the *Public Purse*. What you call your *King's Bounty*, or *Queen's Bounty*, is no Bounty from either of them; it is twelve shillings and two pence a year of the public money, which no-one can withhold from you; it is allowed you by an Act of Parliament, while you are taught to look upon it as a present from the King or Queen! I feel an indignation at this I cannot describe. – I would have you consider the nature of your situation, I would have you know that you are not the servant of *one man* only; a British soldier never can be that. You are a servant of the whole nation, of your countrymen, who pay you, and from whom you can have no separate interests.[7]

Cobbett's assertion that the nation consists of all its inhabitants, and not merely of its rulers, is a precursor to his later organic Radicalism which stresses the collective character of 'Old England', and is also the basis for his Radical arguments in favour of universal manhood suffrage and Catholic Emancipation. But Cobbett's early and late unswerving Radical loyalty to the nation, refusing to identify 'Britain' with its rulers, also provides us with a neat and early example of the instability of rhetorical meaning, as we will see next that in the America of the 1790s his patriotism signifies something different. What is less clear is the ideological significance of Cobbett's consistent patriotism in changing circumstances. Does this contextual change of meaning mirror an ideological shift, or conceal an ideological consistency?

Cobbett arrived in Philadelphia in 1792 to find that the revolution debate, to which he had contributed in London with *The Soldier's Friend*, was also raging in America. As in Britain the debate – apparently about a foreign event – was really concerned with domestic politics. The pattern of response to the Revolution followed broadly similar lines in both countries, beginning with enthusiastic welcome, and ending with the ruling class in each turning against the French when it became clear that their Revolution was not merely an attempt to emulate the English or American system, but a radically new departure which in turn might be emulated by their own disaffected publics. Moreover, key texts from the English debate were absorbed into the American one and reworked for American purposes. It is unsurprising that the debates should be so closely related. Not only was America's independence from British rule only sixteen years old in 1792, but the two main texts of the British debate were written by politicians who had supported the American Revolution.

Burke's *Reflections on the Revolution in France* came as a shock to those who had expected him to support the French rebellion. Burke argued however that the American emulation of British governmental structures had granted it a stability which French Jacobinism could never provide.[8] He was also alienated from French Jacobinism by the possibility that it would be imitated in Britain. The immediate catalyst for the publication of the *Reflections* was the appearance of a sermon by the Dissenter Richard Price, entitled *A Discourse on the Love of Our Country*, which argued that cornerstones of the British constitution should be abandoned in imitation of the French model.[9] Burke's perceived betrayal of the Revolutionary cause meant that the *Reflections* in turn elicited numerous replies – the most successful of these being Paine's *Rights of Man*. Burke's assertions that the mainspring of human action should not be reason but feeling and that Enlightenment philosophy robbed power of its beauty; and his emotive picture of the sufferings of Louis and Marie Antoinette led Paine famously to complain that 'he pities the plumage, but forgets the dying bird'.[10]

This conflict between two important commentators on the American Revolutionary struggle dramatized urgent American conflicts, since for Americans the choices posed by the French Revolution were particularly piquant, coming at a time of existing uncertainty and debate over the future of the American state. In the years between the Revolutionary war and the French Revolution the major political battle in the United States had been between the Federalists and Republicans over the ratification of the Federal constitution. This had finally been signed in 1787 only two years before the storming of the Bastille. Written by Federalist politicians led by Washington, the constitution was seen by many to move away from the State independence and democracy of the Revolutionary period, and to emphasize instead executive power and centralization. During the 1790s Federalist constitutional, political, philosophical and imagistic assumptions were coming under attack from Republicans who saw them as part of a centralist counter-revolution against the looser Articles of Confederation which had characterized the Revolutionary period.[11] On 6 March 1794 the Republican *Aurora or General Advertiser* wrote of the Federalists and their constitution as follows:

The question of adopting the new federal constitution of government, formed a Party among us, of such a mind, as will probably subsist in all free states, wherein the power of the Executive is made adequate to the ends, for which such a department can usefully exist. Some well meaning men, of minds and tempers fitted to lean with fondness towards splendour and patronage, or tainted from early life with monarchy, to a degree, of which they were perhaps insensible, or justly alarmed at the hazardous impotence of the existing Congress, thought they saw no danger in anything, but in dissention, anarchy and disunion. Others, of intentions equally good, of minds more erect, active and irritable in respect to their rights, thought they saw no small danger in the constituted and foresaw much more in the constructive powers, that would result, in practice, to all the departments of the new government. Which side was the right side, experience must determine.

It is clear from this extract that the *Aurora*, like Burke, sees the Federal constitution as indebted to British Governmental models, but that for them this is not a desirable state of affairs. While the Federalist Government presented itself as determinedly neutral in its attitude to Britain, and claimed allegiance to the republican ideal, the Republicans accused them of hankerings after aristocracy. An earlier and less measured passage from the *Aurora* of 3 January 1794 had asserted that Congress should examine 'the conduct of that aristocratical Junto with which the Executive is surrounded and which, perhaps against its natural inclination, has made it adopt the tone, the style and the manners of arbitrary sovereigns':

They will examine the mysterious schemes of that faithful copyist of the British ministry, who by his inverted politics has contrived to create a monied aristocracy, give individuals an opportunity of accumulating immense fortunes, which it would have been more expedient and more conformable to republican principles to have divided among the many, who has formed our system of finance on the odious model of that of England, with loans, banks, excises; an embroiled, expensive, unjust and oppressive complication which a free people who cherish their independence ought to have guarded against with the greatest care.[12]

In this state of affairs, the French Revolution and subsequent conflict between France and Britain became potent symbols for Americans. The Republican hostility to British Governmental models was heightened and dramatized by increasing Anglo-American discord on the outbreak of the Revolutionary war in Europe. The British blockaded French ports, captured neutral

Early writings 1792–1800   39

American merchant ships, impressed American citizens of British extraction into the British Navy, refused to remove troops stationed on American territory, and were accused of aiding the American Indians.[13] Domestic and foreign policy consequently became entangled as Republicans argued for intervention in Europe on the French side and for the extension of the American revolution along Jacobin lines, while Federalists stressed the necessity of neutrality, of preserving liberties already achieved, and of avoiding the anarchy and bloodshed which were increasingly characteristic of the French experience.

These arguments and loyalties are reflected in the styles available to and exploited by newspapers of varying political persuasions. The *Columbian Centinel* (which would become perhaps the most respected of the Federalist papers) illustrates this neatly, as it undergoes an ideological change of heart which is clearly reflected in the argumentative tactics and images it adopts. Like most newspapers, it greeted the French Revolution initially with enthusiasm, and wrote on 4 January 1792 in terms which identified the French and American revolutions as part of the same rebellion against tyranny, and which characterized aristocracy as the common enemy of liberty:

> In the preceding year, we have seen the *termination* of the labours of a Body of Patriots, who, illumined by the rays of the *Sun of Liberty*, which arose in the *United States*, have made discoveries of the *Rights of Man*, unparalleled in the History of the World: – We have seen a Monarch, whom *Americans* love and respect, misguided by ambitious counsellors, flying with his family from his kingdom; – and we have seen the citizens of *France*, with a magnanimity superior to all we have read of, in *Romans*, conduct, in safety, that Monarch back to his palace: – We have since seen him, after dismissing those advisors, appear before the assembled Nation, and formally ratify that CONSTITUTION, which forms the basis of his glory as a Patriot King, and the palladium of his, and the Rights of all Frenchmen ... From a picture, so agreeable, we with pain turn to one delineated by the *sombre* pencil. THE COUNTER REVOLUTIONISTS, by whom we mean the refugee Princes and Nobles of *France*, the Princes of the Empire, and the dignified Clergy of *Italy* who drew revenues from *France*, appear by the last accounts, still to menace the tranquillity of *France* ... but these freemen are possessed of the idea that they are invincible – & such we trust they will prove themselves.

In this extract the paper draws on a familiar kind of chiliastic Enlightenment rhetoric which dwells on progress, the triumph of reason over despotism, and the inevitable victory of justice. As well as expressing itself in this Enlightenment tone, the *Centinel* also deploys standard republican and Jacobin words and phrases, like 'sun of liberty', 'rights of man', 'palladium of... Rights' and, later, '*Truth is eternal*'.

The attack on aristocracy in this passage is a characteristic expression of republicanism at this time: hatred of aristocracy is as ingrained in American writing of the period as is the preoccupation with vulgarity and refinement in its British counterpart. Cobbett would taunt his Democratic opponents by filling his bookshop window with aristocratic and royal portraits, for example, while the *Aurora* supported the execution of Louis XVI, printed reports of the trials of French aristocrats, and reprinted on 31 December 1794 the following satirical French attack on counter-Revolutionary writings:

The scribblers form the advanced guard of the aristocrats, a cowardly and effeminate army; some of these gallant troops are now detached to harass the enemy on all sides under favour of the night; unhappily the different parties met each other on the road, and struck with a panic at the appearance of something like men, they fire some shot in the air, and abandon the supposed field of honour with the utmost precipitation...

Given this general abuse of aristocracy, the effect of the execution of Louis on the *Columbian Centinel* is interesting. The paper's support for Louis XVI is clear from the first extract quoted above, and is representative of the views of many Americans. Louis had intervened in the American Revolutionary war on the American side and, in *A Bone to Gnaw for the Democrats*, Cobbett would observe the paradox of American citizens celebrating the execution of Louis on Independence Day: 'a number of Americans assembled to rejoice on account of this blessing, called to the universe at the same time to witness their joy at the murder of him who conferred it!'[14] The execution of Louis leads the *Columbian Centinel* away from support for the French Revolution. And since Burke's is the most powerful conservative voice in the period it is perhaps unsurprising that from this point onwards the *Centinel* begins to adopt Burkean rhetoric and methods of argument. In contrast to its previous rhetoric in celebration of reason, for example, on 4 May 1793 it deploys heavily emotive prose in order to describe 'the Last Twenty Four Hours of the Life of Louis XVI'.

Its defence of the recently ratified Federal constitution similarly recalls Burke's constitutional arguments in favour of the status quo, as it speaks of the constitution as 'the present glorious temple of liberty',[15] as though it were the work of a classical and heroic age, and makes a Burkean analogy between the state and a living organism. Burke had argued that 'a state without the means of some change is without the means of its conservation',[16] and that the Revolution Settlement of 1688 had been an example of beneficial change which yet accorded with the organic nature of the British state – a body which

> is never old, or middle-aged, or young, but in a condition of unchangeable constancy, moves on through the varied tenour of perpetual decay, fall, renovation, and progression. Thus, by preserving the method of nature in the conduct of the state, in what we improve we are never wholly new; in what we retain we are never wholly obsolete.[17]

On 16 January 1796 the *Centinel* makes a similar point, with a similar stress on the value of the status quo, and in a similarly grand style:

> The wise framers of our constitution were not unthoughtful of the dangers of alteration. They have provided for amendments in an orderly way. This part of our system has been generally admired. But however beautiful the theory of amendment may be, a man must be blind to the springs of human action, to the solemn testimony of experience, and to the instructive tragedies of *France*, if he does not mingle some stubborn apprehensions of consequences with his applause of the principle. He will compare the body politic with the body natural, and will feel that you cannot stop the movement of either, like a watch, to mend them. For that stoppage is not remedy but death.

Again like Burke, with his emphasis on the stability granted by the Revolution Settlement of 1688, the *Centinel* stresses the need to conserve gains won and to avoid civic unrest:

> Let not Americans be the dupes lest they should become the victims of a sanguine opinion, that they could pass a second time unharmed through the fire of a revolution. We have now more liberty to lose and less to gain than any nation; we ought, therefore, if we have good sense, to be of all people, the latest and most loth to begin this work...

Burke is not just important for Federalist writers, however. A letter to the Republican *Aurora* of 30 December 1793 recognizes Burke as the voice of British tyranny, and declares his language 'calculated for the meridian of St James, and the suppleness of a commoner'. Similarly, the Republican *National Gazette* seems to rework Burke's observation that the Jacobin agitators in Britain resemble 'half a dozen grasshoppers' who 'make the field ring with their importunate chink, whilst thousands of great cattle, reposed beneath the shadow of the British oak, chew the cud and are silent',[18] when it conversely declares: 'Let not the little buzz of the aristocratic few and their contemptible minions of speculators, tories and British emissaries be mistaken for the exalted and generous voice of the American people'.[19] Again, roles are reversed, as 'aristocrat' becomes a habitual term of Republican abuse.

In America, then, Britain (and Burke as its representative) is a symbol of either moderation and stability, or of the rejected past of tyranny. Republicans look to France and, to a lesser extent, Federalists to Britain in a polarization which, since Britain and France are merely symbols of alternative American futures, disallows any new democratic figuration of Britain. For America, in other words, 'Britain' and 'France' *mean* their existing political constitutions.

This discursive difference between cultures, where the image changes its scope of possible meanings in different contexts, inevitably changes the nature and significance of Cobbett's patriotic rhetoric. In this American context it effectively means alliance with the Federalist conservatives, whose attempt to ratify the unpopular Jay's Treaty with Britain attracted Peter Porcupine's support. The immediate occasion for Cobbett's first American pamphlet however was the arrival of Joseph Priestley in the United States. Priestley's arrival added one more to pro-French, Republican voices, while his comments about British justice served to confirm American prejudice against Britain. Cobbett's attack on Priestley makes clear that his purpose is to assert and defend particularly British interests and to argue for Anglo-American co-operation.

With this publication, then, Cobbett continues the patriotic rhetoric of *The Soldier's Friend* but by doing so he allies himself with an ideological position at odds with the one he has previously held. As we have seen, in the context of the surrounding American debate, Britain represents oligarchy. So even if Cobbett – lately the Radical of *The Soldier's Friend* – is seen here once more to be adopting a patriotic stand, by defending Britain in the United States he is manoeuvred into support of the British Government which he had so lately denounced. These paradoxes seem to be reflected in Peter Porcupine's style as his writings retain the colloquial and witty style conceived with *The Soldier's Friend*, but combine this with pro-aristocratic sympathies and discursive forms in such a way as places him within the transgressive space I ascribed to him in my introductory chapter. So if Cobbett's ideological position is vexed, in other words, it nevertheless creates the conditions for the establishment of his characteristic style. Why Cobbett prefers comedy and personal invective to rational debate with his opponents will, however, raise questions about how defensible Cobbett felt his own position as Peter Porcupine to be.

In order to place Cobbett's transgressive methods in context, we need to begin by sketching in the nature and debts of American journalism. Despite its hostility to conservative rhetoric, both Federalist and Republican journalism closely resembles the press of the aristocratic British state in this period, drawing on several shared journalistic traditions. Given the youth of the American Republic it is unsurprising that its journalism should be indebted to British models, but it is often strange to notice that while the Republican press champions plebeian French democracy, in format and literary style it is as refined as Dr Johnson, and as restricted to readers with certain educational attainments. But the class prejudices which go along with such usage in the English context are missing in America. While its use of language is appropriate for educated readers, for example, the Federalist *American Minerva* boasts in its first issue of 10 December 1793 that Americans of all social status fit this description. In this context (regardless of whether this was really the case) the reader with Jacobin sympathies is not assumed to be illiterate or foolish, nor can Federalist papers adopt a position of powerful condescension towards them. On 2 January 1796 the *Columbian Centinel*, despite its Burkean language, talks across and not down to readers with opposing political views:

Citizens of United America! as you value your present enviable lot, rally round your own good sense! expel from your confidence men who have never ceased to misadvise and deceive you. Be just, be prudent. Listen impartially to the unadulterated language of truth; and above all, guard your peace with anxious vigilance against all the artful snares which are laid for it.

But while the great majority of American newsprint in the period adopts this refined style, its political debate occasionally draws on other less polite traditions shared with Britain. The Federalists would draw increasingly on the model of Swift, portraying French and Republican theories about human nature, the State, and scientific discovery, as Laputan excesses.[20] Stinging personal abuse had been a feature of American journalism from the earliest Colonial period[21] – a tradition polished in Britain by Pope, who enjoyed a large readership in the United States,[22] and also exploited by Wilkes in *The North Briton*, and Junius in his outrageously insulting letters. While Wilkes had described a political opponent as 'the most treacherous, base, selfish, mean, abject, low-lived and dirty fellow, that ever *wriggled* himself into a secretaryship'[23] and Junius had famously informed Lord Mansfield that 'our language has no term of reproach, the mind has no idea of detestation, which has not already been happily applied to you, and exhausted',[24] the death of Benjamin Franklin Bache, editor of the *Aurora*, elicited the following obituary from his opponents: 'The Jacobins are all whining at the exit of the vile Benjamin Franklin Bache. So would they do if one of their gang was hung for stealing. The memory of this scoundrel cannot be too highly execrated.'[25]

Cobbett's contributions to this style of invective have often been criticized, but it is clear that they are part of a shared English and American tradition. If Cobbett's use of invective seemed excessive on his return to Britain, it is perhaps an indication that British political rhetoric of the early nineteenth century was becoming more respectable, in the ways identified by Ian McCalman. Indeed it is interesting that when Cobbett reissued his American writings in a British edition, he felt obliged to tone down certain passages. For example, in *A Bone to Gnaw for the Democrats* he had described Republicans as 'cus-nus': the American edition adds the helpful footnote 'This in the vulgar tongue; means; Bare— A—es',[26] while the English edition remains discreetly silent. Later, the American edition of the pamphlet dramatized the crew of a captured English ship rejecting the offers of friendship proffered by their French captor: '"No," said they, "you French B—r, we are none of your brothers."'[27] The English edition replaces 'B—r' with 'dog'.[28] The extremism of Cobbett's personal attacks was shocking to his American audience nevertheless, as outrageous invective became his trademark in the pamphlets and newspapers he published in the United States.

Cobbett's first American publication was *Observations on the Emigration of Dr Joseph Priestley, and on the Several Addresses Delivered to him on his Arrival at New York*. Priestley had been the main target of a 'Church and King' riot in Birmingham in 1791. A Dissenter and a scientist, he had also supported the French Revolution, and had been involved in plans to celebrate the storming of the Bastille with a dinner in Birmingham on 14 July 1791. This celebration was cut short by a mob (probably incited by reactionary interests) who attacked first the venue of the celebratory dinner, then the city's Dissenting chapels, and finally the homes of the dinner's prominent participants. Priestley's library, and his collection of virtually irreplaceable scientific instruments and priceless manuscripts were destroyed. After a period of official inactivity order was finally restored and two of the mob were hanged. The trial was unsatisfactory, however, as the hanged were obviously scapegoats and the issue of official collusion was not addressed. Though compensated for his personal belongings Priestley was not compensated for his manuscripts. Three years later, when he had settled his affairs, he emigrated to the United States.[29]

Cobbett's attack on Priestley has usually been seen as an unjustifiable and vitriolic one. Despite its rapid notoriety, the *Observations* is a patchy and often disappointing piece of writing from both a political and a literary point of view. It won Cobbett the fame which set him on his pamphleteering path mainly through the extreme choler of its personal attack. Cobbett accused Priestley of wishing to see Birmingham razed to the ground, of preaching anarchy and bloodshed, and of sending his son to France to ask for citizenship at the height of the Terror. While these accusations were extreme, unfounded and often unconvincing, occasionally they struck home in ways which anticipated Cobbett's later and more successful writings, and this is the main interest of the *Observations* for us. The pamphlet's elegant opening, for example, speaks of Priestley's emigration in a way which instantly alerts us to the satirical duplicity of Cobbett's style, where we can take nothing at face value:

When the arrival of Doctor Priestley in the United States was first announced, I looked upon his emigration (like the proposed retreat of Cowley to his imaginary Paradise, the Summer Islands) as no more than the effect of that weakness, that delusive caprice, which too often accompanies the decline of life, and which is apt, by a change of place, to flatter age with a renovation of faculties, and a return of departed genius. Viewing him as a man that sought repose, my heart welcomed him to the shores of peace, and wished him what he certainly ought to have wished himself, a quiet obscurity. But his answers to the addresses of the Democratic and other Societies at New York, place him in quite a different light, and subject him to the animadversions of a public, among whom they have been industriously propagated.[30]

Here, the understated insults imply that Priestley is a foolish old man who should be grateful for the tolerance of Americans rather than seeking to contribute to political life. The long-suffering writer, though magnanimously willing to put up with Priestley's senile vanity, finds himself reluctantly obliged to respond to its unreasonable excess. Since Cobbett's main grudge against Priestley is that he is associated ideologically with France, this subtle attempt to present him as deranged seems similar to the Federalist tendency to identify French principles, philosophy, and science in general, with Laputan madness. In a coarser vein Cobbett would elsewhere nickname Benjamin Franklin the 'lightening-rod man', reducing his experiments with electricity to the level of farce.[31]

If the treacherous gentility of this opening subverts itself in a way hostile to Priestley, the pamphlet is elsewhere in danger of undermining its own procedures by the use of sophistical arguments. Dr Priestley, Cobbett declares, wishes to make the people free against their will: 'if the English choose to remain slaves, bigots, and idolaters, as the Doctor calls them, that was no business of his: he had nothing to do with them.'[32] Once established, however, this extremely dubious argumentative position allows Cobbett cleverly to turn against the Jacobins their own phrases and ideas – of the kind which we earlier saw the *Columbian Centinel* expressing:

'The sunshine of reason will assuredly chase away and dissipate the mists of darkness and error; and when the majesty of the people is *insulted*, or they feel themselves oppressed by *any set of men*, they have the power to redress the grievance.' So the people of Birmingham, feeling their majesty insulted by *a set of men* (and a very impudent set of men too), who audaciously attempted to persuade them that they were '*all slaves and idolaters*,' and to seduce them from their duty to God and their country, rose '*to redress the grievance*.' And yet he complains? Ah! says he, but, my good townsmen,

'————you mistake the matter:
For, in all scruples of this nature,
No man includes *himself*, nor turns
The point upon his own concerns.'

And therefore he says to the people of Birmingham, 'You have been misled.'[33]

The tongue-in-cheek awareness of its own argumentative impudence makes this passage particularly appealing, as does the burlesque of its comic use of Jacobin ideas – for example, where

Cobbett turns the abstract idea of the sovereignty of the people into a physical attribute, so that the mob can feel its 'majesty insulted' like a kick in the pants.

The pamphlet occasionally achieves satirical brilliance. Of the several addresses to Priestley which Cobbett discusses in the *Observations* he remarks, laconically and wittily: 'it is no more than justice to say of these addresses, in the lump, that they are distinguished for a certain barrenness of thought and vulgarity of style, which, were we not in possession of the Doctor's answer, might be thought inimitable'.[34] The pamphlet's use of comedy is patchy, however. In later writings, as we shall see, Cobbett successfully deploys literary criticism as another comic means of attack on his enemies. His early attempts at this style of criticism in this pamphlet misfire as often as they hit home, however, as for example he reproduces a perfectly inoffensive passage from Priestley as an unconvincing example of bad writing and bad grammar.[35]

The pamphlet which followed this first attempt was entitled *A Bone to Gnaw for the Democrats*, and its procedures are far more sure. In this pamphlet Cobbett hones the technique of mixing refinement with vulgarity with pyrotechnic results, and it becomes clear from reading it that Cobbett's primary rhetorical method in America is to place humour above truth.

As with the *Observations*, the *Bone to Gnaw* makes its arguments by entering into a dialogue with opposing writers. Here his principal antagonist is James Callender, author of a pamphlet entitled *The Political Progress of Britain: or, an Impartial History of Abuses in the Government of the British Empire*. This pamphlet had appeared in Scotland in 1793, and was republished in America the following year where its author had fled in expectation of prosecution. Callender's pamphlet opens as follows:

The people of Scotland are, on all occasions, foolish enough to interest themselves in the good or bad fortune of an English prime minister. Lord North once possessed this frivolous veneration, which hath since been transferred to Mr William Pitt; and the Scots, in general, have long been remarked, as the most submissive and contented subjects of the British crown. It is hard to say what obligations have excited that universal and superlative ardour of loyalty, for which, till very lately, we have been so strikingly distinguished.[36]

Here it is instantly apparent that we are in the same stylistic territory as the majority of American newsprint. This is political debate conducted at a high level of earnest refinement. Compare the Preface to *A Bone to Gnaw for the Democrats*:

READER,
If you have a Shop to mind, or any other business to do, I advise you to go and do it, and let this book alone; for I can assure you, it contains nothing of half so much importance to you, as the sale of a skein of thread or a yard of tape. By such a transaction you might possibly make a net profit of half a farthing, a thing though seemingly of small value, much more worthy your attention than the treasures under the State house at Amsterdam, or all the mines of Peru. Half a farthing might lay the foundation of a brilliant fortune, and sooner than you should be deprived of it by this work, though it may be called my offspring, I would, like the worshippers of Moloch, commit it to the flames with my own hands.[37]

This extravagant disclaimer, which is simultaneously an extravagant *claim* for the treasures it contains, is calculated to amuse and attract its reader. The exuberant colloquialism is toned down for a few sentences at the beginning of the pamphlet proper, but soon re-emerges. Why, Cobbett asks, should the author of *The Political Progress of Britain*

come a' the wa' from Edinburgh to Philadelphia to make an attack upon poor old England? And, if this be satisfactorily accounted for, upon principles of domestic philosophy, which teaches us, that froth and scum stopped in at one place will burst out at another, still I must be permitted to ask; what could induce him to imagine, that the citizens of the United States were in any manner, whatever, interested in the affair?[38]

The author of *The Political Progress*, Cobbett tells us, is fully aware of this problem, and for this reason has written that the Republican leader Thomas Jefferson, among others, has approved of the work and has encouraged its publication, Jefferson declaring that 'it contained the most astonishing concentration of abuses, that he had ever heard of'.

And did he, in good earnest, imagine that mixing with such company would render his person sacred and invulnerable? He should have recollected, that though one *scabby* sheep infects a whole flock, he does not thereby work his own cure.

As to *Mr Jefferson*, I must suppose him entirely out of the Question; for no body that has the least knowledge of the *morality* and *refined taste* of that Gentleman, will ever believe, that he could find any thing worthy of *respect* in a production, evidently intended to seduce the rabble of North Britain. Besides, upon looking a second time over the words attributed to *Mr Jefferson*, I think, it is easy to discover, that the quotation is erroneous: the word *abuses*, I am pretty confident, should be *abuse*; and thus, by leaving out an *s*, the sentence expresses exactly what one would expect from such a person as *Mr Jefferson*: 'that the work contained the most astonishing concentration of *abuse*, that he had ever heard of.'[39]

Cobbett's use of colloquial language both shocked and entranced his American audience.[40] The outrageous application of phrases like 'froth and scum' and 'scabby sheep' are brilliantly insulting, while the comments on Jefferson are incisively double-edged and the rewriting of his comment on the *Political Progress* is inspired. This testimonial from Jefferson becomes a recurring theme throughout the pamphlet: later, Cobbett sums up the contents of the measured and restrained *Political Progress* in the following entirely unjust terms:

it contains the most sophistical and ill-digested account of the national debt, the wars, taxes, and expences [*sic*] of government in Great Britain, that has ever yet appeared; in short, the piece, altogether, forms one of the most complete Whiskey-boy Billingsgate libels, or as *Mr Jefferson* emphatically expressed it, 'the most astonishing concentration of abuse,' that ever was seen, or heard of.[41]

As well as turning Jefferson brilliantly against Callender, this is surely a good tongue-in-cheek description of Cobbett's own outrageously extreme and libellous methods.

If this is one style of political argument, the intensely genteel manner which Cobbett also occasionally affects invokes the commoner tradition of refinement with which he is surrounded. In so far as his pamphlet is framed as a response to another, Cobbett is a reviewer, and he consequently exploits the traditional authority of the reviewer as the 'Greybeard'. He stresses the maturity and authority of written opinion of which – it is implied – his is an example, and which grants him an unforgiving eye for the failings and evasions of others:

When a person sits down to write, his mind must be in some sort composed; time is necessary for the arrangement of his ideas: what he has written must be examined with care; he augments, curtails, corrects and improves. All this naturally implies the most mature reflection, and makes an assertion or an opinion in print be justly regarded as irretractable.[42]

We shall see in the next chapter how his conservativism relates to that of Dr Johnson. Here it is worth noticing the portentous Johnsonian gravity of Cobbett's remarks on composition – especially in contrast to his own methods.

In the passages from the *Bone to Gnaw for the Democrats* quoted here, then, Cobbett creates for himself a character at once aristocratic and vulgar, as he deploys ideas of refinement and vulgarity and indirectly questions Jefferson's right to the title of 'Gentleman', while at the same time expressing these ideas through startlingly coarse imagery. This pamphlet swings between colloquialism and Johnsonian diction, insult and an exaggerated concern with gentility and refinement. The result is exhilarating and disarming: it seems that, while his aims may be serious, his method is to raise laughs at the expense of his enemies and, crucially, at his own expense, as the ludicrous insults and accusations of libellous extravagance in others seem to be self-referentially tongue-in-cheek. When his enemies published a cartoon depicting Peter Porcupine spewing out vitriolic hatreds, while Liberty and the American eagle sat by and wept, Cobbett retorted: 'I believe most of those who have read my essays will do me the justice to say, that I have endeavoured to make America laugh instead of weep.'[43] The implication of this statement, taken together with his American pamphlets, is that, however damaging and extreme his invective, the function of his comic attacks is not to reveal truths. But nor is it merely to create a basis of goodwill and collusion between himself and the public he entertains. Cobbett's comedy is challenging and subversive as it attempts to seduce readers into *traitorous* laughter, treacherously at the expense of their own beliefs.

If his persona's class is changeable according to the occasion, then so is his nationality. His stress on refinement and vulgarity makes him sound British, but he takes pains explicitly to dramatize himself in the pamphlet as an American citizen of long standing. He reports Republican demands to remove a statue of George II from a church in Philadelphia as follows: 'The church is full as well without it, as with it. I have frequented Christ Church for near about thirty years, without ever observing that such a thing was on the walls of it'.[44] This recalls Cobbett's claim in the *Observations* that an anti-British prejudice is 'not only excusable, but almost commendable, in Americans', of which he counts himself one: 'I am one of those who wish to believe that foreigners come to this country from choice, and not from necessity. America opens a wide field for enterprise ... this is what brings foreigners amongst us ...'[45]

This pragmatic self-presentation, and the sophistry of his arguments lead him into usages which have attracted criticism. The *Observations*, for example, breaks into an allegory which is clearly indebted to Jonathan Swift's *Battle of the Books* and which is also apparently anti-abolitionist:

> *The Pot-Shop, a Fable.*
> In a pot-shop, well stocked with ware of all sorts, a discontented ill-formed pitcher unluckily bore the sway. One day, after the mortifying neglect of several customers, 'Gentlemen,' said he, addressing himself to his brown brethren in general, 'Gentlemen, with your permission, we are a set of tame fools, without ambition, without courage; condemned to the vilest uses, we suffer all without murmuring: let us dare to declare ourselves, and we shall soon see the difference. That superb ewer, which, like us, is but earth; those gilded jars, vases, china, and, in short, all those elegant nonsenses, whose colours and beauty have neither weight nor solidity, must yield to our strength, and give place to our superior merit.'
> This civic harangue was received with peals of applause, and the pitcher (chosen president) became the organ of the assembly. Some, however, more moderate than the rest, attempted to calm the minds of the multitude; but all those which are called jordens, or chamber-pots, were become intractable; eager to vie with the bowls and cups, they were impatient, almost to madness, to quit their obscure abodes, to shine upon the table, kiss the lip, and ornament the cupboard.[46]

This story works on two levels. First, it is an allegory for the class war of the French Revolution, as the obscure and unglamorous sections of china society overthrow their betters. As such an allegory, the choice of china to symbolize human beings is one which fits neatly with the conservative message that certain sections of society are intended for labour and some for privilege, and that to overturn these relationships is laughable or dangerous.

In its context in the pamphlet, however, this allegory is not directly about the French experience, but is actually an argument against the abolition of slavery. The 'brown brethren' who labour and rebel represent the slaves on whose behalf Priestley has appealed upon his arrival in America. Of Priestley and his like, immediately before the fable of the '*Pot Shop*', Cobbett declares 'So! These gentlemen are hardly landed in the United States before they begin to cavil against the government, and to pant after a *more perfect state of society*!' Americans will sort out abolition for themselves, and in their own time, he adds.[47]

It is apparent from the wider context of Cobbett's American journalism that this argument about slavery is pragmatic however. With its fable of the '*Pot-Shop*', the pamphlet seems to appeal to American Jacobins to recognize the inconsistency of their own position, as their expressions of belief in equality are contradicted by their ownership of slaves. In this pamphlet the implication is that Cobbett and his Jacobin readers will at least agree that slavery is in the natural order of things, like the natural inferiority of chamberpots to fine china, and that a slave rebellion will lead to catastrophe as the china rebellion leads to a pile of broken pots. This granted, the implication seems to be that the reader will be obliged to rethink his support of the French Revolution for the same reasons.

This fairly conciliatory attitude to the American Jacobins and their slaves is contradicted by the pamphlet which followed. In *A Bone to Gnaw for the Democrats* Cobbett highlights the hypocrisy of American Jacobinism in a way which seems implicitly critical of slavery. After quoting a series of Jacobin toasts, reported by an unnamed newspaper, he declares:

To these extracts I shall take the liberty of adding two others, both from the same Newspaper; one of them is an elegant account of the close of a Civic feast, and the other, though not absolutely on the same subject as the first, certainly adds to its beauty. The first is the precious jewel, and the last the foil: I shall therefore place them as near as possible to each other.

'After this the Cap of Liberty was placed on the head of the President, then on each member. The Marseillois hymn and other similar songs were sung by different French citizen members. Thus chearfully glided the hours away of this feast made by congenial souls to commemorate the happy day, when the sons of Frenchmen joined the sons of America to overthrow tyranny in this happy land.'

'"FOR SALE", TWO NEGRO LADS ONE ABOUT TWELVE AND THE OTHER ABOUT FIFTEEN YEARS OLD – BOTH REMARKABLY HEALTHY; – THE YOUNGEST IS NEAR FOUR FEET NINE INCHES HIGH, AND THE OLDEST ABOVE FIVE FEET. – ALSO A NEGRO WENCH FOR SALE, COMING EIGHTEEN YEARS OLD, AND FAR ADVANCED WITH CHILD – BUT VERY STRONG AND CAPABLE OF ANY KIND OF WORK.' !!![48]

Such variation between – and even within – pamphlets on the issue of slavery, along with Cobbett's later English declaration that less time should be spent worrying about slaves abroad, and more about starving labourers at home,[49] indicates the pragmatism with which he approaches the issue. It seems to be the case that his printed views on slavery alter simply as required to score maximum points over his adversaries. Such pragmatism about issues on which we expect consistency has won Cobbett much criticism. But like his pragmatic willingness to change even his nationality for rhetorical effect, this inconsistency seems clearly to be an example of artifice rather than thoughtlessness, freeing him to make the best argument available for the particular audience and particular issue he is addressing. This may undermine the credibility of his arguments intellectually but, as we have already seen, Cobbett's tactic is not the logical persuasion of his readers. Like his seductive comedy, this intriguing and at least rhetorically impressive flexibility of principle may be more likely to slip under the intellectual guard of hostile readers than clear, consistent and therefore answerable arguments.

The entertaining pragmatism, inconsistency and apparent opposition for opposition's sake of Cobbett's early journalism is neatly demonstrated by the obvious pleasure he takes in a 'bear garden interlude'[50] entitled *A Kick for a Bite; or, Review upon Review ... in a Letter to the Editor, or Editors, of the American Monthly Review*. Here Cobbett counter-attacks a recent critical review of *A Bone to Gnaw for the Democrats* not in ideological but in personal and literary-critical terms.

> In addressing myself to you, on the present occasion, I feel a considerable embarrassment on account of your number. I do not mean the number of your shop, but the number of your person. From certain circumstances, which shall here be nameless, I was led to suppose you of the singular; but your Review for February seems to contradict this supposition. However, whether you are one, and have only made use of the plural pronoun *we*, and its correspondent *our*, in imitation of the style royal; or whether, like Legion, you are really many, I hope, no charge of impoliteness will be brought against me for addressing you as an individual; since it may be fairly presumed, that no more than one person can have been employed in the composition of one page, and since it is very clear, that there is but one page of original composition in all your Review.[51]

Bearing in mind the general detestation of aristocracy that we have already noted to be general in American journalism, Cobbett's insinuation that the Editor of the *Monthly Review* has royal pretensions and sympathies is particularly mischievous. Moreover, as it is juxtaposed to a reference to the Editor's 'shop', the blow is compounded by Cobbett's snobbery. The passage continues by lulling the reader into a sense of security by seeming to consist of social small talk, until the paragraph ends with the smartest blow of all, its attack on the *Review*'s unoriginality.

Cobbett's main weapon in the article is the application of his grammatical skills to the Editor's review article of *A Bone to Gnaw for the Democrats.* The full joke is concealed from his immediate audience, as at this stage they are ignorant of Cobbett's true identity, and that his first occupation on reaching the United States was as an English teacher to French émigrés. But that the Editor is having an essay marked in public is clear despite this. Cobbett marks it well, explaining the article's grammatical failings clearly and making them seem glaringly obvious, rather than making himself seem pedantic, but the assessment is made at the expense of the Editor's dignity.

'Well, but what *are* the *means?...* Simple *laughter.*' And nothing else Sir? Nothing but simple laughter? *Are* the *means* simple *laughter?* Why then, simple *laughter are* the *means*; and if it be good english to say, that simple *laughter are* the *means,* so it is to say, that a simple *Review are* the *books.*

You seem, my dear Sir, to be very anxious to scrape acquaintance with me; observe then; if you should see a person with one ear hanging down upon his cheek, like the ear of an old sow, that is PETER PORCUPINE, at your service. – For, you must know, when I was a little boy at school, this self same phrase 'simple *laughter are* the *means,*' happened to come blundering into my translation; for which the enraged brutal pedagogue ... after having loaded me with half a score dunces and numskulls, seized me by the unfortunate ear, and swinging me in the air, as huntsmen do young hounds, to see if they are of the right breed, left me in the condition above described. From the indignation that I cannot help expressing at this treatment, you may easily imagine, Mr. Reviewer, that I cannot wish to see the same happen to you.[52]

Little needs to be said of the bulk of this passage, the humour being obvious and self-explanatory. But the grotesquely fantastical anecdote Cobbett tells is an instance of his frequent use of satirical methods associated with Hogarth and Cruikshank. This image of Cobbett hanging by the ear from the fist of his enraged schoolmaster is political cartooning in words,[53] and his readiness to depict himself in this grotesque and ludicrous way perhaps implies a sense of superiority that can afford to indulge in self-mockery in order to achieve its political point. Yet the genuine humour of the passage, even apart from its scurrility and snideness, suggests a zest for the form which also overrides concern with personal dignity. Cobbett undoubtedly took his political role in America extremely seriously – claiming in an open 'Letter to the Rt Honourable William Pitt' of 1804 that his 'exertions ... were such as hardly to be credited, if they were fully described, and the effect they produced cannot possibly be conceived by any one who was not a witness of them'[54] – but his preferred stylistic tactic is to abandon serious argument in favour of comic transgression of discursive norms, mingling opposing linguistic usages in *A Bone to Gnaw for the Democrats*, or, as in *A Kick for a Bite*, using a courteous and refined form at odds with its insulting content.

Cobbett's terms of reference in *A Kick for a Bite* are determinedly refined ones, as he presents his subject as that of correct grammar and portrays it in metaphors drawn from the law: 'the *Bone to Gnaw, for the Democrats*, has awakened in you the dormant powers of criticism: you have, at last, entered on the exercise of your censorian function, and the offending production has been summoned to your bar'. But while the manner and the preoccupations may be refined, the use of satire and sarcasm in productions like this one is by no means genteel. We can see a movement during the first paragraph of the pamphlet from his teasing interpretation of the Editor's use of the plural pronoun 'we', through the ceremonial apologies for the possible incorrectness of his mode of addressing the Reviewer, to a direct insult at its conclusion. Cobbett continues to make no bones about his contempt for the Editor's intellect, as he declares his aim is to 'prove ... that you are totally unqualified for judging of that, or any other literary performance'.[55] The adoption of a patronizing tone of mock concern towards the Editor, and a blissful unawareness that the Editor might be intending him harm as he benevolently worries that his opponent might damage *himself*, also make the insults very funny: 'When I see you flourishing with a metaphor, I feel as much anxiety as I do when I see a child playing with a razor.'[56]

Upon the subject of rhetorical figures, Cobbett discourses with a verbal grace, and a stress on balance as the hallmark of beauty, worthy of Pope and his Augustan contemporaries: 'Bold figures are sometimes graceful and every way becoming; but in a cool *critique* none ought to be attempted, except such as tend to illustration; such as light, without dazzling. The figure that has taken up so much of our time, is so far from being of this description, that it absolutely throws an obscurity over the whole passage.'[57] Here the *Essay on Criticism* seems to combine with *The Dunciad*. And cleverly, Cobbett turns on his opponent for misuse of verbal techniques that his Augustan tone suggests he might recommend, as he criticizes the Editor's tautological use of 'mirthful laughter' merely to balance 'ferocious grin'. Cobbett suggests that the Editor might be driven to such infelicities by a desire to please the 'fair sex', who he claims enjoy such a 'see-saw' or 'up-and-down style'. Whatever may be the indelicate implications of attributing such enjoyments to 'ladies', he phrases his disapprobation in genteel language, seeming to mimic even the thoughts and values of the upper class: 'but, though pleasing the fair sex ought to be a capital consideration with every one who puts pen to paper, yet it is certainly unseemly in a grave Reviewer, to affect the silly lisping style of a writer of love-letters. A downy chin covers a multitude of sins, which a grey beard serves only to expose'.[58]

While this sentence is characterized by the same literary paralleling and balance that Cobbett has been discussing – 'downy chin ... grey beard' – it seems to signal a turning away from the social inanities that he has been previously uttering, moving like the opening paragraph from a position of politeness to one of insult. In fact this seems to be a constant feature of the pamphlet as a whole, as the gestures of geniality are repeatedly subverted by sharp and self-consciously courtly satire. For example, Cobbett feigns concern at the Editor's lack of literary talent, and attempts 'helpful' suggestions as to alternative employment. After canvassing – and rejecting – the possibility that the Editor may be fitted for manual work, Cobbett appears to despair: 'You will say that you must live, some how or other; to which I shall answer in the words of a French courtier, to whom a certain libellist addressed the same observation: "*Ma foi, je n'en vois pas la necessité.*"'[59]

This courtly reference draws our attention to the counter-revolutionary self-confidence of Cobbett's American journalism which identifies him with earlier aristocratic American writers like James Rivington who wrote during the 1770s and 1780s. Rivington affected scarlet, gold and lace in his clothing, projected himself as urbane and cultured in his paper, and had his shop smashed by the mob in reply.[60] With his first publications Cobbett drew similar threats from Republicans and, as I have already noted, also drew accusations of aristocratic origins. It is interesting then that his extremely scurrilous invective seems to work in the same way as the exuberant writings of the Cavaliers a century and a half earlier. Representing established power, whose traditional confidence is expressed by the fact that it perceives itself as divinely ordained, the Royalists' writings were characterized by self-confidence, apparent enjoyment in deriding their opponents, and extremely vicious personal insults. While their opponents trod carefully, the Royalists launched broadsides against Cromwell himself: G. A. Cranfield

Early writings 1792–1800

quotes the continuous stream of personal jokes: 'he was, variously, "Noll-Nose", "His Nose-shippe", "King Nose", "Coppernosed Noll", or, more elaborately, "High and Mighty Cromwell, King of Cruelty, Lord of Misrule... and NOSE almighty"'.[61] Obscenity was also a favourite means of attack: 'that right reverend Father in Rebellion, Lust and Lies, Hue Peters... tickles up his Welch Buttocks at Milford-haven, levells his Petard, gives fire, and makes breaches between the Hamms of the Welsh Runts, reducing to the obedience of his Lust-y Masters at Westminster sometimes half a dozen in a day'.[62] Cranfield suggests that the obscenity of the seventeenth-century Royalists associated them dangerously with the salacious street literature of the 'mob', and that the enfranchized nation's fear of that class was partly responsible for the subsequent elimination of such obscene vulgarity from political debate in the eighteenth and early nineteenth centuries.[63] This is interesting as it indicates the dual nature of this kind of invective: at once self-confidently aristocratic, yet expressed through the populist language and preoccupations of the people.

Perhaps Cobbett's mixture of aristocratic and plebeian styles which, like the writings of the Cavaliers, implies a cheerful certainty of his superiority made him particularly infuriating. The revelation of his entirely plebeian, impeccably non-aristocratic, origins a year later with the publication of his agricultural autobiography *The Life and Adventures of Peter Porcupine* must have compounded his opponents' irritation. It certainly made him difficult to attack without betraying his opponents' latent snobbery, which ill accorded with their ostensible political position. James Quicksilver for one is caught out in this way in his review of *The Life and Adventures of Peter Porcupine*: 'If to be descended from an illustrious family reflects honor on any man, as Porcupine judiciously observes... it is certainly a pity that he should have been born in a cottage with two windows only, and that he should be the humble son of an obscure, mulish farmer'.[64] This attack seems particularly ill-judged, as by deriding Cobbett's origins and ancestry Quicksilver is in danger of deriding a large proportion of his readers. Agricultural interests are strongly represented in American newspapers of the 1790s. The Federalist *American Minerva* devoted large sections of its paper to matters likely to be of special interest to its farming readers – for example, the edition of 18 December 1793 is largely given over to an essay 'on the management of the DIARY, [*sic*] particularly with respecting to the MAKING and

CURING OF BUTTER.' Moreover, the figure of the farmer is a recurring one in the tradition of republican American political journalism. Over the winter of 1793 'A Farmer of the Back Settlements' contributed a series of articles to the *Aurora* which discussed the political events of the day. More famously, during the struggle for Independence twenty-five years earlier, John Dickinson had contributed a series of letters to the *Pennsylvania Chronicle and Universal Advertiser* under the collective title *Letters from a Farmer in Pennsylvania to the Inhabitants of the British Colonies* which had been a decisive influence on the Revolutionary debate. These famous letters give the figure of the farmer a cachet in American political journalism which makes James Quicksilver's gibes seem particularly inappropriate.

Dickinson's letters are also interesting for us, as the opening of the first letter of the series seems to provide a model for Cobbett's autobiographical writings in *The Life and Adventures of Peter Porcupine*. Here is Dickinson:

My Dear Countrymen,
I am a FARMER, settled after a variety of fortunes, near the banks, of the river *Delaware*, in the province of *Pennsylvania*. I received a liberal education, and have been engaged in the busy scenes of life: But am now convinced, that a man may be as happy without bustle, as with it. My farm is small, my servants are few, and good; I have a little money at interest; I wish for no more: my employment in my own affairs is easy; and with a contented grateful mind, I am compleating the number of days allotted to me by divine goodness.[65]

The occasional colloquialism, the willingness to introduce the self before entering into political discussion, and the depiction of the writer's surroundings as a kind of tranquil touchstone for the disinterested nature of his views: these are all in some way recalled by the opening to Cobbett's *Life and Adventures of Peter Porcupine*:

To be descended from an illustrious family certainly reflects honour on any man, in spite of the sans-culotte principles of the present day. This is, however, an honour that I have no pretension to. All that I can boast of in my birth, is, that I was born in Old England; the country from whence came the men who explored and settled North America; the country of Penn, and of all those to whom this country is indebted.

With respect to my ancestors, I shall go no further back than my grandfather, and for this plain reason, that I never heard talk of any prior to him. He was a day-labourer; and I have heard my father say, that he worked for one farmer from the day of his marriage to that of his death, upwards of forty years. He died before I was born, but I have often slept beneath the same roof that had sheltered him, and where his widow dwelt for several years after his death. It was a little thatched cottage, with a garden before the door. It had but two windows; a damson tree shaded one, and a clump of filberts the other. Here I and my brothers went every Christmas and Whitsuntide to spend a week or two...[66]

Written in response to accusations about his past as wildly inaccurate as many of Cobbett's own slurs on others, the *Life and Adventures* asserts the discomfitingly plebeian nature of his background, challenging to democratic adversaries. This self-revelation, like Dickinson's, seems to vouch that his views are disinterested; and, like Dickinson's, the autobiography allows the development of a new more comfortable relationship between the writer and his reader. This adoption of tactics associated with a respected figure in American republican history for the purpose of granting his own pro-British writings credibility, along with the mix of colloquialism and gentility in his earlier writings, anticipates some of the most successful transgressive methods of Cobbett's Radical maturity.

During the late 1790s Cobbett continued to produce a large amount of material characterized by more or less the same exuberant style. Cobbett began his daily newspaper *The Porcupine Gazette* in 1797, with a blunt statement of its principles. Unlike other papers, whose political loyalties are determined by 'the caprice of the multitude, the length of the purses of certain wholesale subscribers, &c. &c.':

My politics, such as they are, are known to everyone; and few, I believe, doubt of their continuing the same.
Professions of impartiality I shall make none. They are always useless, and are besides perfect nonsense, when used by a news-monger: for, he that does not relate news as he finds it, is something worse than partial... To profess impartiality here, would be as absurd as to profess it in a war between Virtue and Vice, Good and Evil, Happiness and Misery.[67]

This stands in stark contrast to the similar statement of principles which had been made by the *American Minerva* upon its inception on 10 December 1793. The *Minerva*'s editor, though politically aligned with the party Cobbett would support, conceived his task as a far more judicial one:

The Editor will endeavour to preserve this Paper *chaste* and *impartial*. Confidence, when secrecy is necessary or proper, will never be violated. Personalities, if possible, will be avoided; and should it ever be deemed proper to insert any remarks of a personal nature, it will be held an indispensable condition, that the name of the writer be previously left with the Editor.

Cobbett's paper increasingly represents everything that the *Minerva* vows to avoid. While his writings had always dealt with personalities and been framed in terms of personal invective, his later newspaper writing – as many critics note – became more acrimonious, and eventually a good deal less enjoyable and effective. Indeed, it would be due to accumulating libel cases that he would eventually leave the United States and return to England in 1800. His principal opponent in these years was Dr Benjamin Rush whose draconian treatment of the yellow fever which swept Philadelphia at regular intervals, Cobbett (rightly) claimed cost many lives. Rush prosecuted Cobbett for libel and won – a success which made emigration a necessity for financial reasons. But Cobbett was not always the innocent and injured party. The tone of the *Gazette* is uniformly shrill and extreme and, though he was undoubtedly the victim of much similar abuse, passages such as the following redefine his previously funny if abrasive persona, turning Peter Porcupine into a violent, vindictive and maniacal presence:

Ha! ha! ha! ha! – Do you know what I am laughing at, Tench? – To think of your publishing your negro-like defence in *Bradford's paper*. To see you flying for shelter under the wing of Tom Bradford, has diverted me more than anything that this farcical world ever exhibited to my view. – Why, man, it was this very Tom Bradford, that first gave me information respecting you! It was he that gave me *notices* for your history; it was he that told me all about your famous *triumphal entry*; and, O lud! how he used to grind his tusks and curse, in telling me, that you had been rewarded with a fat office, under the Federal government, to the exclusion of some good honest whig like himself.[68]

It could be argued that with the birth of the daily *Porcupine Gazette* Cobbett's American writings lost much of their verve, as they ceased to be occasional and became routine. But it might also be true that these flawed and disturbing texts merely highlight an uneasiness implicit in their more successful predecessors, concerning the potential intellectual bankruptcy of their reliance on comedy and invective as opposed to argument.

The successful qualities of Peter Porcupine's pamphlets – their inspired and witty insults, their mixture of genteel and colloquial language, and their turning of opponents' styles and arguments back upon those who espouse them – will re-emerge in Cobbett's Radical English prose, but in a much subdued form and with different significances in so far as their changed political context again changes their meanings. The sheer pragmatic exuberance of these American writings is never recaptured. Certainly, as we shall see in the next chapter, Cobbett was obliged to modify his literary style upon his return to England in 1800 in order to conform to the prevailing assumptions, images and available discourses of early nineteenth-century English journalism.

CHAPTER 2

A version of reaction

Cobbett returned home from America in 1800, famous for his pro-British, anti-democratic writings as Peter Porcupine, to a welcome from Pitt's Tory administration and offers of control over various newspapers sponsored by the government. Refusing these offers (but accepting private financial help from the Tory William Windham) Cobbett began his independent *Weekly Political Register* in 1802. As Asa Briggs points out, however, Cobbett was fortunate in the timing of the first issue. Addington had taken over from Pitt as Prime Minister in 1801, and under his leadership the Peace of Amiens had been achieved. Cobbett, objecting to this compromise with Bonaparte, adopted a tone far from sycophantic towards his former allies. Thus, having made his name in America as a dissenting voice, here too he 'could be both patriot and critic at the same time', criticizing the peace as undermining national honour, security, and martial traditions.[1]

Cobbett's early English writings are thus not in any simple relationship to the status quo. This chapter will explore the language and methods of his version of reaction, beginning by exploring the literary environment into which he enters on his return to England in 1800 and ending with close readings of three *Political Register* articles from 1802. As Cobbett perceives his place as being firmly within the mainstream of enfranchised political debate in this period, an initial examination of broadly 'refined' writings is appropriate. This contextual exploration will allow us to see the nature and interest of Cobbett's apparently conservative writings. As we shall see in the ensuing analysis, while he skilfully reproduces the stylistic practices of his peers his early writings are, nevertheless, frequently problematical and self-contradictory and often betray anxiety as to the nature of his real and his preferred audiences. These tensions are interesting in the light of his imminent ideological switch towards Radicalism. The way in which they are manifested will also be relevant to our later examination of Cobbett's radical style.

Since at this Tory stage in Cobbett's career we are most interested in mainstream English writing, representing enfranchised voices, it is necessary to look back to eighteenth-century journalistic models. This is the case because to understand refined political discourse in the period it is necessary to appreciate its traditional self-sufficiency. This is neatly demonstrated by the example given by James Boulton of an exchange between two political opponents of the 1780s, Dr Johnson and John Wilkes. Tory Johnson is notorious for a use of lexis and syntax designed to specify his readership as a refined one and to assert his membership of the intellectual and political elite.[2] Johnson's language use exposes him to ridicule from 'Radical' Wilkes, and at first this seems to be an example of political conflict which plays by the rules of refinement and vulgarity described by Olivia Smith. Thus the opening paragraph of Johnson's *False Alarm* develops a comparison between superstition and fear of government and ends with the assertion that the populace is now no more afraid of government than it is of signs and portents. In Johnson's words: 'The sun is no more lamented when it is eclipsed, than when it sets; and meteors play their coruscations without prognostic or prediction.' Wilkes responded with glee, seeming to highlight Johnson's verbal snobbery and to assert the contrary value of clarity: 'Believe me, Sir, the *intellectual sight* of ordinary freeholders is liable to be *offusqued* by a *superfluous glare* of erudition. The dimension of OUR understanding is not of the proper magnitude to admit of *sesquipedalian documents*. OUR undisciplined taste is apt to be nauseated by the reduplicated *evomition* of unknown idioms'.[3]

But it is obvious from a closer look at this exchange between government and opposition writers that it is in fact a world away from the kind of conflict between classes that Radical historians describe and which Olivia Smith presents as the problem which Paine, Hone and Cobbett among others attempt to address. Regardless of Wilkes's role in the history of Reform, this is a literary exchange firmly restricted to fellow members of the elite. The humour of Wilkes's attack depends upon our understanding of the words Wilkes uses, since the joke is that he is describing his own inability to understand long words in language more obscure than Johnson's. In this way, mainstream political writing whether ministerial or oppositional shares a common style which in turn encodes certain elitist assumptions about its readership and, by extension, about what kinds of readership are appropriate to political discourse in general.

These stylistic features persist in conservative writings of the 1790s and beyond, but in the climate of plebeian self-assertion created by the French Revolution the assumption that political debate will be dominated by the enfranchised and educated is no longer so implicit. As several critics have noted, for writers of the 1790s the display of educational and social superiority becomes a self-conscious weapon against lower-class presumption. Thus, for example, James Boulton identifies the deep coherence of Burke's *Reflections* on a stylistic and conceptual plane, where not only does the repetition of primal images of home, family and nature manipulate the emotional responses of the reader and extract his concurrence, but the stylistic procedures enact the ideological matter, and the text becomes a self-validating document.[4] Olivia Smith elaborates on this view of Burke's stylistic tactics, by pointing to the way in which his sense of a necessary tradition and hierarchy is supported syntactically by his use of adjectives coupled with nouns, to imply the necessity of the status quo, in so far as it implies that 'there is one way in which we are compelled to respond to things.' Smith also points to the way in which verbs in the *Reflections* are 'hardly noticeable', only able to 'augment the power of objects'; implicitly denying 'the possibility of choice or action'.[5] This self-conscious enactment of philosophical and cultural values is also apparent in the 'Prospectus' to the *Anti-Jacobin*, a paper written largely by Government ministers. Expecting certain things of its readership, and assuming its own superiority, the paper can afford to reverse the moral value of its assertions, smugly confident that the reader will set it back to rights: 'We confess, whatever disgrace may attend such a confession, that We have not so far gotten the better of the influence of long habits and early education ... but that We have our feelings, our preferences, and our affections, attaching on particular places, manners, and institutions, and even on particular portions of the human race'.[6] This opening declaration from the Prospectus clearly recalls Burke, and his celebration of the 'little platoon'[7] from which we develop our wider affections. It also follows Burke in stressing the centrality of tradition, socialization and prejudice. The *Anti-Jacobin* goes on to confess itself '*prejudiced*' and uses the term mock-pejoratively, but the implication is clearly the same as Burke's, that prejudice represents the wisdom of the ages.[8] In other words, what is and has been is good; innovation is an unpredictable and unnatural mutation on the prevailing order.

'In MORALS We are equally old-fashioned. We have yet to learn the modern refinement of referring in all considerations upon human conduct, not to any settled and preconceived principles of right and wrong, not to any general and fundamental rules which experience, and wisdom, and justice, and the common consent of mankind have established, but to the internal admonitions of every man's judgement or conscience in his own particular instance.

The invocation of concepts like experience and wisdom implies that morality, like the law, is based on 'the common consent of mankind' established over long ages. This is explicitly preferred to 'the internal admonitions' of every individual. In the context of this strong sense of the rightness of the cause conferred by antiquity, the *Anti-Jacobin* wilfully disregards the possibility that the new concept of covenant between a freely-chosen government and its electors may hold some value. The Jacobin doctrine

is formed not on a system of reciprocal duties, but on the supposition of individual, independent, and unconnected rights; which teaches that all men are pretty equally honest, but that some have different notions of honesty from others, and that the most received notions are for the greater part the most faulty...[9]

Here the paper adopts a vulgar tone with 'pretty equally honest' and by doing so suggests that there is an ignorant naiveté to Radical thought, as it implies a slipshod and inadequate reasoning faculty.

In the fifth number of 11 December 1797 the paper parodies Southey's 'The Soldier's Wife'. The paper introduces the poem as an example of Jacobin selfishness in contrast to its claim to benevolence. The paper quotes the first three stanzas of Southey's poem as follows:

THE SOLDIER'S WIFE
DACTYLICS

Weary Way-wanderer, languid and sick at heart,
Travelling painfully over the rugged road;
Wild-visaged Wanderer! Ah! for thy heavy chance.

Sorely thy little ones drag by thee barefooted,
Cold is the baby that hangs at thy bending back –
Meagre and livid, and screaming its wretchedness.

> Woe-begone mother, half anger, half agony,
> As over thy shoulder thou lookest to hush the babe,
> Bleakly the blinding snow beats in thy haggard face.

'We think that we see him fumbling in the pocket of his blue pantaloons' the paper declares, and goes on to reprove the poet's non-intrusive narrative viewpoint where, it claims, instead of helping her, the poet-figure 'leaves her to Providence'. The paper proposes to prove this rule of Jacobin selfishness by offering an exception, claiming to quote another poem which describes 'one of those cases in which the Embargo upon Jacobin Bounty is sometimes suspended'. Despite this emphasis on the issue of charity, what follows is an attempt to discredit political opposition as much by stylistic as by ideological ridicule:

> THE SOLDIER'S FRIEND
> DACTYLICS
> Come, little Drummer Boy, lay down your knapsack here:
> I am the Soldier's Friend – here are some books for you;
> Nice clever Books, by TOM PAINE, the Philanthropist.
>
> Here's Half-a-crown for you – here are some Hand bills too –
> Go to the Barracks, and give all the Soldiers some.
> Tell them the Sailors are all in a Mutiny.[10]

The brilliance of the parody lies in the caricature of the Radical speaker – who is a composite of Southey, Paine and also of course Cobbett, the anonymous *Soldier's Friend* – implying that Radical writing (and thus Radical thought) is by definition clumsy and unimaginative, and that the Radicals' designs on the poor are either patronizing or sinister, with 'Nice clever Books'. This stylistic mirroring of historical authority (or lack of it) draws on shared assumptions about the nature of such authority which are inimical to working-class self-confidence. Marilyn Butler makes the same point when she says of the paper that its early numbers were 'highly mindful of their own elegance, classical correctness, and ease: good literature, the message goes, is for, and by, the upper orders only. Cleverness and wit are intimidating qualities, not comforting to the socially inexperienced reader, but demanding his respectful assent.'[11]

The writings of Burke and the *Anti-Jacobin* are canonical representatives of opposition to the French Revolution and English

Jacobinism. But in addition to these enduring writings, there is a wealth of ephemeral but influential comment appearing in the daily press. This genre is significant for our purposes, not only because ephemeral writings represent the reality of daily political discussion, but also because Cobbett identified himself with the daily newspapers on his entry into English journalism in 1800.[12]

Any attempt to make generalizations about this genre, however, is fraught with danger. The papers are numerous, written by many hands, and changing over time. So, for example, despite the fact that by 1815 Cobbett could characterize *The Times* as 'the trumpet of all the haters of freedom; all those which look with Satanic eyes on the happiness of the free people of America; all those who have been hatched in, and yet are kept alive by, Bribery and Corruption',[13] it nevertheless approached the early stages of the French Revolution with a cautious welcome, seeing it as a French attempt to emulate British freedoms.

21 July 1789 is the second day of reliable news reports from France since the fall of the Bastille a week earlier. In the editorial of this edition *The Times* preens itself on its early and accurate reporting by comparison with its rivals, and reports that the French rebellion is more or less over. The King has seen sense, sacking Necker his finance minister, issuing pardons to the newly-released prisoners from the Bastille, and promising to talk with representatives of the bourgeoisie. The people's natural love for their monarch has been restored by these actions and cries of '*vive le roi*' have once more been heard on the streets of Paris. The paper clearly approves of this returning stability, but its support for the enemies of despotism is also apparent:

> Austria will in all probability be the next arbitrary Government against which the arm of liberty will be uplifted. The people of that country have long groaned under the laws of oppression, and when they see the consequences of a French rebellion, will no doubt think it high time to make an attempt at raising the banners of freedom over the sceptre of despotism.
>
> Never did the once infatuated votaries of priestcraft, travel with greater pleasure to display the cross in PALESTINE, than the Pilgrims from French Tyranny flock to the new Parisian standard of liberty; and they go with equal ardor, – for there is a holy zeal in freedom as well as in religion.

Here the tone is clearly approving, but interestingly this effect seems to be achieved by syntactical and connotational means which 'refine' the potentially vulgar, and play down the violent realities of revolution. Thus the 'arm of liberty' is depersonalized: the force for change, it implies, is irresistible and based on a philosophical good quite detached from the actions of, and not embodied within, any individual. Further, the use of the passive 'will be uplifted' implies not only that the struggle for liberty is an inevitable response to an intolerable state of affairs, but also evades the human activity implicit in an active verb. That is, in both these ways – the metonymic arm, and the passive verb – the reference to liberty avoids any suggestion of an angry mob physically overthrowing the established government, but instead concentrates on the principle of liberty and its moral force. This is repeated with the euphemistic and similarly metonymic prediction that the Austrians will be the next to raise 'the banners of freedom over the sceptre of despotism'. It is interesting to note that David Aers, Jonathan Cook and David Punter have identified exactly the same features in Coleridge's early poem 'The Destruction of the Bastille'.[14] Whether or not Coleridge had read the reports in *The Times*, this coincidence suggests that such depersonalizing images and pacifying grammar represent Revolution in a way congenial to liberal Englishmen in this period. The morality of the rebellion is reinforced for *The Times* by the assertion that 'holy zeal' characterizes the rebels, while the reference to 'priestcraft' implies – possibly condescendingly – that the French are progressing towards a British style of enlightened constitutional government and away from the superstition and ignorance of divine monarchical rule.

By 1791, however, 'liberty' has come to signify something else, due to a change in the prevailing notions of what constitutes 'arbitrary' or 'legitimate' government, and of the political rights and abilities of the 'refined' and 'vulgar' respectively. If monarchs are to be 'cashiered for misconduct' as Richard Price would have it,[15] for failing to represent all sections of society adequately, then 'liberty' becomes a dangerous and effectively different concept. *The Times* is further incensed by Paine's application of French principles to the British system. In response to these various attacks the paper responds by vilifying the concept of the 'Rights of Man'. And interestingly, in contrast to the stylistic practices of the earlier article in support of the Revolution, the paper now makes its attack by stressing the contingent and passionate vulgarity of Radical thought.

That this ideological shift is reflected in the paper's style is evident from the edition of 8 July 1791. This edition contains a mock Bill of Rights which begins with the bald statement 'Man is born free, and has a right to act as inclination leads and nature directs.' The conclusions drawn from this premise assume that inclination will lead, and nature direct, to the perpetration of selfish, bestial, and anti-social acts. This seems in a direct conservative line of descent from Hobbes's vision of life in the state of nature as 'solitary, poore, nasty, brutish, and short', and from the Christian conception of original sin. This being so, a nightmare vision of unfettered human society is easy to construct, and *The Times* supports its vision with examples from history to validate its claims and, like Burke, to enact the sense of history and culture which it perceives as under threat:

> He is therefore warranted by natural right to dethrone a king, and usurp the regal authority, as Oliver Cromwell did –
> To set a city on fire, and murder his mother, as Nero did –
> To stab his reputed father, and assassinate his best friend, as Brutus did –
> To trample on religion, annihilate all distinction in Church and State, level his Sovereign to a plebeian, and overturn the constitution of an empire, as the French have done –
> To deny the existence of any power which one man should have over another, for the benefit of Society, as PAINE has done –
> To make no distinction as to property, and when one man wants money, to force it out of another man's pocket, as highwaymen do –
> To give equal applause to vice as to virtue, and to encourage evil as well as good; each being the natural disposition of man, and of course equally his right –
> To allow universal toleration of evil – as one of the first principles in the human heart, when by law; and to permit the passions of the mind to exercise the fulness of their wish, unchecked by the fear of punishment –
> This is the true Rights of Man –

This passage is interesting for its invocation of horrors particularly piquant for a landed and monied readership, such as the abandonment of ideas of personal property. The disruption of other 'natural' values is also suggested with the image of the mutilation of parents which recalls Burke's *Reflections*, and his reference to the French as 'those children of their country who are prompt rashly to hack that aged parent in pieces, and put him into the kettle of magicians...'[16] The horrors invoked by *The Times* are similarly couched in classical references: in both cases the classical allusion perhaps emphasizes the antiquity and learning of the culture under threat. The choice of violent images also provides emotionally appealing horror.

In direct contrast to the earlier passage on Austria, the sense of individual action in *The Times*'s article is strong. The forceful act of claiming liberty is conveyed through forceful, active verbs: 'murder

... stab ... trample ... force ... pull down ... destroy ... level'. We can draw a parallel and contrast here with the methods of the *Anti-Jacobin* which we saw adopted Southey's style for the purposes of parody. If the 'vulgar' is defined as material, passionate, and practical, as Olivia Smith suggests, then this article adopts the language of vulgarity, not to amuse and reassure, but to shake and disconcert its refined reader.

The Times is also capable of the kind of attack by ridicule practised by the *Anti-Jacobin* however. A fortnight later, on 26 July 1791, it describes the Revolutionary dinner given by Joseph Priestley which resulted in his flight to America. We have already seen the treatment given him by Cobbett upon his arrival there; *The Times* introduces the subject with a kind of mock playbill describing the entertainment to follow:

>FORTUNATE RECOVERY
>OF
>THE CANONIZED REMAINS
>BELONGING
>TO
>MISS PRESBYTERIA DEMOCRACY,
>WHO SUDDENLY FELL
>AN UNWILLING SACRIFICE
>TO
>AN UNEXPECTED STROKE
>OF
>THE GRIM KING OF TERRORS,
>AT DINNER,
>AFTER THE FIRST COURSE
>OF
>A GRAND PUBLIC FESTIVAL
>GIVEN BY HER
>TO
>THE BRITISH DISCONTENTED AND DISSENTING
>IN
>THE TOWN OF BIRMINGHAM,
>ON THURSDAY,
>THE FOURTEENTH OF JULY, 1791 §

The article is structured as an elaborate conceit upon this personification of Radicalism as 'Miss Presbyteria Democracy'. The corpse is laid out in Priestley's library 'on some corrected proofs of THE RIGHTS OF MAN', among statues of Cromwell and Voltaire and under a ceiling painted with scenes of Dionysus teaching republicanism and atheism, and Tom Paine '*chopping off the limbs* of the British constitution in order to make it fit the bed he made for the RIGHTS OF MAN'. The paper describes the storming of Priestley's library by 'Britannia' and the consequent roamings of the funeral party in search of a safe resting place for the corpse. Runneymead has been finally chosen, the paper concludes, 'where it is to be interred under the REVOLUTION PILLAR; and in tomorrow's Paper we shall give a full account of the whole cavalcade, hymns, chorusses, orations, &c, &c, &c. that have been sung, said, and muttered on this glorious occasion.'

Articles from 1800 show a different side to the paper's language use. By this stage *The Times* is in support of the Ministry, and now dramatizes itself as a paper in the political know. The following dignified language, of 10 July, is typical:

Whatever conduct the EMPEROR [of Austria] may hold upon this occasion, he has not the plea of necessity for abandoning the Alliance. It is more by personal character and the conduct of his Cabinet upon another occasion, than by any judgement of the present state of affairs, that these persons are guided who prognosticate his implicit concurrence with the dictates of General BONAPARTE.

If we turn to oppositional papers at the turn of the century, we have to be aware that general comparative statements about the differences between oppositional and ministerial writing are problematic. First of all, of course, the ministry and the opposition swap around at regular intervals; secondly, and more importantly, there are good and bad writers on both sides. Jeremy Black notes that a simplistic reading of the eighteenth century could suggest that opposition papers sought to import popular idioms into their writing, while ministerial papers did not. He points out that this is a tempting reading but an inaccurate one. Conservative papers often adopted a popular style; opposition papers often indulged in 'lengthy essays whose tone of high seriousness and moral outrage became repetitive and whose vindictive abuse could not compensate for a general humourlessness.'[17] In the end we return to the point which I have been making so far: that all mainstream journalism of the period plays by the rules of the political status quo, conforming more or less to the traditions of enfranchised reaction or opposition. For example, on 25 June 1795, *The Morning Chronicle*'s opposition to the Tory government, and to its policy against the French, displays complexity and refinement of vocabulary and syntax. It defends as follows its remarks on the price of bread earlier in the week:

This observation is stigmatized as originating in the true spirit of French jacobinism; as a foul slander; as tending and intended to excite commotions, and instigate the mob to the most atrocious outrages. We have long known that not to praise all and singular, the measures of Ministers, is, in their language, disaffection, and to find fault with any of them, rank jacobinism.

Between 1800 and 1804 *The Courier and Evening Gazette* swings from the approvingly unannotated reproduction of speeches by Fox, towards support of the Ministry and towards an audience which demands certain delicacies, refinements of expression, and flattery of its insider status:

Lest we should be suspected of having spoken lightly, and without information, upon a subject of equal delicacy and importance, to which we alluded on Tuesday and Wednesday, we now state that we have every reason to believe that the visit of an illustrious person to Bath, was to consult a Noble Lord, who DID give that opinion which we quoted on Tuesday. The visit may indeed have had another object in view, relating also to the question of guardianship. But that object was of minor importance, and as it is not all of a political nature, we shall [not] allude to it more particularly. Those who are at all acquainted with the subject know what we mean.[18]

We will return to enfranchised oppositional discourse in the next chapter. For the purposes of this chapter, the important conclusion to be drawn from these examples of political comment of the period is that, whether Tory or Whig, the political discourse of the enfranchised is refined in its stylistic usages, and often self-consciously so. Refinement, in other words, comes to mean something in itself, and to be used as a weapon against popular agitation. The daily press shares the tactics and preoccupations of its canonical peers and, in so far as Cobbett identifies himself with this literary genre, his entry into British politics means an entry also into this highly self-conscious and self-affirming environment.

Cobbett is never tactful enough to be described as diplomatic, but in the early numbers of the *Political Register* he comes close to a statesmanlike tone which implies a sense of personal responsibility and power. He may dismiss the readers of the *True Briton* and the *Sun* as people 'whose powers of perception we should not suppose to rise much superior to those of the more intelligent species of quadrupeds',[19] but on the whole his tone is restrained at this point. In the following extract from the 'Summary of Politics' for 15 May 1802, we can see his skilful ability to reproduce appropriate rhetorical styles as required. The change in tone from the American pamphlets we examined in the last chapter is almost total, and this if nothing else should answer doubts about Cobbett's stylistic self-consciousness:

> Lord Grenville's speech we had the good fortune to hear, and we hope that the public will be furnished with an opportunity of reading it; not in the garbled state in which it must necessarily find its way into a news-paper, but at full length, and as near as possible in the same order and the same words in which it was delivered... His arrangement was new and uncommonly perspicuous; his language was elegant, his manner dignified, and his arguments were irresistible.[20]

With this we are faced with the careful elegance and dignity of the politician or refined journalist of the period. But it is not enough to say that Cobbett merely parrots the prevailing discourse of authority upon his entry into English political debate. As I will show in the rest of this chapter, he is stylistically ambivalent in this period – sometimes conforming to this model, at other times transgressing its rules, assumptions, and implied readership. As a result his writings evince increasing tensions, as can be seen from the following examination of three articles from the *Political Register* of 1802.

As early as February 1802 Cobbett is attacking the quiescence of the government and its apparent willingness to concede Napoleon's superior military strength. In the 'Summary of Politics' of 27 February, Cobbett exploits a range of rhetorical methods in an attempt to arouse 'national spirit'.[21] Although its stance seems oppositionary, it is nevertheless expressed, by and large, in a manner which we have seen to be characteristic of mainstream political debate. Interestingly, however, in as much as he uses similar methods during his Radical years, Cobbett is already presenting himself in the role of teacher, purveying the 'truth' to his more or less reluctant pupils – or, perhaps more appropriately, as a pastor preaching to a recalcitrant flock. The article opens with a quote from the Bible which Cobbett takes as his text for the ensuing sermon:

> As a strong mark of the frivolity and blindness of the Ante-diluvians, we are told, in Holy Writ, 'that they ate, they drank, they married wives, and were given in marriage, until the day that Noah entered into the Ark, and the flood came, and destroyed them all;' so, at the present time, ninety-nine

hundredth of the people of this infatuated city appear to be totally occupied in discussing the rival pretensions of private and public theatres, in deciding upon a choice of amusements, at the very moment when themselves and their children are threatened with the overwhelming domination of France; a chastisement not much less tremendous than that which was inflicted upon the thoughtless and degenerate contemporaries of Noah.

'There is a time for all things;' Cobbett continues – and here we must hear an echo of Ecclesiastes, the preacher, 'to everything there is a season, and a time to every purpose under the heaven',[22] – 'and whichever way we turn our eyes, whether to the east or the west of our Island, whether we contemplate the state of our foreign or domestic concerns, everything we see or hear tells us that this is the time to be serious.' Following from the depiction of the English as frivolous and blind, infatuated and thoughtless, and in the context of his demand that they *look* 'to the east or the west', this also seems to echo St Paul in his first letter to the Corinthians.[23] Cobbett is demanding that his readers 'put away childish things' and assume an adult responsibility for their country, and a greater political awareness. Cobbett addresses the London theatre-going public, and he strives for pedagogic authority by means of religious allusion.

Despite the fact that the Bible is, as we have noted, an authoritative discourse for all classes, Cobbett's use of it here is strictly conservative. Cobbett is using a standard reactionary device of presenting the French Revolution and Napoleonic conquest as a punishment inflicted on civilization by God rather than a holy crusade for liberty and equality.[24] We can see that this assumption drives Cobbett's analogy between the 'overwhelming domination of France' and the overwhelming biblical deluge, and it resurfaces later in the article as he depicts Napoleon as an apocalyptic 'vulture' descending on the timorous 'chickens' of nations. In this way, Cobbett is allying himself, however critically, with the audience he addresses, wishing them to regain their traditional strength of purpose and ready to teach them how to accomplish this. So at this stage, in other words, Cobbett is playing by refined discursive rules.

Co-existing with this pedagogic and prophetic tone is an emphasis on rationality and clear argument. Having demanded that his readers look up from their trivial concerns and engage with the major political events of the day, Cobbett seems to be attempting their enlightenment by self-consciously measured and progressive arguments, with conclusion following example, and example conclusion:

It is stated in the French papers, that the Prince of Orange has arrived at Paris, to solicit from the Chief Consul permission to enjoy his private property in Germany. This circumstance fully proves how completely that prince has been abandoned by the powers of Europe, and it also proves, that Buonaparte is the absolute master of the Empire and of all its princes, who hold nothing, no not even their lives, but by his consent. The nations of the earth are crouching down under him like chickens at the approach of the vulture. The only check to his ambition and rapacity seems to exist in France itself, where he and his comrades are certainly not popular. His journey to Lyons, and his proceedings there, have excited much discontent amongst the people of France, who perceive in those daring projects of aggrandisement the seeds of new wars, and new miseries, fresh dissentions in the interior of France, and fresh pretexts for the exercise of that execrable tyranny, on which the existence of the Republic essentially depends. The government is by no means ignorant of the disaffection which prevails; but, in order to prevent its effects, great care is taken to stifle the voice of all those, who, by their disposition and their talents, are likely to become formidable to the Consul and his associates. Since the journey to Lyons, more than sixty persons have been seized and imprisoned, charged with no other crime than that of disliking the government, and detesting those by whom it is administered. While these acts of tyranny have been practised at Paris, others, of a nature more cruel, have been committed in the departments, and that too on persons, whose fate will excite compassion in every honest and loyal heart: we allude to the royalists of La Vendée, many of whom have lately fallen a sacrifice to the ferocity of their persecutors.

Towards the end of this passage the argument switches from being self-consciously logical to self-consciously emotive. This seems directly reminiscent of Burke and resonant of high romance. When Cobbett declares that 'every honest and loyal heart' would pity the victims of tyranny, Burke's vision of the 'ten thousand swords' leaping from their scabbards to the defence of the French queen seems subliminally present.[25] Like Marie Antoinette in Burke's *Reflections*, the Royalists here are presented as passive sufferers. The echo of Burke sanctions this emotional argument and implies the whole rich vein of Burke's writings on the organic state and, increasingly importantly as the article progresses, his celebration of chivalry and honour as a part of that social system.

This becomes important because the following paragraph casts Cobbett, and champions of free speech everywhere, in a heroic light. If this recalls Burke's defence of chivalry then it can only aid Cobbett in his attempt to present himself as a truer patriot than the Government ministers, who have agreed to the Peace of Amiens, and to stir the 'national spirit' with which this article is so much concerned:

> Not a word of these things do we hear through the channel of the French press, which is in that state of abject subjection, to which Buonaparte would wish to reduce the press of this country. The press of Great-Britain and that of America are, indeed, the last refuge of the liberties of the world; and, we may be well assured, that no exertion of stratagem or of force will be spared to stifle their enquiries. In America, the accomplishment of this object will be very difficult, but, however humiliating the acknowledgement, we sincerely believe that the difficulty will be less in this kingdom; a belief in which we are persuaded our readers will participate, when they observe the language of those English prints, which are under the influence of the ministry, and when they are informed, that silence, with respect to Buonaparte, has been, by authority, already imposed on the *Journal de Peltier*. To suppose that the liberty of the British press is, at last, to be destroyed by the person whom Lord Hawkesbury so lately styled a 'Corsican adventurer;' to suppose, that we are no longer to find protection in those courts, which have ever been the safe-guard of ourselves, and the admiration of the world; to suppose these things possible is, in some sort, to renounce one's nature; but, so humble, so base are we become, and such is our propensity to sink, that it is beyond the powers of the mind to conceive the depth of degradation to which we shall finally descend.

Cobbett's closing comments here, painting Napoleon as a 'Corsican adventurer' rather than an extraordinary military hero, emphasize the extent of the degradation with which the country is threatened by the frivolity of its people and the weakness of its government. This invective against British degeneracy seems to colour the final paragraph of the article, which is characterized by an uneasy mixture of patriotism and contempt for those in power.

Cobbett begins by noting that 'during the last week ... some faint gleamings of national spirit have appeared'; here the phrase 'faint gleamings of national spirit' seems to hold two opposing conceptions of Britain in one focus: raising the idea of national spirit in the process of denying its strength. Cobbett continues with similarly two-edged ironic applause for those who have realized that 'it is better to fight a little longer than instantly to die', while his contempt for the rulers of the country he claims to revere is obvious with the conversational observation that 'nay, in some instances, they have actually, though with quivering lips, pronounced the tremendous monosyllable *war*'. This movement towards the colloquial is interesting in so far as it coincides with combative oppositional sentiments, but the piece quickly swings back to refinement with the gracefully constructed observation that 'Buonaparte is too profound a politician to be influenced by these feeble exertions of expiring hope'.

This ambivalence of tone spills over into the 'Summary of Politics' for 6 March, the following week.[26] Cobbett takes up his argument where he left off, and acknowledges that in the intervening week national spirit has been increasing. He sees the new tone of belligerence from government sources as 'compelled' by this change in public opinion:

> It is with great pride that we perceive this [national] spirit daily rising; nor should we be without some hopes, that the disgrace of the last six months, great as it is, might yet be wiped away ere the year has expired, were we not fully persuaded, that Buonaparte and his associates are too sensible of the advantages, which they have already obtained by the weakness of our ministers, and too well assured, that a treaty founded on the basis of the preliminaries, cannot fail to effect the destruction of England. There are, indeed, some very difficult points to be arranged: the conceding, the yielding, the humble, the crouching, the crawling, the prostrating propensity of our Cabinet, might encourage the Consul to demand the Isle of Wight; but those, who, if we may judge by their past conduct, would willingly yield even that island to his grasp, will not, we think, in the present temper of the country, dare to leave him in possession of the islands of Malta and Elba.

The invective against ministers here is brilliantly achieved, with the comic graduation of insult from 'conceding' to 'prostrating'. The assertion that public opinion is responsible for the government's change of heart, along with the comedy of the invective, draws Cobbett's readers into collusion with him by setting them up as the standard by which government acts, and by inviting them to laugh at and despise those in authority over them.

But Cobbett does not allow his readers to go unchallenged. In what follows he examines the rise of national spirit as well as the government's change of tone, and his conclusions are not comfortable ones. Having praised 'spirit' as an emanation of honour the previous week, he now attributes its re-emergence to ignoble motives:

> We wish that truth did not oblige us to attribute this change to the disappointment of those who foolishly relied on a decrease in the price of provisions and an extension of trade; we sincerely wish we could attribute it to some more dignified and honourable sentiment, arising from some national quality, on which we might, at last, safely depend for deliverance

from the misery and degradation with which we are menaced. The decline, the rapid decline, of trade, the stagnation in manufactures and commerce: this it is that has opened the eyes of the ignorant and the selfish; and we shall, probably, now hear of *national honour* from those very lips, which, six months ago, were constantly employed in uttering eulogiums on the framers of the Preliminaries of Downing Street, by whom that honour has been trampled underfoot. In the joyous illuminations of the 10th of October (which we shall ever ascribe to the folly of the Ministers), it was not uncommon to see the motto of '*Peace* and *Commerce*', as well as '*Peace* and *Plenty*'. These ideas were not of much longer duration than the candles which exposed them to the eyes of the ignorant and infatuated rabble. If, amongst the numerous herd, who adopted these mottos, there be one man of sense to be found, what must be his shame and remorse, now, when he sees the manufacturers, the merchants, the ship-owners, the tradesmen of every description, mingle their complaints with the clamours of the hungry, the idle and the turbulent poor; when he sees his country plunged at once into poverty and dishonour, and staggering along, like the Ass of Isacar, between two burdens, the burden of War and the burden of Peace!

We can note points in this passage at which Cobbett disrupts the received stylistic practices of his conservative peers. When he asserts that 'the manufacturers, the merchants, the ship-owners, the tradesmen of every description mingle their complaints with the hungry, the idle and turbulent poor', he seems to be identifying a commonality of oppositional interest between classes of society not usually identified together in refined political discourse. It could be that Cobbett is deploring this state of affairs, and that the chagrin of the 'man of sense' among the peacemongers is at the unnatural disruption of class brought about by the cessation of hostilities. But it is not this simple. When Cobbett refers to the 'rabble' or 'herd' in this passage these terms do not necessarily denominate the lower classes. Contrary to this common usage, Cobbett here disruptively applies these terms to those of all classes who welcomed peace.

The disruptive character of this procedure is illuminated if we compare this passage to another from 22 September 1804. Cobbett ends the 'Summary of Politics' for that week with a discussion of the likely election of the aristocratic Radical Sir Francis Burdett:

No one can have forgotten, that, in answer to all our statements against the ignominious peace of Amiens, we were reminded that the *people*, the *nation*, had decidedly expressed their approbation of it ... But, now, behold, when joy at the supposed success of Sir Francis Burdett is expressed by two or three hundred thousand voices, the people are no longer the *people* and the *nation*, but the *mob* and the *rabble*! In the cause of Burdett and Independence it will not be asserted, that there was any base and cowardly; yet those who join in that cry are called rabble, while the name of *the people* and *the nation* are given to the vile and infamous herd, who, though they knew that LAURISTON brought the confirmation of their country's ignominy, harnessed themselves to his chariot, forced him through the ranks of the guards, and drew him in triumph ... But, the shouts of that worse than brutal rabble were convertible to ministerial support; those plaudits were in favour of a measure, for which the ministers stood in need of a justification; then, therefore, the applauders were the people and the nation, but now they are rabble and mob.[27]

The care with which Cobbett spells out the contested nature of the terms 'people' and 'rabble' shows that he is concerned that his readers should be aware of the political investment of such denominations. At the same time he offers a practical lesson in the creation of such political imagery by turning the terms back against the supporters of Lauriston. For present purposes the interest of this extract is that it shows that Cobbett is aware of the tendency of the ruling class to use these terms pragmatically against the lower orders. If so, his reversal of this tactic, in the article of 1802, looks consciously disruptive. Cobbett pragmatically applies the terms 'rabble' and 'herd' to members of the rising commercial elite. Indeed, from this point in his career onwards, Cobbett tends more and more to equate the 'mob' with the numerous 'hirelings' of State. Such imagistic usages build up a system of relations and identity between classes which resist their polarization even at this early stage of reaction. This is reinforced when Cobbett identifies as his ally and ideal reader the 'one man of sense', regardless of class, who can see and comprehend the catastrophic results of the peace.

In the context of Cobbett's pedagogic stance this refusal to categorize by class is important. As in the previous week's article, the implication is that *all* the readers of the *Political Register* stand in need of guidance regardless of class or status. In this context, the article's closing series of rhetorical questions about the dangers posed by France demands the concurrence of all its readers:

shall we, at this day, be told, that there is no terror in her threats? When she has driven us up into a corner, and has got her knife at our throats, shall we be pacified, by the empty sound of capital, credit, and confidence, uttered from the lips of cowardice and imbecility? That our resistance will be in vain is possible; but is such a possibility any reason why we should not resist? Because we see our danger, must we not attempt to avoid it? Are we bound to expire with a locked jaw, lest we should chance to expectorate on the instrument of our destruction? We, for our parts, acknowledge no such obligation, and we yet hope to see the day, when our sentiments will be sanctioned by the unanimous voice of the country, which we hope will at last prove itself to have been deluded rather than debased.

The framing of these violent images of personal danger in the form of questions demands that the reader answer each with a vehement negative – ironically, Cobbett in this way exploits the self-interest he has previously castigated. But with the reference to the British as either 'deluded' or 'debased' in the final sentence of the article, the reader is offered an escape-route from any humbling sense of inadequacy. That is, the reader is more likely to choose the first of these alternatives, and by doing so is obliged to accept Cobbett in the pedagogic role he has created for himself.

These two articles share several features then. Overall, they conform to refined grammatical and lexical usage, and by doing so conform to the expectations of the audience they are addressing. But there are some problems. Cobbett's ideological ambivalence, as his former allies ratify the Peace of Amiens, is conveyed through the use of irony, of invective, and of disrupted classifications – for example, where Cobbett redefines the nouns 'rabble' and 'herd' for oppositional purposes.

Potentially problematic, also, is the assumption that the readership of the *Political Register* needs a political education. If we compare this to the *Courier*'s deferential treatment of its readers, then we need to ask whether Cobbett is playing with dangerously vulgar forthrightness, or whether this is an indication that he is in an uncomfortable relationship with his audience. Perhaps in this period of political conformity Cobbett differs from papers like the *Courier* by failing to share his audience's assumptions and values.

That issues of readership and style are a problem in this period of Cobbett's journalism is obvious if we turn to an article written three months later and published on 26 June.[28] This article deals with issues relating to the recent dissolution of Parliament, and in particular a coincidental resurgence of agitation for democratic reform. Cobbett's task in the article is to discredit these agitators and to warn his enfranchised readership against the arguments for Reform made by the Whigs. This being so, the assumptions and images employed are calculated for that audience, resulting in certain unavoidable but crucial anomalies. Cobbett argues against parliamentary reform by asserting that, unsatisfactory as it may be, the present parliamentary system is the best that the disenfranchised can get. This is a view very much from a position of power, but it is complicated by the oppositional nature of his political stance, his preoccupation with 'truth', and his apparent urge towards the colloquial style with which he began his career, and to which he would return in 1816.

The article begins with a dismissive description of the constitutional doctrine which Cobbett would, ironically, be later endorsing. As so often, Cobbett offers his comments in a pedagogic spirit as he notes that the recent publication of 'two factious addresses' have, with their deployment of words like 'representation and elective franchise ... done much towards confusing the brain and corrupting the hearts of His Majesty's subjects'. Cobbett adds that 'though we have not the vanity to suppose, that we possess the power of dissipating the fatal delusion, it is our duty to contribute our mite in the attempt'. He begins his tuition by acknowledging the legitimate grievances of the disenfranchised if their premise that representation equals power is granted. Cobbett does not accept this premise, however, and he argues against it from various angles. First, he invokes the pernicious example of the United States. Then, in the following passage, he employs the bullying pedagogic tactics that we have identified in the previous two articles: assuming that his conclusions are universally agreed, with constructions like 'of course', and leaving the reader no third alternative beyond agreement with Cobbett on the one hand, or infamy on the other:

> Our famous countryman, SWIFT, has compared the people, who choose popular assemblies, to those silly worms, which exhaust their substance, and destroy their lives, in making habits for beings of a superior order. With all due deference to such an authority, we beg leave to say, that the latter part of the comparison will not bear the test of experience. That the people, in the exercise of their imaginary rights and privileges, do exhaust their substance and sometimes, destroy their lives, is most certain; but, that they do this for the sake of *beings of a superior order* will be believed by no one, who has paid any attention to the objects of their choice, and who must, of course, have observed, that that choice does not infrequently fall upon *bankrupts, swindlers, quacks, parasites, panders, atheists, apostates*, in a word, upon the most infamous and the most despicable of the human race; wretches whom no prudent tradesman would trust alone in his shop, and with whom any honest man would blush to be seen in conversation.

Here Cobbett simultaneously damns and praises the judgement of the presently disenfranchised. This inconsistency is compounded by an irresistible temptation for the reader to draw comparisons with the British government. Despite Cobbett's assertions, we are bound to remember his previous characterization of the British cabinet as the 'conceding, the yielding, the humble, the crouching, the crawling, the prostrating' appeasers of tyranny. When Cobbett declares that popular choice 'does not infrequently fall ... upon the most infamous and despicable of the human race' it is hard to take this as applicable only to *popular* assemblies.

But Cobbett intends that we should limit our reading in this way, an intention facilitated by the assumption that his audience will be with him on this subject. He moves on to describe American elective practice and to argue, seemingly directly with the disenfranchised, that reform is an evil. This implied reader is not an entirely unlikely one, in that the rising but disenfranchised middle class may be reading him, but Cobbett speaks to them in the voice of enfranchised paternalism. His final tactic in the following passage is to argue that power is, in any case, something no disenfranchised person could responsibly wield and which they should not even desire:

Men of sense know, that the people can, in reality, exercise no power which will not tend to their own injury; and, therefore, if they are honest men, as well as men of sense, they scorn to foster their vanity at the expense of their peace and happiness. Hence it is, that in States, where the popular voice is unchecked by a royal or any other hereditary influence, that voice is, nine times out of ten, given in favour of those fawning parasites, who, in order to gratify their own interest and ambition, profess to acknowledge no sovereignty but that of the people, and who, when they once get into power, rule the poor sovereign, that has chosen them, with a rod of scorpions, affecting, while the miserable wretch is writhing under their stripes, to call themselves his '*representatives*!'

It is odd that a man of sense can be at the same time so politically naive as Cobbett here implies. In the context of his overall endeavour to teach his readers to judge and to observe this passage sits very oddly, and seems a convenient judgement if he is addressing those who currently do hold power. The instability of his argument seems to be elided, however, by his increasing use of emotive biblical imagery towards the close of the passage.

Cobbett's increasingly millennial tone culminates in his depiction of 'the tyranny of an elective assembly', which seems like a nightmare version of Burke's immemorial State. Like Burke's organic State,[29] Cobbett's democratic tyranny transcends the individual and neutralizes individual power:

Of all the tyrannies that the devil or man ever invented, the tyranny of an elective assembly, uncontrouled by regal power, is the most insupportable. When the tyrant is an individual, the slaves have the satisfaction of knowing their oppressor; they have the consolation of hearing him execrated, and, amidst their miseries, they are now and then cheered with the hope, that some valiant hand will bear a dagger to his heart. But, an uncontrouled elective assembly is an indefinable, an invisible, and an invulnerable monster; it insinuates, like the plague, or strikes like the apoplexy; it is as capricious, as cruel, and as ravenous as death; like death too, it loses half of its terrors by the frequent repetition of its ravages, and, such is its delusive influence, that every man, though he daily sees his neighbours falling a sacrifice to the scourge, vainly imagines it to be at a distance from himself.

Like Burke, Cobbett also makes his argument in this article through images rather than explicit, rational debate. Having identified the democratic assembly with forces of destruction and darkness in the extract above, he concludes with contrary images of monarchy that conjure ideas of light and splendour, fountains and sunlight:

'Stick to the *Crown*, though you find it hanging on a bush,' was the precept which a good old Englishman gave to his sons, at a time when the monarchy was threatened with that subversion, which it afterwards experienced, and which was attended with the perpetration of a deed that has fixed an indelible stain on the annals of England, blessed be God, we are threatened with no such danger at present; but a repetition of the precept can never be out of season, as long as there are Whigs in existence, and as long as there are men foolish enough to listen to their insidious harangues. The crown is the guardian of the people, but more especially is its guardianship necessary to those who are destitute of rank and wealth. The King gives the weakest and poorest of us some degree of consequence: as his subjects, we are upon a level with the noble and the rich; in yielding him obedience, veneration, and love, neither obscurity nor penury can repress our desires, or lessen the pleasure that we feel in return; he is the fountain of national honour, which, like the sun, is no respecter of persons, but smiles with equal warmth on the palace and the cottage; in his justice, his magnanimity, his piety, in the wisdom of his councils, in the splendours of his throne, in the glory of his arms, in all his virtues, and in all his honours, we share, not according to rank or to riches, but in proportion to the attachment that we bear to the land that gave us birth, and to the sovereign, whom God has commanded us to honour and obey.

This method of arguing through images seems useful as a way of appealing to emotion, and thereby avoiding the problematics of more rational debate. But problems and anomalies within the argument are nevertheless apparent. We can see this by examining the way in which the reciprocal relationship between the monarchy and the people is presented in the final sentence as a version of matrimony. For Cobbett, the people are the bride to the monarch's bridegroom and the implication is that, like Cinderella, the people will be elevated by the noble condescension of the king.

In his description of this elevation, Cobbett identifies himself with the 'weakest and poorest', claiming that the king gives 'us' consequence: 'as his subjects, we are upon a level with the noble and the rich'. This identification seems inappropriate to the readership of the *Political Register* at this stage in the paper's conservative history. But the sentiments expressed are equally inappropriate to Cobbett's imagined working-class readership. The invocation of the marriage service and the subliminal presence of the fairy-tale are both ways of presenting what is essentially a power relation as an emotional bargain and bond. Cobbett asserts that by 'yielding [the monarch] obedience, veneration, and love,' the subject may expect in return 'pleasure...justice...magnanimity...piety...wisdom...splendour'. This bargain, Cobbett reiterates, is not a financial or political one, as we benefit 'not according to rank or to riches, but in proportion to the attachment that we bear to the land which gave us birth, and to the sovereign, whom God has commanded us to honour and obey.' But at least marriage in the period entitled women to some financial support.

Again the parallel with Burke's emotive argumentative methods seems clear. The parallel is extended if we compare Cobbett's depiction of the monarch as the 'fountain of national honour' which in turn is a universally warming 'sun', with Burke's panegyric on Marie Antoinette which we have already had occasion to invoke:

It is now sixteen or seventeen years since I saw the queen of France, then the dauphiness, at Versailles; and surely never lighted on this orb, which she hardly seemed to touch, a more delightful vision. I saw her just above the horizon, decorating and cheering the elevated sphere she just began to move in, – glittering like the morning-star, full of life, and splendor, and joy.[30]

Cobbett's monarch is perhaps slightly more useful than Burke's, in so far as he is at least a warming sun, whereas Marie Antoinette is a

A version of reaction 85

beautiful but functionless star. This indeed seems to be offered as compensation for the non-practical nature of the gifts the monarch bestows upon his bride. However dubious these benefits may seem, such ideas have been used before in Cobbett's American writings. Thus, for example, he described his feelings upon seeing the British fleet at Spithead, in *The Life and Adventures of Peter Porcupine*: 'My heart was inflated with national pride. The sailors were my countrymen; the fleet belonged to my country, and surely I had my part in it, and in all its honours.'[31]

However, the intangible benefits which Cobbett here offers to the disenfranchised labourer seem profoundly unsatisfactory when looked at from the labourer's perspective. Cobbett can get away with this here only because, as we have already noted, he is not actually addressing the labouring class. That this is the case becomes even more apparent if we compare this passage from the *Political Register* with an address to the masses written the following year. In that address, commissioned by the government and distributed by the Church, Cobbett's arguments for civil obedience and patriotism were far more practical. There Cobbett used the tried and tested formula of crude atrocity stories against the French to convince the poor of their own interest in British victory and the status quo. Towards the end of the address, Cobbett describes the French invasion of Germany in 1796 to 1798, prefacing his remarks with the observation that, following French assurances, 'some of the poorer classes regarded the French, not as enemies, but as their deliverers from taxes and labour'. That these French promises were hollow is soon made clear, as is the universal suffering bound to follow from a French victory over England:

> No sooner, however, had the invasion taken place, no sooner had the French become masters of the country, than they spread themselves over it like beasts of prey, devouring and destroying every thing before them. They spared neither cities nor towns, neither villages nor hamlets, nor solitary houses; from the church to the cell, from the castle to the cottage; no state of life, however lofty or however humble, escaped their rapacious assaults; no sanctity excited their veneration; no grandeur their respect; no misery their forbearance or their pity. After having plundered the houses of the gentry, the clergy, and the tradesmen; after having pillaged the shops, warehouses, and manufactories, they proceeded to the farm-houses and cottages; they rifled the pockets and chests of the inhabitants, cut open their beds, tore up the floors of their rooms, dug up their cellars, searched the newly-made graves, and broke open the coffins in hopes of finding secreted

treasure. They sometimes threatened people with immediate death, sometimes put them to the torture, sometimes lacerated and crippled them, in order to wring from them a discovery of their little pittance of ready money ... towards women of all ages and all conditions, they were guilty of brutality never before heard of: neither extreme youth nor extreme age; neither weakness nor deformity, nor the most loathsome disease; neither the pangs of labour, nor the agonies of death, could restrain them: cries, tears, supplications, were of no avail; and where fathers, husbands, or brothers interfered, murder seldom failed to close the horrible scene. To spread nakedness and hunger, to introduce misery and disease amongst all ranks, seems to have been their uniform desire; but the lower orders of the people, the artisans and the labourers, were the objects of their direst malignity; against them was directed the sharpest bayonets; for their bodies the choicest torment, for their minds the keenest anguish was reserved. From one end of the country to the other, we trace the merciless ruffians through a scene of conflagration and blood; frequently we see them butchering whole families, and retiring by the light of their blazing habitations; but amongst the poor alone do we find them deferring the murder of the parents, for the purpose of compelling them to hear their children shriek amidst the flames![32]

The almost ludicrous malignity of the French here is a far from subtle way of enlisting working-class support for the British government, and in this context it is clear that Cobbett would not seriously offer 'honour' and 'splendour' as sufficient rewards to a genuine labouring-class reader. For some reason, in other words, Cobbett's self-dramatization as a patriotic pauper is consciously aimed at his refined readership in this article of June 1802.

But why should Cobbett purport to speak in the voice of the disenfranchised – a tactic then at odds with his political allegiances, his audience, and his own social status? By invoking Hannah More's tracts of the 1790s which Cobbett admired during his conservative phase, and which we shall examine at more length in Chapter 7, we may arrive at some answers.[33] Hannah More's vernacular pamphlets preached submission in the language of those to whom they were addressed, but perhaps predictably her stories of working-class misery and gratitude for upper-class charity were more popular with the rich than with the poor to whom they were distributed. We can see in Cobbett's article of 1802 the reasons why More's methods should appeal to him in his conservative phase. In Chapter 7 we shall see how her methods (especially her failures) still provide Cobbett with material in his Radical phase.

More's most famous work was *Village Politics*. In this pamphlet of

1793 Jack Anvil the blacksmith counsels Tom Hod, a mason infected with Jacobin principles, as follows: 'Tom! I have got the use of my limbs, of my liberty, of the laws, and of my Bible. The two first, I take to be my *natural rights*; the two last my *civil and religious*; these, I take it, are the true *Rights of Man*, and all the rest is nothing but nonsense and madness and wickedness'.[34] In the linguistic battlefield depicted by Olivia Smith it seems odd that we are here presented with truth from the mouth of the vulgar blacksmith. But More is of course drawing on the ancient and refined literary mode of pastoral, which sees wisdom in the mouth of the old shepherd, folly in the corruptions of civilization: 'Sir, I am a true labourer: I earn that I eat, get that I wear, owe no man's hate, envy no man's happiness, glad of other men's good, content with my harm; and the greatest of my pride is to see my ewes graze and my lambs suck'.[35] Privileging these working-class values and lifestyles, or in Cobbett's case, speaking in the voice of the poor and weak, can be in this way a profoundly conservative procedure. The pastoral mode, after all, relies on those who recognize it, and those that do are accustomed to take the portrayal of lowly virtues pretty lightly. Moreover, the contented swain or Cobbett's patriotic pauper represent no threat to the status quo. On the contrary, representing the feudal hierarchy, they represent a lost age of social harmony and stability. Perhaps it is comforting to the refined reader of this panegyric to imagine and identify himself with a suffering but patriotic and grateful worker in a period of social unrest at home, and war abroad.

What is most interesting about this imagery, in the light of what is to come in Cobbett's later Radical career, is that it demonstrates the dependence of the meaning of a piece of writing on matters such as the nature of the assumed reader, the price of the paper in which it appears, and the context of political arguments in which it is embedded. Organic imagery will be used often in the course of Cobbett's Radical career, but then it will mean something very different to its meaning in the passage from 1802 which we have been examining. In his later Radical writings the disruption of class, with Cobbett addressing the upper classes in the character of the lower, becomes subversive rather than hierarchical. In 1802, when the *Register* is priced at nearly a shilling, aimed specifically at an audience educated in pastoral imagery and its significances, and when its use of pastoral is couched in an article arguing for the inability of the disenfranchised to engage intelligently with political issues, the portrayal of contented poverty is profoundly conservative, reinforcing rather than challenging the assumptions of its readership.

It is common to argue that Cobbett's political conversion to Radicalism begins with the clash between his idyllic conservative vision of England and the reality of rural poverty which met him on his return to the country in 1800. From the tensions and contradictions we have identified in Cobbett's conservative writings we could construct a formal parallel to these biographical comments. We could argue that his pastoral images draw attention to the disjunction between their ideal landscape and the realities of rural life and that, as a consequence, his refined pastoral vision leads inevitably to the language and ideas of the ancient constitution which asserts that this social bliss only existed in the past.

But this assumes a lack of literary self-consciousness on Cobbett's part that ill accords with his deployment of refined usages. It assumes that Cobbett uses pastoral images simply because he believes in them, and that his subsequent disillusionment drives him towards opposition. From our examination of his literary context, and the discursive world he inhabits, it seems more likely that he uses the pastoral because it is an *available* and powerful conservative discourse, in the same way that he later adopts constitutionalism because it is the current Radical language and not because of a coincidental discovery of a heartfelt belief in his Saxon heritage. In this way we can turn the argument round, and argue that Cobbett is in control rather than at the mercy of his literary practice. The next chapter will continue to examine Cobbett's use of such prevailing discourse, in the period of his ideological transition between 1804 and the birth of his twopenny *Register* in 1816.

CHAPTER 3

Oppositional styles 1804–1816

To represent him with fidelity, it is necessary to premise, that we must consider him, like every other Harlequin, under a multitude of dissimilar shapes; sometimes as an impassioned Royalist; at others, as a fanatical Citizen; then successively as a maniac, a prophet, and a recorder of lies; one moment the admirer, the next the reviler of the greatest enemy of our country; to-day, the strenuous advocate, tomorrow the libellist of Mr Pitt; and in the same style of ludicrous versatility, the defamer and panegyrist of Charles Fox. In short, he surpasses all men in barefaced impudence, and is equalled by none in dullness and stupidity.[1]

Thus wrote Coleridge in *The Courier* of 1805, in an article entitled 'A Political Harlequin: William Cobbett'. The article was introductory to a series of articles published over the winter of 1805 which aimed to refute his arguments. This undertaking is itself testimony to Cobbett's perceived influence in the period, which belies the epithets 'dull' and 'stupid' with which Coleridge attempts to brand him. The passage is interesting because it makes clear the mainstream nature of Cobbett's nascent opposition in this period, in that he is identified with Charles Fox rather than Thomas Paine; and it is useful as it reminds us of his open willingness to change his political stance. This chapter looks at Cobbett's period of ideological transition from 1804 to 1816, identifying changes from and continuities with his earlier conservative writings, examining his use of available discourses, and exploring the stylistic characteristics of his address to the poor in 1816.

The Peace of Amiens broke down in 1803, and war with France was resumed. Cobbett was pleased with this development, but the government's attempt to reward him for his writings in favour of war is often seen as a reason for his movement towards opposition.

Appalled by the general acceptance of such financial rewards and favours, Cobbett began an investigation into the state of the British economy which led him to Paine's *Decline and Fall of the English System of Finance*. As a result of this reading, Cobbett conceived an enduring contempt for the financial markets which he saw as perverting the British economy. Having been a ferocious critic of Paine, Cobbett from this point onwards pays him homage.

While many critics note that the period 1800 to 1806 was one of a sort of wilderness for Cobbett, as he returned to England an ostensible supporter of the status quo and soon found himself in opposition to it, Ian Dyck has been the first to identify one crucial moment of conversion to an unequivocal stance of opposition. He identifies this moment as being Michaelmas week 1804, on the authority of later testimony to this effect by Cobbett, who referred in 1821 to a formative visit to Horton Heath which convinced him of the suffering of the agricultural poor and the harmfulness of supposed improvements like enclosure.[2] And, perhaps significantly, it is precisely this same week of 1804 which sees in the *Political Register* the beginning of a long-running series of open letters to William Pitt, Cobbett's former ally, through which his increasingly oppositional views are expressed. The literary tactics employed in the letters vary, but a handful of examples will show how Cobbett's ideological shift demands a change of style in order to deal with the increasingly inappropriate nature of his audience.

Significantly, the first two letters of the series contain Cobbett's first major English statement of autobiography. We have seen that Cobbett's American autobiography, the *Life and Adventures of Peter Porcupine*, acted as self-defence from the accusations of his opponents in America. More than this, it constituted Cobbett's first public revelation of his real identity. If the symbolic value of the act of publishing the *Life and Adventures* was a metaphorical taking-off of the jacket before settling a dispute with the fists, then Cobbett's open 'Letter 1 to the Right Honourable William Pitt on the Causes of the Decline of Great Britain', of September 1804, seems to repeat the action, this time in response to the entrenched powers of England.[3] Cobbett justifies his autobiography by noting the differences between argument and opinion, where the latter is the defining characteristic of politics:

In estimating arguments, relating to any subject, and particularly to measures and events, in which the writer has taken no part, personal considerations with regard to him ought never to intrude; but, Sir, this intrusion, so inimical to the cause of truth and of justice, experience has convinced us that nothing can prevent in the case of political discussions; where, though the reasoning have no possible connexion with the character, conduct, motives, or views of the reasoner, though the door be barred against them by every principle according to which men, in other cases, form their judgement, intrude they will; and powerful indeed must be the talents of him who can with safety bid them defiance! Greatly and justly diffident in this latter respect, feeling the full weight of the task I have ventured to encounter... I shall, I hope, be excused... if, previous to my entering on the important subject before me, I endeavour to guard against the foul hostility of personal considerations, whatever degree of conviction my reasoning may have the good fortune to produce.[4]

Cobbett fulfils this aim of guarding against 'the foul hostility of personal considerations' by giving an autobiographical account of his career and ideological development, specifically concerned to justify and detail his change of opinion away from support, towards criticism, of Pitt and his policies. Thus, he begins by explaining his entry into politics; identifying the real-life events which acted as a catalyst, and narrating the 'facts' of his influence and importance as an American pamphleteer. Cobbett thus describes his early occupation as an English teacher to French émigrés, and the moment which plunged him into his literary career:

One of my scholars, who was a person that we in England should call a Coffee-house Politician, chose, for once, to read his newspaper by way of lesson; and, it happened to be the very paper which contained the addresses presented to Doctor Priestley at New York, together with his replies. My scholar, who was a sort of republican, or, at best, but half a monarchist, appeared delighted with the invectives against England, to which he was very much disposed to add. Those Englishmen who have been abroad, particularly if they have had time to make a comparison between the country they are in and that which they have left, well know how difficult it is, upon occasions such as I have been describing, to refrain from expressing their indignation and resentment; and there is not, I trust, much reason to suppose, that I should, in this respect, experience less difficulty than another. The dispute was as warm as might reasonably be expected between a Frenchman, uncommonly violent even for a Frenchman, and an Englishman not remarkable for *sang froid*; and, the result was, a declared resolution, on my part, to write and publish a pamphlet in defence of my country, which pamphlet he pledged himself to answer: his pledge was forfeited: it is known that mine was not.

This autobiography and that which follows seems propelled by a desire to present his career to date as a series of spontaneous emotional and intellectual responses to external circumstances and inner feelings, over which he has little control. So, in this passage, he presents the dispute with his pupil and the Priestley addresses as the occasions for a first, spontaneous publication which springs in an unmediated way from his natural national chauvinism. If we look further into the article, polemical reasons for the partial nature of this account emerge. After a description of his American influence which makes large claims for the importance of his writings, Cobbett describes his return to England in 1800 and alludes bitterly to recent accusations from the government, which then welcomed him, that he is an '*American* and a *traitor*'. This immediately accounts for the previous stress on spontaneity, and his assertion that love of his country, rather than a love of literary fame, spurred his first efforts:

I was actuated, perhaps, by no very exalted notions of either loyalty or patriotism; the act was not much an act of refined reasoning, or of reflection; it arose merely from feeling, but it was that sort of feeling, that jealousy for the honour of my native country, which I am sure you will allow to have been highly meritorious, especially when you reflect on the circumstances of the times and the place in which I ventured before the public.

This self-projection has helped to create the Cobbett myth, but in this article it is clearly deployed in a calculating manner, in order to counter accusations that his new opposition to Pitt is unpatriotic in a time of war. By stressing his emotional identification with England, which makes him take criticism of it personally, and by demanding that Pitt admire this feeling, Cobbett turns the tables, implying that if Pitt attacks him then it is indeed Pitt who is a traitor to his country:

I believed you, when you so confidently and so solemnly declared, that 'the war might be carried on for any length of time without the creation of new debt,' and that 'it would not be difficult to provide taxes for eight years;' ... if *desertion* be a proper word to employ, it will be allowed that I did not desert you, but that you deserted me.

But, though thus deserted, I might, say your friends, have avoided going over to your political opponent. Here too, Sir, I shall, I hope, find very little difficulty in showing, that, though, in this case, the path pointed out by reason and by honour, by loyalty and by patriotism, was strewed with thorns, I have, in no single instance, deviated from it.

Despite these polemical gains, Cobbett's letters to Pitt are also interesting in the light of the criticisms made by his contemporaries that he changed his views in order to boost his sales or that he was an inveterate opponent who wrote well only from positions of opposition. When Cobbett conceals his earlier literary ambitions in this letter to Pitt he does so partly because *The Soldier's Friend* was considered seditious by the Establishment and would be easily cited as evidence for his treasonable views. But it is also true that Cobbett's famous persona was only born with his American writings, and that in America – at least until 1794 – his pen had yet to find its focus, its interest and its party. If it is invariably when Cobbett finds his enemies that he finds his voice, then this partial account of his entry into politics is in some symbolic sense true, as it marks the real beginning of his career. It is therefore interesting that he should express his disaffection from the English Tories by remembering (and misremembering) this moment of enabling opposition.

This method of arguing through autobiography is an oblique one. Such obliqueness is repeated on 15 December 1804, in 'Letter VI to the Right Honourable William Pitt on the Causes of the Decline of Great Britain',[5] where Cobbett makes his oppositional points by omission and analogy, as though direct assertion is at this stage too difficult to be attempted. Cobbett quotes comment in the ministerial press which predicts that the people of France will soon rebel against the tyranny of Napoleon, and in the same breath reports the 'tranquillity' of Ireland, and the 'sincere and ardent sentiments of loyalty' now evident there towards the British government. Cobbett wants to draw attention to the contradiction between these two statements. He points out that Ireland is now under martial law, and that if its inhabitants are really tranquil and loyal then this suggests that the sanguine hopes of a French rebellion against Napoleon are unlikely to be realized. In a curious passage headed and ended by long dashes which separate it off from the rest Cobbett adds: 'This argument, however, drawn from the experience of Ireland, is, it must be confessed, worth nothing, the radical position being shamelessly false; and, I have only introduced it in order to shew how completely destitute these writers are of principles where on to reason'. What makes this comment particularly odd is that while he hastily adds that the Radical argument is 'worthless', the arguments which follow reach more or less the same conclusion: that organizational and ideological control are not reasons for rebellion, but rather are effective means at the disposal of Napoleon (and, by analogy, the British government) for suppressing Dissent.

Cobbett again quotes from conservative promises that French rebellion is imminent, and again rejects them: 'thus, Sir, are the people of this country deceived; thus are duped; thus are their spirits buoyed up upon false hopes, by a reliance upon anything rather than their own national exertions.' Here Cobbett seems to repeat his conservative arguments as he deplores the lack of national spirit displayed by the English government and people, but now his presentation of Napoleon is far more positive than in the articles from 1802 which we examined in the last chapter:

It is not against a renowned military chief that a people rebels; it is not against such a chief that a people murmurs: no, Sir, they murmur and they rebel against rulers of an exactly opposite description. Such a chief may be tyrannical; but from this cause the great mass of the people will feel not much inconvenience. 'To men remote from power' his tyranny will hardly be known; while the glory which his military achievements shed upon the country, will illumine even the meanest hut, and will endear him to every one to whom nature has not denied the capacity of feeling that he has a share in that glory: and, of those who do not so feel, the enmity may be safely despised. Besides, the soft, the silent, the cat like paw of corruption and of perverted law; the exercise of tyranny under the name, and in the phrases, of justice and liberty, such as I have witnessed in America, for instance, is much more deleterious to society, as well as more grating to the soul of the individual, than the random bolts, the partial blows, of a single despot, which, at least, leave to the sufferer the consolation of being pitied.

The mix of ideas, and Cobbett's apparent anxiety in opposition, is obvious and intriguing here. The stress on the benefits of national glory for the common man seems part of the conservative discourse that we examined in the last chapter, yet at the same time the growing radicalism of his writing is evidenced by the distinction he draws between the political nation of the enfranchised and the mass of the population, as he points out that the majority of the population have nothing to do with political issues. Such a distinction puts the ministerial papers – and the refined reader – firmly in their place, as it points out their numerical insignificance. Again, the description of the greater evil of disguised tyranny seems to be making an oblique point about Britain, especially with her role in Ireland. But this obvious and satirical point is itself hedged about with disguises: Cobbett distracts our attention from the British analogy by invoking America as an example of such tyranny. This manoeuvre is repeated as Cobbett recants his former characterization of Napoleon as a 'Corsican adventurer':

The aversion to upstarts, I grant, is powerful and highly laudable: it has its rise in the most just and noble sentiments of the mind. But, Sir, those who have risen, however suddenly, by deeds of arms, are not upstarts. The term upstart will never be applied to the hero of the Nile. Extraordinary talents, exerted in rendering great public services, whether in the cabinet or the field, are a fair foundation for rank and power. Men exalted by such means may be an object of envy amongst their less meritorious or less fortunate rivals, but the mass of the people will seldom fail to acknowledge the justice of their claims. The upstarts whom good men hate are such as have risen by low and base arts, or who have grown up out of the follies or vices of their particular patrons, or of the government and governing system in general. They have been well denominated mushrooms; for they spring from the rotten part of the state, and the soil that bears them will seldom bear anything else. Crawling sycophants, labourers in the dirty work of corruption, with all the endless list of jobbers of every description, such as I have seen in America, for instance. Such are the upstarts; men who, having, as it were, stolen fortunes from the public treasure; that is to say from the labour of the people, become, by the means of those fortunes, the possessors of the land, making slaves of those whom they have already pillaged and impoverished: such are the upstarts, whom every honest and honourable man must hate, and to whose sway he can never submit without impatience.

Again, Cobbett obliquely characterizes Britain – and here in terms that will become familiar in his later unequivocally Radical writings, as he reviles 'sycophants', 'jobbers' and parasites upon the public purse. In the first letter to Pitt, we remember, Cobbett's self-portrayal as a patriot implicitly branded Pitt as a traitor. In this sixth address he declares that it is placemen and pensioners who are the real upstarts, not men of arms. In an interesting anticipation of his later preoccupations, Cobbett also appeals to a populist judgement on political rulers, as he avers that military heroes will always win the approbation of the masses. But again, just as the parallel with Britain is becoming clear, he invokes America as his explicit example. This oblique method of argument implies a profound anxiety about the reader he is addressing, who may not concur with his arguments and who may even prosecute him.

Such anxiety about the reader also seems to be signalled by his assessment of Napoleon. When Cobbett defends Napoleon's rise he declares that the term 'upstart', with its dismissive suggestion of vulgarity, can never be applied to men who have risen through military exploits, or who have done great public service for their country. If the real upstarts are parasites upon the public purse like Pitt, then Cobbett's own career seems to parallel those aspects of

Napoleon's progress which are stressed here. Cobbett gained his first social elevation through the army, rising to the rank of sergeant-major, while in the first letter of the series he justified his authority as a commentator, and defended his ideological switch, by appealing to his own great service to Britain during his time in America:

> In that city, where, when I started on my career, an Englishman was ashamed to own his country; where my life had been a hundred times threatened unless I desisted to write against France; where the name of his Majesty was never mentioned unaccompanied with some epithet too foul and calumnious to repeat; in that city I lived to see a public celebration of Lord Nelson's victory over the French, and to be serenaded with the tune of 'God Save the King!' What a change! Certainly not to be entirely ascribed to me. But, it was a change which I had a considerable share in producing; I staid the mischief; I prevented that which would have prevented us from profiting from the events which time was hastening along. My American friends give me all the credit of this change: I claim no such thing; but I know, that I deserve, and that I shall have, the lasting gratitude of both countries. The services, of which I have been speaking, have not ceased their operation: they are still active: the people of America cannot, even if they would, forget what they have learned against France; nor, which is, indeed, of more importance, will they again be silenced with regard to the merits of Great Britain. The time of my writing will be looked back to as a memorable epoch, not only in American politics, but in the political mind of America. I untied the tongue of British attachment: by an extraordinary exertion I broke the shackles in which the public mind had been held from the commencement of the revolutionary war, and once more opened a way for the workings of nature and of truth.[6]

This egoistic self-projection infuriated his opponents, but it is interesting in conjunction with the later stress on public service as a sign of honour which Cobbett identified as a feature of Napoleon's career. If Cobbett's authority is challenged by his defection into opposition, and if his social status is now increasingly likely to be used as a weapon against him by government supporters, then his defence of Napoleon, which parallels his previous self-celebration, may also be a self-defence. This goes some way to explain the political value of Cobbett's growing admiration for Napoleon, which Coleridge derided in the passage with which this chapter began.

Cobbett's attempts to communicate his changed vision of British society are framed in ways which often resemble the strategies of his conservative writings. As ever, Cobbett's declared aim in this period is to enlighten his readers, so that they can act in an informed manner. 'I wish to see people, of all ranks and degrees, ready and resolutely resolved to defend their country, to repel and to chastise the foreign foe; but I wish not to see them the dupes of the weak or wicked men, whose misconduct has exposed them to the inroads of that foe.'[7] But in this period of transition towards Radicalism the nature of the 'truth' to be conveyed becomes contested, while Cobbett also experiments with different discursive practices through which to express it. In the remainder of this chapter we shall see him experimenting with the discourses of deism, Dissent and the ancient constitution by turns, as though he is searching for a discourse adequate to his Radical needs.

Cobbett's use of discourse associated with varying religious positions is particularly interesting since his written statements on religion are notoriously pragmatic. Cobbett usually dramatizes himself as a staunch Anglican. Even in his intensely pro-Catholic, medievalist *History of the Protestant Reformation*, he still makes this attachment plain:

Born and bred a Protestant of the Church of England, having a wife and numerous family professing the same faith, having the remains of most dearly beloved parents lying in a Protestant churchyard, and trusting to conjugal or filial piety to place mine by their side, I have in this undertaking had no motive, I can have had no motive, but a sincere and disinterested love of truth and justice.[8]

Accounting for this loyalty to Anglicanism, most biographers note his political concern with tradition, and the symbolic value of religious faith. Anglicanism is seen as synonymous with conservatism, which accounts for his loyalty to it in his Tory phase, while John Carswell notes that Anglicanism was as much a feature of the agricultural countryside as Methodism was a phenomenon of the city.[9] In this case, as an essentially agricultural Radical, Anglicanism still seems the obvious choice for Cobbett even after his change of loyalties. This pragmatism is generally recognized, and frees us from the necessity of trying to make ideological sense of his simultaneous use of deist and Dissenting rhetoric in the period from his imprisonment in 1810. Instead we can account for this phenomenon as yet more evidence for the self-consciously rhetorical nature of Cobbett's journalistic practice.

Deists asserted that the existence of God was a rational necessity but rejected revealed religion. A part of the general Enlightenment attempt to replace superstition and bigotry with reason, deism was unrespectable as it rejected the moral certainties which we saw the *Anti-Jacobin* defending in the last chapter, and was associated with French Jacobinism which had replaced Christian worship with the worship of Reason during the 1790s. Publishing Paine's *Age of Reason* and D'Holbach's *Ecce Homo*, which both attempted to discredit revealed Christianity, were activities subject to prosecution. In a series of letters and articles in the *Political Register* of 1813 to 1815 Cobbett experiments with these deist ideas – this apparently uncharacteristic episode in his career has been researched by Ian McCalman,[10] and is interesting for us as a clear example of the artifice and experimentation of Cobbett's radical style. Indeed, this pragmatic experimentation might be seen as *characteristic* of the self-consciously rhetorical Cobbett we are constructing in this study. We shall note two main points from this episode. Firstly, it gives an interesting stylistic twist to Cobbett's habitual preoccupation with 'truth', as in order to purvey a deist truth he is obliged, paradoxically, to write in disingenuous ways. Secondly, and more importantly, this experimentation with a rationalist, Painite type of Radical discourse runs concurrently with the exploitation of opposing Radical styles and is abandoned when it fails. In this period it seems that Cobbett is experimenting with varying Radical styles in order to reach his reader in the most effective way.

This enlightening debate began with Cobbett's discussion of the Trinity Bill, introduced to Parliament by William Smith, which proposed toleration of Freethinking Christians and Unitarians who rejected certain aspects of Christian doctrine. Cobbett observed in the *Political Register* that he found total acceptance or total rejection of Christianity acceptable, but not the halfway position favoured by rational Dissent. At the same time, George Cannon – a prominent member of the blasphemous underworld depicted by McCalman – began to contribute articles and letters to the *Political Register* purporting to be written by scholarly divines. All seemed to support Christianity, but 'their real purpose was to exacerbate the religious doubts of Cobbett and his readers by ridiculing the Established Church and the Christian religion.'[11] From this point Cobbett became involved with a group of Radical deists who met at the large London house of businessman Timothy Brown, and the deist campaign in the *Political Register* gathered pace with Cannon's 'disingenuous' portrayal of biblical incidents, and 'unctuous' presentation of religious doctrines, aiming to undermine religious authority.[12]

Cobbett himself joined in this disguised argument for deism by commenting upon the debate in his editorials and entering into argument with various real or fabricated correspondents. His writings on these matters at times resemble Cannon's satirical contributions, at others he writes more plainly. In an article of 20 November 1813, he gleefully reports on a letter (actually from Cannon[13]) received that week which praises his defence of Christianity but criticizes his inclusion of blasphemous letters in the *Register*. Cobbett defends this policy by arguing that his cogent arguments in favour of revealed religion can only gain weight from the inadequate reasoning of his foes:

> I am much flattered to perceive, that my correspondent, A. B. approves of the way in which I answered the *whys* and *wherefores* of Mr Fordham and Ecce Homo. They asked, *why* God should die; *why* he should choose to pass through the process of impregnation, delivery, swaddling clouts, circumcision, temptation by the Devil, buffeting, and, finally, hanging by those miscreants, the Jews; *why* he could not have saved men without all this. – To this cavil I answered by putting to them the question: '*Why* a chicken came out of an egg, instead of being littered as young dogs are.' – This it was which so much pleased my correspondent. Indeed it was a *clencher*; and, as A. B. observes, '*completely* silenced these poor, foolish, impertinent sort of inquirers.'

This verbal slapstick is amusing enough, but a few lines later Cobbett observes 'if the old maxim be true, that *Truth*, the more she is rubbed the brighter she will appear, *discussion* must always be in favour of those, who have *Truth on their side*; and, as we churchmen have truth on our side, discussion must be in *our* favour.'[14] The disjunction between this avowed aim of weighing varying views fairly, and the concealed derision of established religion motivating Cobbett's procedures, recalls the ambivalence of the 'Letters to Pitt' with their sidelong attacks on the British government. Such equivocation sits uneasily with his more characteristic pedagogic stance which is illustrated in the 'Summary of Politics' of two weeks later. Here Cobbett seems, more characteristically, to be speaking plainly – a fact perhaps signalled by the extraordinarily conversational tone of the following extract:

> The truth is (and I am not ashamed to avow it), that the reading of Ecce Homo, which I have performed with great care, has given rise to *difficulties* in

my mind. There are parts of that work, which, I confess, I am quite unable to answer; and which, nevertheless, I must see *answered* before my mind can be settled upon the subject. – It is, therefore, my intention to state the *difficulties* which I experience, in the hope that some one will clear them up for me. We are a pretty large family here; and, it is of importance that we should think rightly upon a matter of such vast consequence... It is very certain, that, where there are so many sects, all calling themselves *Christians*, and all differing from one another, *some of them must be in error*. They cannot *all* be right. Some of them must be teachers of falsehood. And from the teaching of falsehood, surely, no good can possibly arise. – It shall be my object to elicit the *truth*, as far as my inquiries go.[15]

Two months later however, in February 1814, Cobbett again writes at length in the disingenuous style described by Ian McCalman.[16] What 'truth' is, in this shifting context is unclear. It seems ironic that Cobbett's inclination towards reason seems obliged to voice itself in this treacherous rhetoric of disguise. Cobbett's starting point in this article is a declaration of support for the view that plunder is the soldier's 'legitimate harvest'. Cobbett had, in an earlier article, made this argument by taking biblical precedent as his authority. He repeats his assertion here, and cites 'an instance, wherein God himself, through his instrument, Moses, had warranted such plunder, particularly in the case of the unfortunate Midianites, who were first stripped, by God's chosen people, of all their goods and chattels, and were then, by the command of Moses, the servant of the Lord, all slaughtered, men, women, and children'. The significance of the juxtaposition of phrases like 'God's chosen people' and 'the servant of the Lord' with the barbarity of the acts described is obvious. Cobbett has revived this topic in the article in response to a 'Correspondent' who quibbles with this authority on technical rather than moral grounds, with a selective approach to the Bible which marks him as a Dissenter:

He says, that 'the form of the Jewish government, was that of a real *Theocracy*, that is, a government under the immediate superintendence of God himself, who was the ruler of the Jews, not under the simple title of governor of the universe, but was, strictly speaking, the *temporal* sovereign, who gave them a code of laws, which was the sole direction of their political conduct, and every authority, whether ordinary, or extraordinary, received its delegation immediately from him.' Therefore, says he, there can be no similarity in the cases on which to ground a parity of reasoning.

This theological hair-splitting subverts itself, as the lack of humane outrage evinced by the correspondent undermines the moral authority of Christianity. The absurd conclusion which Cobbett draws from this argument is that it entails the denial of the authority of *all* biblical teachings, on similarly technical grounds:

If this be the case, away goes at once all the Old Testament, at any rate; and all these copies of the Bible that are circulated about, and all the searchings into them, which poor boys and girls are desired to be incessantly making, must tend to the producing of great and general mischief. The people constantly hear sermons, founded on texts of this book. They are constantly exhorted to look on it as their guide; to resort to it, in short, as the means of procuring to themselves everlasting salvation; they are told that it is the word of God; they are told, that if they diligently read it, they can scarcely fail to do well in every act of life ... And, yet, in the midst of all this, directly in the teeth of all this, after all the soldiers have had Bibles put into their hands, and have, doubtless, in obedience to the wishes of their commanders, carried them in their knapsacks on foraging as well as other expeditions, up starts my correspondent, and with front of ten-fold brass, tells me, and tells the public through me, that we are not, as to cases of plunder, to take the Bible for our guide, because, forsooth, the government of the Jews was a government by God himself!

The tone of righteous indignation against the Correspondent's arguments becomes increasingly convincing throughout this passage. But at this point Cobbett deliberately undermines his own position, and the usual stress on the value of biblical teachings which he has been defending, by reminding the reader of the untenable stance with which he had begun:

If this be the case, if we are not to look upon the Bible as a sure guide in this respect, why are we to look upon it as a sure guide in any respect; why are we to consider it as any guide at all? – My correspondent very slily observes, that he *believes* me to *assent* to the *inspiration* of the scriptures; and that he *hopes* that I am acquainted with the history of the Jewish people. To be sure I assent to the inspiration of the scriptures; and to the inspiration of the *whole* of them too, and not to that of bits and pieces of them. I take them all together, and I take them, too, in the fair meaning of the words that are made use of. And, now, that I have made this avowal, let me ask my correspondent, why I am to look upon the ten commandments as any rule of conduct for me, unless the soldier is to be guided by the example of plunder in the case of the Midianites?

At this point Cobbett follows his argument through to its logical conclusion, arguing that if biblical authority is so selective, then commentaries should be provided with the Bibles given to the poor in order to advise them about what to accept or ignore. From this, Cobbett suggests that perhaps the Catholics had the right idea in keeping such problematic material from their flocks.

This article seems like a defence of biblical authority, then, but its real effect is to draw its reader's attention to problems of biblical interpretation, and to moments when Christian teachings seem morally unacceptable. In this way, like the writings of George Cannon, Cobbett's apparent defence of Christianity is actually a veiled attack upon it. With the suggestion that Catholicism is a wiser religion than Anglicanism, Cobbett's arguments add popery to blasphemy.

The radicalism of such procedures is obvious, as Cobbett associates himself with the French Enlightenment of atheism and reason, which rejected revealed religion as a superstitious bar to the free exercise of the rational faculty which alone could institute social justice. But this kind of radicalism is dangerous. For McCalman it belongs to the marginal underworld; while, as we have seen, the *Anti-Jacobin* both ridiculed and reviled the Jacobinical rejection of revealed moral codes. The taint of such deism enabled conservative writers to demonize Paine. I suggested above that this episode in Cobbett's career demonstrated his conscious choice of populism: we can support this suggestion by pointing out that Cobbett abandoned his flirtation with deism when it became clear that by doing so he was alienating his readers.[17] More significantly, in the light of his imminent address to the working class, the rejection of religion problematically entails the rejection of one of the only discourses readily available to them.

That Cobbett is aware of the potential radical power of biblical discourse is indicated by the fact that during the same period which saw the deist writings we have been exploring so far, he was also experimenting with the apocalyptic language of Dissent. The fact that Cobbett explores this discourse also makes his discursive pragmatism particularly clear, since he himself notoriously loathed Dissent in all its forms.

The discourse of religion is heterogeneous. Within the broad movement of Dissent alone there is the rational Dissent of the Unitarians and their like, Calvinist Puritanism, Wesleyan Methodism, and what E. P. Thompson called the 'poor man's Dissent' of Bunyan and the Primitive Methodists. The political roles of these groups and their discourses are often contested. Unitarianism can be seen as dangerously rational and assertive, while the Methodism of the poor – whether Wesleyan or Primitive – is deferential and pacific. This is E. P. Thompson's reading.[18] On the other hand, we might follow Marilyn Butler, seeing the Unitarianism of Richard Price, whose *Discourse on the Love of our Country* provoked Burke's *Reflections*, as sounding more extreme than it actually was.[19] Ian McCalman differs from E. P. Thompson by seeing Methodism as a door to an underworld where breakaway groups and inspired prophets like Richard Brothers and Joanna Southcott presented a real alternative of plebeian Radicalism.[20]

Dissent had, of course, been associated with Radicalism from the Civil War. E. P. Thompson suggests that its apocalyptic language is the medium through which 'minority groups have articulated their experience, and projected their aspirations for hundreds of years.'[21] David Hall similarly notices that Dissenting discourse is one which has slipped its leash and become the language of the people.[22] Olivia Smith, as we have already seen, portrays biblical language as one of the only authoritative discourses available to the disenfranchised, and one, moreover, which confounds class distinctions and promises justice and peace for the suffering.[23] Regardless of the nuances of belief and practice among different groups Dissenting rhetoric sounds automatically subversive as its characteristic use of millennial language promises the imminence of total change.[24] In Richard Price's writing, this is combined with a stress on reason and truth which is reminiscent of the Enlightenment:

What an eventful period is this! I am thankful that I have lived to it; and I could almost say, *Lord, now lettest thou thy servant depart in peace, for mine eyes have seen thy salvation.* I have lived to see a diffusion of knowledge, which has undermined superstition and error – I have lived to see the rights of men better understood than ever; and nations panting for liberty, which seemed to have lost the idea of it...

Tremble all ye oppressors of the world! Take warning all ye supporters of slavish governments, and slavish hierarchies! Call no more (absurdly and wickedly) REFORMATION, innovation. You cannot now hold the world in darkness. Struggle no longer against increasing light and liberality. Restore to mankind their rights; and consent to the correction of abuses, before they and you are destroyed together.[25]

Marilyn Butler notes of Price that while his actual political aims were modest this tone makes him sound like an extremist. The second paragraph, stressing reformation rather than innovation, makes his moderation clear, but the final phrases envisage the overthrow of power in apocalyptic language which conversely makes revolution seem imminent. Ultra-Radical Robert Wedderburn, member of the violently Radical underworld, actually sounds more pacific than Price in his depiction of the Spencean Utopia to come:

Will not priests follow their princes and sing the solemn dirge of tyranny and corruption falling into contempt, and hail the Kingdom of Christ forwarded by Spence, and experience the new birth, 'for a nation shall be borne in a day'. Then shall the worthless kings who thirst for human blood to support their tottering thrones turn their swords and spears into ploughshares and pruning hooks, then will it be said, and not before, as the apple tree amongst the trees of the wood, so is my beloved sovereign amongst the sons. I sat down under its shadow with great delight, and its fruit was pleasant to my taste.[26]

As E. P. Thompson points out, Joanna Southcott's prophecy of impending doom is vague enough to accommodate religious or political interpretations. Her imagery and preoccupations resemble both Price and Wedderburn, indicating that this discourse, like that of the pastoral or the ancient constitution, is one propelled by convention:

O England! O England! England! the axe is laid to the tree, and it must and will be cut down; ye know not the days of your visitation... The midnight-hour is coming for you all, and will burst upon you. I warn you of dangers that now stand before you, for the time is at hand for the fulfillment of all things. 'Who is he that cometh from Edom, with dyed garments from Bozrah; that speaketh in righteousness, mighty to save all that trust in him; but of my enemies I will tread them in mine anger, and trample them in my fury; for the day of vengeance is in my heart, and the year of my redeemed is come.'[27]

The conventionality of this discourse makes its tone as easy to reproduce as those of the pastoral or the ancient constitution. Like them, its use implies a whole political and moral perspective, as well as positing a particular kind of reader. Unlike the language of pastoral, however, the audience indicated is defined by its very breadth. That is, if the use of pastoral implies a well-educated audience, the use of apocalypse implies a more or less Radical readership drawn from all classes. It is interesting, then, that Cobbett increasingly explores the resonance of apocalyptic language in the period after 1810 when the radicalism of the *Political Register* is confirmed and extended. There is a sense in which the usage reflects

Cobbett's own sense of oppression and powerlessness in his state of imprisonment, but it also seems significant as a means by which to break out of the constraints of enfranchised political discourse.

Imprisoned in 1810 for speaking out against military flogging – for having spoken 'the truth' – Cobbett's tone during this period becomes increasingly prophetic, and at times he sounds like a seventeenth-century martyr. He develops a demonology of the Establishment press, where they are habitually designated the 'MEAN, MERCENARY and MALIGNANT crew,'[28] placemen and pensioners are 'the sons and daughters of Corruption,'[29] and the *Political Register* is often headed by evangelical texts from the Bible: for example, 'The hope of the HYPOCRITES shall perish.'[30] An article of 2 January 1811 is a good example, where the apocalyptic insults rise to a surreal crescendo: 'those vile men who deal in and fatten upon corruption... the people's enemies... the venal and corrupt crew; that tribe of hypocrites... these corruption mongers, these publishers of fawning paragraphs, these flatterers of the Princes, these varnishers of their faults, these hypocritical and canting slaves, these MEAN, MERCENARY and MALIGNANT men...'[31] This rhetoric of Dissent does not represent a turning-away from the preoccupation with the discovery of 'truth' which, I have suggested earlier in this chapter, continued to characterize Cobbett's writings of ideological change. Existing contemporaneously with the deist writings we have already explored, Cobbett's prophetic role is still to enlighten and to inform his readers.

Cobbett addresses the leading article of the *Political Register* for 14 January 1815[32] to Major Cartwright, the venerable advocate of constitutional Radicalism in the period. It concerns the treaty of Ghent of 24 December 1814 which concluded the Anglo-American war raging since 1812. Cobbett's subject is the misinformation and inconsistency of the ministerial papers:

We now come to the most important and most interesting part of our subject; namely, THE CONSEQUENCES of this peace, made at such a time and under such circumstances. Considered as to its probable and almost necessary consequences, it is, in my opinion, an event of infinitely greater importance to the world than any that has taken place since the discovery of the Art of Printing. But I will not enter further into the subject, 'till I have laid before you, or, rather, put upon record, for the sake of reference, some of the overflowings of gall, which this event has brought from the throats of the sworn enemies of freedom.

Characteristically, then, Cobbett is proposing to enlighten his readers, and he goes on to indicate the appropriate response to the materials he quotes. The hyperbole of his opening estimation of the importance of the treaty of Ghent sets the scene for his imminent switch into the language of apocalypse as it indicates that the circumstances with which he is dealing are of grave importance to the future of the nation and the world.

Cobbett continues by quoting the attitudes of the conservative press towards America, with whom England is now at peace, attempting to damn them out of their own mouths, by picking out phrases which he will return to again and again throughout his attack:

There are several of our public prints, indeed, a very great majority of them, in country as well as in town, which have urged the *justice* and *necessity* of extinguishing the American Government; that '*ill-organised association*;' that '*mischievous example* of the *existence* of a Government, founded on *Democratical Rebellion.*' This peal was rung from one end of the country to the other. But the print, which led the van in this new crusade against liberty, was that vile newspaper, the *Times*, to which paper we and the world owe no small portion of those consequences which will result from the peace of Ghent, followed by such a war.

It is at this stage (signalled, perhaps, by the reference to the 'crusade' of *The Times*) that Cobbett launches into his apocalyptic denunciation. Suddenly Cobbett is a prophet, crying out the truth in a wilderness of misinformation and exulting at the overthrow of corruption:

– This print was, upon this occasion, the trumpet of all the haters of freedom; all those who look with Satanic eyes on the happiness of the free people of America; all those who have been hatched in, and yet are kept alive by, Bribery and Corruption. To judge of the feelings excited in the bosoms of this malignant swarm by the peace of Ghent; to enjoy the spectacle of their disappointment and mortification; of their alternate rage and despondency; of the hell that burns in their bosoms: to enjoy this spectacle, a spectacle that we ought to enjoy, after having endured the insolence of their triumph for so many years; to enjoy this spectacle we must again look into this same print; hear their *wailing*, view the *gnashing of their teeth*, see now the foam of revenge, and then the drivel of despair, issue from their mouths, teeming with execrations. With the *help of the Ministers*, we have, for once, beat the sons and daughters of corruption; and if we bear our success with moderation, let us, at any rate, hear and laugh at the cries of our always *cruel*, and, until now, insolent enemy.

With this vision of corruption overthrown, there are strong echoes of biblical punishments from that of Sodom and Gomorrah to the overthrow of Babylon and its wealthy but corrupted citizens; there is also an echo of John's vision of the 'three unclean spirits like frogs [which] come out of the mouth of the dragon, and out of the mouth of the beast, and out of the mouth of the false prophet'.[33] The reactionary press, in Cobbett's demonology, is the false prophet, the beast, and the dragon. When Cobbett says that 'hell ... burns in their bosoms' we are reminded of Milton's Satan: 'Which way I fly is Hell; myself am Hell'.

The effect of this apocalyptic language is to create a simple but unassailable denomination of sin and virtue: a black-and-white assessment of the moral value of the writings of Cobbett's enemies as falsehood, and his own writings as 'truth': 'As far as I have been able to do it openly through the press, I have, during the war, as you will have perceived, made known the denunciations of these wretches against the liberties of America; and it may not be less useful to make known their wailings, their fears, their despair at the peace...' Definitions of words like 'liberty' which, as we know, were contested in this period, are offered with only one possible interpretation; 'wretches' are clearly defined. The religious language lends this partisan terminology weight and apparent sanction, as the parallels with Babylonian despair, for example, tally neatly with Cobbett's description of the discomfiture of his enemies.

But there are serious problems with this usage. The way in which such apocalyptic language is abruptly introduced, with such an unequivocally and univocally political meaning, makes its designs on the reader uncomfortably apparent. In this way, Cobbett's attempts to cut out alternative definitions of words like 'liberty' and 'wretch', for example, seem not convincingly imperceptible but instead uncomfortably self-announcing. Further, such millennial language can have the opposite effect to the authoritative one desired, and can instead come across to its reader as hysteria and instability. Richard Brothers, for one, was committed to Bedlam. This danger is acknowledged by Hazlitt in his article of the early 1820s, when he remarks indulgently that Cobbett 'is rather too fond of *the Sons and Daughters of Corruption.*'[34] Used incongruously, then, Dissenting discourse can be laughable or alienating instead of authoritative and classless.

A less obvious and more successful use of Dissenting rhetoric can be traced later in Cobbett's career and in more desperate circumstances. As Olivia Smith notes, the rhetoric of Dissent is also a partly conscious referral back to the seventeenth century and, especially in the context of the struggle for a free press, a potent symbol of free conscience. Thus she notes the way in which William Hone relied on his reading of the trials of Foxe, Bunyan and especially Lilburne when taken up himself for blasphemous libel. As an example, Smith points out how Hone's assertion that he is being tried for his life presents him as a seventeenth-century martyr.[35] Smith also notes the way in which Hone, like Lilburne, appeals to the jury directly as Christians who are more charitable than the State which is trying him.[36] Both these points of similarity are expressed by Hone late in his third Trial:

> He felt the most unqualified confidence in the principles and judgement of the Jury, whose attention, he feared, he had too long occupied. But he felt that he was struggling for life, for should he have the misfortune to be pronounced guilty by the Jury, the punishment which awaited him would be equal to the loss of it.[37]

It seems significant and beyond coincidence that, being tried in 1831, on charges of seditious libel, Cobbett appeals successfully to his jury as follows: 'It is their fears which make them attack me, and it is my death they intend. In that object they will be defeated for, thank Heaven, you stand between me and destruction.'[38] The echo of Hone's echo of Lilburne is subtle and effective.

Cobbett's early Radical texts are characterized by the pragmatic exploration of a variety of oppositional discourses. Those we have explored so far in this chapter have been rationalist and Dissenting by turns. Such diversity survives into Cobbett's Radical maturity, in so far as his texts are often a Barthian arena of clashing and mingling discourses, where experimenting, clutching at an appropriate image, and straining towards a mutual language are parts of his task. After late 1816, however, that task does in some sense become easier, as he begins to exploit, rather than to be bound by, his potentially problematic relationship with his audience. His letter 'To the Journeymen and Labourers of England, Wales, Scotland and Ireland' is important not so much because it represents a stylistic turning-point in itself, but because it marks the beginning of this exploitation of readership which soon does facilitate the achievement of his unique stylistic practices.

With this letter, as we know, Cobbett addressed the labouring classes directly for the first time, practically as well as figuratively. That is, not only did he address the leading article of the paper to them, but he also made this an effective communication by publishing the article as a twopenny pamphlet. This circumvented the Stamp Act which demanded that a 'newspaper' pay a tax which artificially raised its price. As comment only, the pamphlet escaped the definition of 'newspaper' and could therefore be circulated at a much lower price.

So the significance of the twopenny pamphlet is its direct address to a nascent and as yet unexploited national audience. By 1816, the *Political Register* is no longer a paper written to the middle and upper classes and read by groups of labourers. With its dual publication it is a paper written first and foremost to a vast labouring-class audience and read by their social superiors. This instantly – albeit perversely – creates the role of maverick which Cobbett relishes, as he renders the political 'ins' outsiders to his enterprise. With the publication of 'To the Journeymen and Labourers of England, Wales, Scotland and Ireland'[39] we see him metaphorically turning his back on his former audience, leaving them to peer over his shoulder into the cosy world established between himself and his new audience. As is clear from the cosiness of the *Courier*'s discussion of royal affairs, quoted in the last chapter, this is what the working-class reader has been obliged to do for generations. To turn the tables in this way is a profoundly radical act.

It is so despite the fact that even at this stage Cobbett's Radicalism is qualified. His famous statement of nostalgia – 'we want *great alteration*, but we want *nothing new*' – originates in this article and, as he does not yet endorse universal manhood suffrage, the audience he addresses in this article is still one which he does not wish to see enfranchised.

FRIENDS AND FELLOW COUNTRYMEN,
Whatever the pride of rank, of riches, or of scholarship may have induced some men to believe, or to affect to believe, the real strength and all the resources of a country, ever have sprung and ever must spring, from the labour of its people; and hence it is, that this nation, which is so small in numbers and so poor in climate and soil compared with many others, has, for many ages, been the most powerful nation in the world: it is the most industrious, the most laborious, and therefore, the most powerful. Elegant dresses, superb furniture, stately buildings, fine roads and canals, fleet horses

and carriages, numerous and stout ships, warehouses teeming with goods; all these, and many other objects that fall under our view, are so many marks of national wealth and resources. But all these spring from labour. Without the Journeyman and the labourer none of them could exist; without the assistance of their hands, the country would be a wilderness, hardly worth the notice of an invader.

Here, as we shall see frequently throughout his Radical career, Cobbett attempts to overturn the refined assumption that the vulgar have no place within the political nation, and no entitlement to human rights. Cobbett points out that the labourer is in fact the essential realizer of upper-class luxury and of the refinement which is seen as a prerequisite to power. Formally, this point is reinforced by addressing the disregarded labourer at all. This enacts the respect and consideration that Cobbett is explicitly arguing should be paid to them. The conversational tone which does not patronize turns the journeyman into the recipient of advice, rather than the object of a sermon or a reading of the riot act.

Not only is the whole stress upon the labourer, and the assertion that he alone is responsible for the greatness of 'Great Britain', but those who think differently – i.e. the political nation, previously presented in abstract terms – are just 'some men'. Not merely is the ruling class dismissed in this way, but Cobbett implies that they are aware of their own insignificance. There seems to be a sidelong snub aimed at the upper-class reader with the suggestion that they merely 'affect to believe' in their own contribution to the national good. Despite the fact, then, that to an important degree the achievement of the text itself is a symbolic one tied up with its low price and wide availability, the stylistic attributes I have identified here point forward to the achievements of Cobbett's later Radical journalism.

With this correct idea of your own worth in your minds, with what indignation must you hear yourselves called the Populace, the Rabble, the Mob, the Swinish Multitude; and, with what greater indignation, if possible, must you hear the projects of those cool and cruel and insolent men, who, now that you have been, without any fault of yours, brought into a state of misery, propose to narrow the limits of parish relief, to prevent you from marrying in the days of your youth, or to thrust you out to seek your bread in foreign lands, never more to behold your parents or friends? But suppress your indignation, until we return to this topic, after we have considered the cause of your present misery and the measures which have produced that cause.

As ever, Cobbett's aim is a pedagogic one, as he explains the 'real' significance of Malthusian population theory, of schemes of emigration, and of poor-law reform proposals.

The kind of language Cobbett employs in the opening paragraphs of the letter seems initially to be a bar to working-class participation. The syntax is still complex despite the apparent urge towards simplification. The sentences are long, though there is a minimum of inversion, a lack of passive verbs, and a reference to the 'soil' which seems a surprisingly concrete attribute of a nation state to come under political discussion. Cobbett similarly lists physical symbols of economic power, such as dresses, furniture, carriages, and ships, and observes, matter-of-factly, that 'without the Journeyman and the labourer none of them could exist'. Nevertheless, the concreteness of one image is countered by the abstractness of another – for instance, the opening sentence elects to portray the powerful classes metonymically as 'rank ... riches ... scholarship' rather than 'proud, rich and educated men'.

Midway through the article, however, the tone becomes noticeably more demotic as Cobbett recasts the message of his opening paragraphs in blunter terms:

You have been represented by the *Times* newspaper, by the *Courier*, by the *Morning Post*, by the *Morning Herald*, and others, as the *Scum* of society. They say, that you have *no business at public meetings*; that you are *rabble*, and that you *pay no taxes*. These insolent hirelings, who wallow in wealth, would not be able to put their abuse of you in print were it not for *your labour*. You create all that is an object of taxation; for even the *land* itself would be good for nothing without your labour.

For historians, the importance of this letter, and the 'Letter to Luddites' which followed shortly after, is that they attempt to politicize the working class and lead them away from aimless violence. For our purposes the interest also lies in this mix of styles, where the different kinds of language used – refined or colloquial – imply different audiences. That is, when Cobbett turns ostentatiously away from his refined readership to address the poor, that ostentation may be a part of the text's meaning. But Cobbett does not marginalize himself from mainstream political culture by turning exclusively to the disenfranchised. His text is still read by everyone, in two editions – one selling for twopence, the other for a shilling and this diversity seems reflected in his linguistic practice. His major achievement is that in this way he mobilizes two apparently exclusive audiences within a single text.

We can illustrate this by returning to the discourse of the ancient constitution, which is the third major style with which Cobbett experiments in this period. In the Introduction I noted that this discourse was one exploited by both Radicals and conservatives, and this sets it apart from the deist, Dissenting and pastoral discourses we have discussed so far, which are more or less exclusively associated with one or the other. One major achievement of the letter 'To Journeymen and Labourers' is its ability to draw out the shared aspects of this general veneration for the past, rewriting the conservative version of the myth, radicalizing the content and the form of its arguments and claiming them for the Radical side; in this way rendering change palatable and less easily suppressed as seditious. This suggestion will be illustrated by identifying the Radical and conservative versions of the myth and showing how Cobbett refuses to choose between them but rather draws on both to create his radical vision.[40]

The Radical ancient constitution is typically a Saxon one, brought to a sharp close by the Norman conquest and the ascendancy of a Norman aristocracy. Cobbett deviated sharply from this wisdom, however, throughout his career. He refused to condemn the Norman period, the monasteries, and some aspects of the feudal social system, and located social perfection not in the arcane Saxon past, but in the England of Edward I, Richard II and Henry VI – even, to some extent, in the 1760s of his childhood.[41] In this way he echoes the conservative version of the myth, which functions in such a way as to lend authority to existing forms of government. In this way, Cobbett seems to reject key aspects of the Radical version of the myth and to adopt parts of the conservative one.

This use of the myth might simply be seen as a confusion which mirrors that of his and any other period – Christopher Hill's essay on the 'Norman Yoke' certainly implies that the concept of the Yoke and the ancient constitution meant different things to different people at different times, and sometimes simultaneously.[42] But I think that by examining the language of Cobbett's ancient constitutionalism and that of his forebears we can say something a good deal more interesting and enlightening. By comparing the classic conservative formulations of Coke and Burke with those of Cobbett, and noticing how they differ imagistically with regard to the value of the individual within the 'organic', non-individualistic state they variously celebrate, we can identify Cobbett's method of making his own Radicalism more respectable, and of showing up the shortcomings of the common stock of conservative images, while doing both in order to draw his working-class reader into possibilities of political action.

Here is Coke describing the individual's relationship to the Common Law, which is the basis of the ancient constitution:

> we are but of yesterday, (and therefore had need of the wisdom of those that were before us) and had been ignorant (if we had not received light and knowledge from our forefathers) and our days upon the earth are but a shadow in respect of the old ancient days and times past, wherein the laws have been by the wisdom of the most excellent men, and in many successions of ages, by long and continual experience, (the trial of light and truth) fined and refined, which no one man, (being of so short a time) albeit he had in his head the wisdom of all the men in the world, in any one age could ever have effected or attained unto.[43]

Stylistically, the convoluted and endlessly qualified sentence which makes up this extract may be merely the product of its age, or of its place in legal literature; but Coke's approach seems significant even in those lights, as it implies the opacity of experience, and the impossibility of making direct statements or judgements about the world. This, indeed, is also the sense of the passage, as it discusses the 'stupendous wisdom' (as we shall presently see Burke describing it) of the Common Law, which no individual can hope to comprehend alone. While the passage is part of a wider attempt to prove the sovereignty of the people as against the monarch, its value as a statement of conservatism is clear, as it rules out the possibility of change within the existing, entrenched bases of power, which exist in a web of tautologies: 'the old ancient days and times past'. These two aspects are of course far from incompatible when we remember that until Cobbett's day 'the people' referred to the enfranchised *political* nation, which constituted only a fraction of the whole.

The stress on collective wisdom and race memory evident in both the passage we have quoted from Sir Edward Coke, and the famous passage from Burke which treats of the temporal and social relationships which make up the English constitution create a sense of quasi-religious grandeur:

> Our political system is placed in a just correspondence and symmetry with the order of the world, and with the mode of existence decreed to a

permanent body composed of transitory parts; wherein, by the disposition of a stupendous wisdom, moulding together the great mysterious incorporation of the human race, the whole, at one time, is never old, or middle-aged, or young, but in a condition of unchangeable constancy, moves on through the varied tenour of perpetual decay, fall, renovation, and progression ... By adhering in this manner and on those principles to our forefathers, we are guided not by the superstition of antiquarians, but by the spirit of philosophic analogy. In this choice of inheritance we have given to our frame of polity the image of a relation in blood; binding up the constitution of our country with our dearest domestic ties; adopting our fundamental laws into the bosom of our family affections; keeping inseparable, and cherishing with the warmth of all their combined and mutually reflected charities, our state, our hearths, our sepulchres, and our altars.[44]

Thus, Coke talks of the 'old ancient days and times past' as a storyteller might begin a tale of Arthur and his knights; and he creates a sense of supernatural wisdom in the collective memory by stressing the ephemeral and limited nature of the individual, including himself: 'we are but of yesterday...our days upon the earth are but a shadow...man, (being of so short a time)...' This is a direct echo of I Chronicles, 29.15: 'For we are strangers before thee, and sojourners, as were all our fathers: our days on the earth are as a shadow, and there is none abiding.' As such, Coke's passage draws an implicit parallel between the eternal nature of God and of society, which in imitation of Him approaches omniscience. Likewise, the insistent repetition of the fact of our mortality seems to mimic the repetitious demise of mere individuals, in contrast to the enduring nature of the collective legal and constitutional race memory. Similarly, Burke not only speaks of the 'stupendous' wisdom of our forefathers, but also implies a divine sanction of the status quo as he speaks of the 'decreed' nature of a 'permanent body composed of transitory parts'. Again, the stress is on the dominance of the permanent whole over the transitory part, as it is 'never old, or middle-aged, or young, but in a condition of unchangeable constancy, [and] moves on through the varied tenour of perpetual decay, fall, renovation, and progression.' For a moment it seems that for Burke the numberless individual deaths of individual members of society become part of a wheeling social growth, of ultimate 'progression'. But this is a wheel that always turns downward again from progression to decay, from individual progression to wider social stasis. Burke's image of the 'image of a relation in blood' signals the frailty of the individual in his scheme. Ostensibly the reference is to blood as in the blood-tie of kinship, but the choice of the word 'blood', along with the later inclusion of 'sepulchres' in his list of items intimately bound up with our way of life, suggests that our way of *death* is also central to our constitutional framework, as it defines the individual as necessarily subordinate to the eternal 'organic' state.[45] For both Burke and Coke, therefore, the only pronoun worth adopting is 'we'.

This choice of pronoun is extremely important when we turn to examine Cobbett's rendering of the virtues of the traditional, immemorial state in his letter 'To the Journeymen and Labourers'. Here Cobbett articulates his reactionary Radicalism as follows, in the context of a rejection of Painite Jacobins:

> Such men, now that they find you justly initiated, would persuade you, that, because things have been perverted from their true ends, there is *nothing good* in our *constitution and laws*. For what, then, did Hampden die in the field, and Sydney on the scaffold? And, has it been discovered, at last, that England has always been an enslaved country from top to toe? The Americans, who are a very wise people, and who love liberty with all their hearts... took special care not to part with any of the great principles and laws which they derived from their forefathers. They took special care to speak with reverence of, and to preserve, Magna Charta, the Bill of Rights, the Habeas Corpus, and not only all the body of the Common Law of England, but most of the rules of our courts, and all our form of jurisprudence... I know of no enemy of reform and of the happiness of the country so great as that man, who would persuade you, that we possess *nothing good*, and that *all* must be torn to pieces. There is no principle, no precedent, no regulation... favourable to freedom, which is not to be found in the Laws of England or in the example of our Ancestors... We want *great alteration*, but we want *nothing new*.

This passage shows the essential differences between the constitutionalism of Coke and Burke, and that of Cobbett. For while Cobbett celebrates the same institutions and rights, he regards them as lost, and in this way his version of the theory is Radical. There again, the implication is that those institutions and rights are either recently lost, or easily re-acquired, as he depicts the recent American Revolution as adopting English traditions of freedom, and asserts that 'we possess' institutions of value. The last famous phrase of the quotation stresses, in fact, the restorative nature of Cobbett's intentions, much more than the revolutionary one.

This is the real interest of this extract. While celebrating traditional, Burkean values, it simultaneously undermines the crucial notion of the 'organic' state holding sway over puny individuals, impotent due to their brief existence. I suggested that for Coke and Burke 'we' is the only worthwhile pronoun: we can see that this might be the case given such a view of the individual, where corporate action and existence are the only ones of import. Equally, of course, in the organic state, only corporate judgements can hold authority, especially judgements matured over several generations. Cobbett, by adopting 'I' and especially 'you', conversely invites the individual reader to consider, to judge, and hopefully to claim the authority to act: to reinstate the political framework he is championing. Politics becomes a dialogue, a discussion between living men, rather than a set of immutable laws matured over a hundred years.

Cobbett's text continues to make this clear, as it goes on to discuss the relative virtues of a passive or an active approach to the issue of rights. He quotes a 'canting Scotchman', publisher of a paper named the *Champion*, who preaches quiescence and 'the virtues of the "*fireside*"'. Cobbett's response is a robust one:

Might we ask this Champion of the tea-pot and milk-jug, whether Magna Charta and the Bill of Rights were won by the fire-side? Whether the tyrants of the House of Stuart and of Bourbon were hurled down by fire-side virtues? Whether the Americans gained their independence, and have preserved their freedom, by quietly sitting by the fire-side? Oh no! These were all achieved by *action*, and amidst bustle and noise. *Quiet* indeed! Why, in this quality, a log, or a stone, far surpasses even the pupils of this 'Champion' of quietness...

There are two points to make here, I think. First, that such a passage clearly reinforces the sense of activity possible to the individual that was suggested by the use of 'I' and 'you' earlier in the text. And second, that by doing so, it also seems to negate the preoccupation with the mortality of the individual which haunts the writings of Burke and Coke. This negation seems implicit in the stress on 'bustle and noise' and the idea that, while within such bustle men may and must have died, their actions prior to death have achieved change and influenced the shape of the society they inhabited. Life for Cobbett, in other words, is more significant than death; whereas for Burke and Coke death, as it stresses the consequent irrelevance of individual actions and desires, is more significant than life.

Here, perversely, the implications of Cobbett's style directly recall Paine's assessment of Burke's argument that the Revolution Settlement applied indefinitely to future generations. While explicitly rejecting Paine in this article, Cobbett's assumptions and formal procedures seem implicitly to echo the following emphasis on the rights and duties of the living from *The Rights of Man*:

> Every age and generation must be as free to act for itself, *in all cases*, as the ages and generations which preceded it. The vanity and presumption of governing beyond the grave, is the most ridiculous and insolent of all tyrannies. Man has no property in man; neither has any generation a property in the generations which are to follow ... Every generation is, and must be, competent to all the purposes which its occasions require. It is the living, and not the dead, that are to be accommodated.[46]

Such perversity is characteristic of Cobbett's Radical writing, and a part of its strength. It is perhaps the incorporation of Paine into Burke, the bringing together of apparently incompatible visions, which constitutes Cobbett's achievement here. With this method he makes Radicalism respectable and reaction subversive.

This is also true of his eclectic version of the ancient constitution. What Cobbett shares with Burke, which makes him seem less straightforwardly Radical in the tradition of that myth, is a belief that the immediately pre-industrial society of the eighteenth century represented a social high-point, and a belief in a multigraded, complex social hierarchy. Cobbett has no levelling urges: what he wants is prosperity for the labourer of the kind which he claims existed in his childhood, expressing a 'peasant radicalism' identified by Daniel Green as concerned above all with 'ancient rights and the bellies of the poor.'[47] But this is where Burke and Cobbett part company again: Cobbett's specific social concern for the real lives of ordinary people is un-Burkean in its specificity, practicality and concern for the socially underprivileged, and humanizes the political theory of the social conservatives, radicalizing the politically acceptable. Cobbett's mixture of discourses turns the images and assumptions of the conservatives back upon them; in Olivia Smith's terms, he adopts the literary images of the refined in order to rework them for the vulgar. Equally, he brings vulgar particularity and emphasis on action into Burke's organic vision. Cobbett's version of the organic communal state is a more 'vulgarly' active place than Burke's, as we have seen, and it is populated with real people from the vulgar classes. Grandad Bloxall, who made the crook that Cobbett carried as a child,[48] his grandmother who knitted his socks even after she turned blind,[49] his father, arguing on the side of American Independence in a local pub[50]: these kinds of characters fill the autobiographical pages of Cobbett's influential writings, while latterday versions of them fill his *Rural Rides*, fleshing out the idea of complex social ties with the people who lived the theory. This mixture of refinement and vulgarity allows Cobbett to discuss popular Radicalism without condemning himself to the margins, or allowing himself to be demonized as a thoroughgoing Jacobin.

The incidents of experimentation and rhetorical artifice explored in this chapter are only extreme examples of what Cobbett has been doing throughout his early career. Chapter 1 saw him calculating the arguments and images most likely to annoy his enemies, while Chapter 2 examined the period of his self-conscious conformity to the refined discursive practices appropriate to his briefly ministerial allegiances. As a conclusion to Part 1, which has been preoccupied in this way with the pragmatism and polemicism of Cobbett's procedures, the next chapter will explore his famous autobiographical writings as rhetorical device, conceived in direct relation to the political myth of the ancient constitution.

CHAPTER 4

Representing Old England

Part I has chronologically explored the rhetorical strategies deployed in Cobbett's writings until 1816, and has noted the changes in discursive practice demanded by his changing political aims during that period. In the Introduction I asserted that an understanding of this rhetorical self-consciousness puts a question mark over traditional critical tendencies to view Cobbett as a hot-headed combatant who writes with instinctive power, but whose instincts also lead him into regrettable intellectual nostalgia and bigotry. I have already explored the contemporary meanings and polemical usages of nostalgia at length. Part II will similarly find itself recurrently preoccupied with his populist rhetoric. I want to end Part I in this chapter by breaking away from chronology in order to suggest some ways in which Cobbett's egoistic persona – the third recurring problem identified in his prose – can be fruitfully related to the discourse of the ancient constitution and can be similarly seen as evidence of his sophisticated rhetorical strategy.

The passage of autobiography from *Advice to Young Men* with which this book began provides an example of Cobbett's problematic egoism, which is compounded as he adds

If such a man be not, after he has survived and accomplished all this, qualified to give advice to young men, no man can be qualified for that task. There may have been natural *genius*: but genius *alone*, not all the genius in the world, could, without *something more*, have conducted me through these perils... [T]hough I do not affect to believe, that *every young man*, who shall read this work, will become able to perform labours of equal magnitude and importance, I do pretend, that *every* young man, who will attend to my advice, will become able to perform a great deal more than men generally do perform...[1]

119

The apparent excess of self-praise here appears differently if we consider the material nature of the publication in which it appears. *Advice to Young Men* first appeared in instalments, at the price of sixpence a part. This self-advertisement appeared in the first number, and bearing this in mind it becomes apparent that the need to sell copies makes the presentation chosen particularly effective. Cobbett advertises his moral authority and exemplary life as something worth buying, something as practically useful as his introduction of 'several valuable trees' and 'the cultivation of the corn plant'. Something, in other words, which will be worth the reader's initial and recurring outlay of sixpence a part.

Similar material constraints operating in a periodical form are recognized by Margaret Beetham. She suggests that the periodical number's simultaneous existence as an individual text and as part of a greater whole puts strains upon it as it is pulled between open-endedness and closure. As a whole, a periodical series must have a recognizable character in order to keep its readers and Beetham identifies certain common characteristics: a constant referral to past and future numbers, an emphasis on serial articles, and a repetition of successful elements.[2] In *Advice to Young Men*, or in the grander context of Cobbett's thirty-three year *Political Register*, his self-promotion may also be a unifying factor, linking his works together and becoming his trademark.

These material requirements coincide conveniently with polemical aims as, for example, the advertising requirement in this passage enables him to stress features of his life and achievements in terms which, in the context we have been exploring, constitute political commentary. In this summary he repeatedly highlights as the ruling characteristic of his life and character the transgression of the boundary between vulgarity and refinement. He stresses the contrast between his lack of opportunities and his large successes, emphasizing the 'vulgarity' of his origins by the construction 'really, for me, high promotion, and with, for me, a large sum of money', which puts the apparent boastfulness of what follows into yet another perspective. Following on from these acknowledgements of his low social status Cobbett's comments seem not so much boastful of, but wondering at, his own achievements. That is, Cobbett seems to be continually stressing the unlikeliness – even the incongruity – of his life-story. The polemical point of such an emphasis is clear, as it asserts that the 'vulgar' can contribute to political and moral debate. In that *Advice to Young Men* was, in its title, addressed to those 'Of the Middle and Higher Ranks of Life', then there is also a polemical point in Cobbett 'egoistically' asserting his right and ability to offer advice at all. By doing so, he implicitly denies the inherent moral superiority of the upper classes, and instead asserts that the working classes may have a thing or two to teach their 'betters'.

Cobbett's egoism is also disliked by his critics because it seems another example of his prejudice and thoughtlessness. Referring political argument endlessly to his own experience smacks of an inability to transcend self in order to gain a wider and clearer view. When Cobbett paints his vision of the mythical golden world of the ancient constitution it is often rendered as the very personal world of his childhood. G. D. H. Cole acknowledged this self-aggrandizement in his famous assessment of Cobbett's egoism:

He had a way, almost like Walt Whitman's, of identifying himself with his countrymen, and of imagining each deed or suffering, all praise or blame, according to him, as given him in a sort of representative capacity.
'Oneself I sing, a simple separate person,
Yet utter the word Democratic, the word En Masse'.
As Whitman felt that he was Young America, Cobbett felt that he was Old England.[3]

Cole's answer to the problem – that Cobbett is speaking for his country and the social relationships he idealizes in a poetic way – seems to acknowledge the polemical demands that I have been exploring, and appears to suggest that his egoism is not a thoughtless mannerism but a literary ploy. To identify himself with Old England is an example of Cobbett avoiding charges of importing foreign political notions into England, while on the 'poetic' metaphoric level identified by Cole, he is also making the return of the golden age a possibility, as it is reincarnated in his own flesh. If Cobbett gains authority from the strength of the myth he taps, that is, then equally by embodying the myth in his writing he grants it a relevance it could not otherwise possess.[4]

This attempt to recreate the ancient constitution in the text is clearly a response to the fact that Cobbett, like all other constitutional writers, sees social harmony as a thing of the past, and the present as the site of disharmony and loss. That is, the ancient constitution as a myth seems successful because it addresses a shared sense of anxiety about the present. For Cobbett the attempt to bring the ancient constitution to life in his autobiographical writings is also an attempt to deny the alienations of the confusing present, described in John Wade's *History of the Middle and Working Classes*, of 1833:

> It is to this extraordinary [industrial] revolution, I doubt not, may be traced much of the bane and many of the blessings incidental to our condition – the growth of an opulent commercial and a numerous, restless and intelligent operative class; sudden alternations of prosperity and depression – of internal quiet and violent political excitement; extremes of opulence and destitution; the increase in crime; conflicting claims of capital and industry; the spread of an imperfect knowledge, that agitates and unsettles the old without having definitely settled the new foundations; clashing and independent opinions on most public questions, with other anomalies peculiar to our existing but changeful social existence.[5]

Cobbett's *Rural Rides* recorded in the form of a diary the events of several journeys around rural England in the 1820s. The most famous of Cobbett's works, it is an apparently artless exercise in self-expression, but an examination of the entry for Friday 27 September 1822 will begin to qualify that judgement.

> From *Lea* we set off this morning about six o'clock to get free-quarter again at a worthy old friend's at this nice little plain market-town. Our direct road was right over the heath through *Tilford* to *Farnham*; but we veered a little to the left after we came to Tilford, at which place on the Green we stopped to look at an *oak tree*, which, when I was a little boy, was but a very little tree, comparatively, and which is now, take it altogether, by far the finest tree that I ever saw in my life. The stem or shaft is short; that is to say, it is short before you come to the first limbs; but it is full *thirty feet round*, at about eight or ten feet from the ground ... The tree is in full growth at this moment. There is a little hole in one of the limbs; but with that exception, there appears not the smallest sign of decay. The tree has made great shoots in all parts of it this last summer and spring; and there are no appearances of *white* upon the trunk, such as are regarded as the symptoms of full growth ... The tree stands upon Tilford-Green, the soil of which is a light loam with a hard sand stone a good way beneath, and, probably, clay beneath that. The spot where the tree stands is about a hundred and twenty feet from the edge of a little river, and the ground on which it stands may be about ten feet higher than the bed of that river.[6]

What is particularly interesting about this passage is the way in which it works simultaneously as a straightforward piece of descriptive writing, and as a symbolic and allegorical one. That the '*oak tree*' is a symbol of England and Englishness is almost too obvious to need stating – it is hard to think of anything more symbolic of Old England than a venerable oak tree – and Cobbett seems to stress that 'the tree' has a significance over and above that attached to any ordinary tree by the repeated use of the phrase 'the tree' instead of an abbreviating pronoun. Another part of its extra significance seems to be that the tree and Cobbett are identified together. Both were youthful together; both now are strong and full-grown – with typical hyperbole, (or, if true, with typical egoism) Cobbett designates the tree the 'finest' that he ever saw. The italicized reference to *white* as a symptom of old age makes the identification even clearer, suggesting symptoms of human ageing. This allegorical matter might even seem heavy-handed were it not for the simultaneously matter-of-fact tone of the passage, dealing as it does with precise measurements, soil types and specific geographical locations. But this factual matter itself also contributes to the symbolism, as it insists that 'Old England' in the shape of the tree and the author, is very much alive and well, and, like the oak tree, living in a very precise location. If Cobbett is concerned to resist the disappearance of the agricultural past and to recreate the mythic golden age, then this mixture of symbolism and specificity is important.

But what perhaps is even more important is the notion of continuity between past and present which promises that all is not yet lost, and offers to redeem the fallen present. The crucial point about the oak tree, and what links it to Cobbett, is that like him it has spanned the vicissitudes of the period, and stands as a visible link to the past. What I want to suggest in now turning to examine specific examples of Cobbett's autobiographical writings is that the best of these are all in some way concerned to find these kinds of links and identifications.

A father like ours, it will be readily supposed, did not suffer us to eat the bread of idleness. I do not remember the time, when I did not earn my living. My first occupation was, driving the small birds from the turnip-seed, and the rooks from the peas. When I first trudged a-field, with my wooden bottle and my satchel swung over my shoulders, I was hardly able to climb the gates and stiles; and, at the close of the day, to reach home, was a task of infinite difficulty. My next employment was weeding wheat, and leading a single horse at harrowing barley. Hoeing peas followed, and hence, I arrived at the honour of joining the reapers in harvest, driving the team, and holding plough. We were all of us strong and laborious, and my father used to boast, that he had four boys, the eldest of whom was but fifteen years old, who did as much work as any three men in the parish of Farnham. Honest pride, and happy days![7]

This passage is taken from *The Life and Adventures of Peter Porcupine*, written in 1796 in America as a response to rumours and accusations circulated by his opponents. Portrayed as various kinds of rogue, Cobbett noted that his working-class origins were never guessed.[8] A large part of his task in this pamphlet, then, is to declare his honest working-class origins, to create as much discomfiture as possible in his Democratic adversaries. As a result the pamphlet is characterized by a good deal of class pride, and a stress on the honourable nature of an agricultural labourer's life and achievements, as we can see from the extract above. And already, despite the fact that at this time Cobbett is largely unaware that the agricultural basis of England is under threat from industrialization, we can see the attempt being made to create identifications and links between Cobbett and the natural landscape and between the past and the present. This is unsurprising: it is in Cobbett's polemical interests in this passage to identify himself with the soil in order to make his claims seem authentic; it is also worth remembering that he is at this time 2,000 miles and thirteen years away from Farnham, yet he has already set himself up as a representative of Old England.[9] Thus, in *Remarks of the Pamphlets Lately Published Against Peter Porcupine*, Cobbett begins with a quote from a letter he is supposedly writing to his father: 'when you used to set me off to work in the morning, dressed in my blue smock-frock and woollen spatterdashes, with my bag of bread and cheese and bottle of small beer swung over my shoulder on the little crook that my old god-father Boxall gave me, little did you imagine...'[10] For different reasons, then, at different times in his career, he is led to find the same kinds of identifications and links between past and present necessary to his rhetorical purpose.

Almost all critics writing about Cobbett note the recurrence of certain images as motifs in his writing. Thus, they will tell us, when we come across anything resembling a 'blue smock-frock' or a 'wooden bottle', we know that we are in for a nostalgic view of agricultural England, and an equally nostalgic glance into the photograph album of Cobbett's memory.[11] This sounds initially like a pejorative judgement, but in fact Cobbett's 'snapshots' are often central to his texts. In the description of childhood employments quoted above, he seems to press his claims for identity with the soil almost literally, as the passage makes him seem an integral part of the natural world. That is, by delineating himself as too small to climb gates and stiles without difficulty, Cobbett seems to depict himself also as too small to grasp these man-made impostures on the land mentally either. Despite the fact that throughout his writings he insists that it is agriculturally fertile nature and agricultural endeavour with which he is concerned, here he seems like a small animal dealing resourcefully with man-made objects but at one, instinctively, with the natural world. And if, throughout the rest of the passage, we are presented with a story of growth and development, of developing skills and understanding of agricultural methods, the previous image I think remains the dominant one. And, as in the much later passage from *Rural Rides* that we have already examined, where Cobbett 'becomes' an oak-tree, this image too is clearly one which seeks not merely to connect but to *merge* Cobbett with the natural landscape that he is seeking to defend.

This suggestion is supported by another seminal moment in the Cobbett photograph album, from *Advice to Young Men*. In the process of arguing against compulsory book-learning for children, he evokes a moment from his own childhood as follows:

When I was a very little boy, I was, in the barley sowing season, going along by the side of a field, near Waverly [*sic*] Abbey; the primroses and bluebells bespangling the banks on both sides of me; a thousand linnets singing in a spreading oak over my head; while the jingle of the traces and whistling of the ploughboys saluted my ear from over the hedge; and, as it were to snatch me from the enchantment, the hounds, at that instant, having started a hare in the hanger on the other side of the field, came up scampering over it in full cry, taking me after them many a mile.[12]

Again Cobbett presents himself as subject to his sense-perceptions, as they hold him in an 'enchantment,' and to compound the non-volitional sense of the passage, he describes the yielding of one enchantment to another as an act of no conscious decision. Thus the hounds come scampering over the field, 'taking me after them'. The lack of a reported decision to follow the hounds is compounded by the use of the non-finite verb form 'taking' which similarly lacks a definite moment of action by a definite agent, rather stressing the opposite qualities of timelessness and non-agency. Cobbett, in other words, seems to yield to an instinct of an animal nature, thoughtlessly responding to the cries and movement. The fact that the passage is an attempt to discourage his readers from imposing book-learning – the epitome of deliberation and rational thought – on their children, seems to reinforce this reading.

When Cobbett's autobiographical writings fail, we can begin to see the reasons for the success they enjoy elsewhere. In the following passage from *Rural Rides* we can see Cobbett attempting to paint a picture of his childhood, which fails to communicate anything of interest:

> As a due mixture of pleasure with toil, I, with two brothers, used occasionally to desport ourselves, as the lawyers call it, at this sand-hill. Our diversion was this: we used to go to the top of the hill, which was steeper than the roof of a house; one used to draw his arms out of the sleeves of his smock-frock, and lay himself down with his arms by his sides; and then the others, one at head and the other at feet, sent him rolling down the hill like a barrel or a log of wood. By the time he got to the bottom, his hair, eyes, ears, nose and mouth, were all full of this loose sand; then the others took their turn, and at every roll, there was a monstrous spell of laughter.[13]

Daniel Green, in his biography of Cobbett, notes that Cobbett 'made much ... of [this] unusual and rather pointless pastime'.[14] This does seem to be an example of nostalgia for the past failing to hold any real interest for us or (one imagines) for Cobbett's children, who had been 'often told ... of this while they were very little' and one of whom is being shown the very spot on this particular rural ride.[15] The passage fails, I think, because it fails in its relationship with its readers, alienating them, rather than demanding their concurrence. Cobbett introduces the incident with an irritating mixture of coyness and solemnity with his reference to legal terminology; he is obliged to go into great detail in order to describe the game; the game itself seems, as Green notes, totally pointless, and the children's explosive laughter leaves us out. Moreover, the attempt to create a kind of sense of oneness with the soil – literally, as 'his hair, eyes, ears, nose and mouth were all full of the loose sand' – fails. There is no room for symbolism as there is in the description of the oak tree – the passage is too one-dimensional for this. For one thing, the anecdote is nothing more than personal recollection and nostalgia. For another, the relationship established in the passage between Cobbett and his environment is one of power, where the natural world is merely a toy to play with, rather than an all-embracing experience. This is also signalled by the fact that this anecdote is social; it is about Cobbett and his brothers, and succeeds only in being nostalgic, whereas Cobbett's recollections of solitary encounters with the land, we have seen, contain symbolic and metaphorical matter which addresses the reciprocal relationship between the individual and his world in the idealized organic state.

Here again, then, we can begin to draw conclusions about the polemical value of this aspect of Cobbett's procedures which, at its best, seems to achieve a symbolic recreation of the ancient constitution in response to the alienations of the present. 'Organicism' has been defined as follows: 'some systems that are not literally organisms are nevertheless crucially like organisms, whose parts can only be understood in relation to their functions in the on-going whole.'[16] Thus, in the organic social world that Cobbett wishes to restore, each individual is linked and subsumed by the whole. Cobbett's self-presentation as merged within the natural world mimics this. His 'egoistic' insistence that all reality should relate to his own experience, however, reflects the corollary of the state of affairs represented by organicism. That is, if each element is linked, then each individual element is potentially a mirror of the whole. In this sense, the simultaneous egoism and self-sublimation of Cobbett's best writing metaphorically recreates the organic world within his text.

This may explain why another important feature of the more effective passages is that they often deal with Cobbett as a very small child. We saw in the passage from the *Life and Adventures* that the dominant image was of Cobbett as an infant; in the passage that we have just examined a part of the problem seems to be that Cobbett is describing the later, social part of his childhood. In the rhetorical context I have just described the primal image of infancy and innocence is crucial. We can explain this by looking at the related issue of primitivism. In her discussion of theories of self in the eighteenth century, Jean Perkins identifies the image of the 'noble savage' as a statement about the optimum relationship between the self and external reality. Like the child or the animal that we have seen Cobbett resembling, and like the individual in the organic state, his state 'does not imply any real consciousness of himself as existing apart from others or even as apart from the outside world; everything appears to him to be immediately related to himself through his senses', and she suggests that Rousseau's writings evince a desire 'to recapture the marvellously passive, completely transparent state of being enjoyed by primitive man.'[17]

As we have already noted in passing, primitivism was certainly very much in vogue during the period as a response to Enlightenment theories of human nature, and to the questions of social progress and industrial sophistication. Images of childhood and of transparent responses to nature are also common currency in Wordsworth's early poetry: thus he idealizes his childhood in the 'Intimations of Immortality', and identifies within that period of his life, in 'Tintern Abbey', a kind of integrated, pre-verbal identification with nature which he has subsequently lost:

> I cannot paint
> What then I was. The sounding cataract
> Haunted me like a passion: the tall rock,
> The mountain, and the deep and gloomy wood,
> Their colours and their forms, were then to me
> An appetite; a feeling and a love,
> That had no need of a remoter charm,
> By thought supplied, nor any interest
> Unborrowed from the eye. – That time is past... [18]

In *The Prelude* the point is made again as Wordsworth describes his childhood behaviour as resembling that of a 'naked savage', and suggests that his relationship with nature is one of 'unconscious intercourse'.[19]

Similarly, John Clare, who resembles Cobbett closely in his labouring-class roots and his self-education, is haunted literally to madness by the loss of his childhood environment. Here we see the same kind of contrast between the golden age of childhood, which resembles closely that of the organic ancient constitution in the poem's imagistic terms, and the dislocations and alienations of the present day. And though his use of environmental changes is clearly acting as a metaphor for emotional and psychological ones, the choice of that metaphor within the text acknowledges the power of the image outside of it:

> Summer pleasures they are gone like to visions every one
> And the cloudy days of autumn and of winter cometh on
> I tried to call them back but unbidden they are gone
> Far away from heart and eye and for ever far away
> Dear heart and can it be that such raptures meet decay
> I thought them all eternal when by Langley bush I lay
> I thought them joys eternal when I used to shout and play
> On its bank at 'clink and bandy' 'chock' and 'taw' and ducking stone
> Where silence sitteth now on the wild heath as her own
> Like a ruin of the past all alone.[20]

Clare's catalogue of abandoned villages, lopped oaks and cultivated commons runs through the familiar aspects of enclosure. His portrayal of his own naiveté and assumptions about the future refers us to a rich vein of emotional concepts: loss of innocence on a personal scale, and the inability of the agricultural communities to foresee the change ahead, with all its accompanying dislocation and disorientation. His image of the change coming like the change in seasons sets up an interesting parallel with Cobbett, as we see that for both Clare and Cobbett (and indeed, for any myth of paradise) the golden age is always summer.

This brings us back to the idea of the integrated, organic state. If Eden and emotional integration with the sensory world is summer, then the loss of those things is winter, and winter is exactly when the possibility of integration is lost. Cold, wet and hungry, winter is when we feel most physically dislocated from the natural world, and sharply aware of our physical individuality. This is another way, then, that the golden age's common images become particularly entangled with images of alienation and dislocation:

O I never thought that joys would run away from boys
Or that boys would change their minds and forsake such summer joys...
Till I found the pleasure past and a winter come at last
Then the fields were sudden bare and the sky got overcast
And boyhoods pleasing haunts like a blossom in the blast
Was shrivelled to a withered weed and trampled down and done
Till vanished was the morning spring and set that summer sun
And winter fought her battle strife and won.[21]

Bearing in mind this literary context we can turn to another of Cobbett's moments in the sun. This shows us perhaps most clearly of all how the myth of the golden age is recreated through his self-centred autobiography in order to imply that it is within the reach of living memory and capable of reclamation.

Early habits and affections seldom quit us while we have vigour of mind left. I was brought up under a father, whose talk was chiefly about his garden and his fields, with regard to which he was famed for his skill and his exemplary neatness. From my very infancy, from the age of six years, when I climbed up the side of a steep sand-rock, and there scooped me out a plot four feet square to make me a garden, and the soil for which I carried up in the bosom of my little blue smock-frock (or hunting-shirt), I have never lost one particle of my passion for these healthy and rational and heart-cheering pursuits, in which every day presents something new, in which the spirits are never suffered to flag, and in which industry, skill and care are sure to meet with their due reward.[22]

When we approach this passage, from *A Year's Residence in the United States of America*, written in 1817 in self-imposed exile from England, yet again we see agricultural activity as an expression of individual oneness with the soil and, here, oneness with the social fabric of the community. This passage is comparable with the *Remarks* which I quoted earlier, with its attempt to build up the sense of a complex of social and family relationships. There, he referred in passing to his 'god father Boxall' as the maker of his 'little crook', the casualness of the reference implying that this is merely a part of a far wider social network to which Cobbett and his family belong. In the passage quoted here, he again refers to his father, stressing the influence of the parent on the child, and thus implicitly denying individualism and invoking the notion of environmental influence. Cobbett is part of a complex social world, in other words, which is the threatened agricultural one.

But when Cobbett comes to indulge in the 'healthy and rational and heart-cheering pursuits' introduced to him by his father, he does so in solitude. He climbs up a steep hill, and literally carves himself a garden out of the rock, carrying up the soil to fill it from the fertile ground below. Not only does this enact Rousseau's myth of the birth of society, to which Cobbett would subscribe later in his career, as he makes his plot his own; but it also seems mythic, in that Cobbett creates it from nothing, and is obliged to undergo physical hardship to do so. The inversions 'scooped me out a '"plot"', 'to make me a garden', seem archaic and add to the sense of the passage as portraying something primeval, mythical and paradisiacal; while carrying the earth in the 'bosom of [his] little blue smock-frock' brings Cobbett into an intimate experience of the soil, and into a kind of communion with it. It is notable that again he is presented as a very young child, and we might also notice that the mythic and archaic nature of the paradisiacal image posits the possibility of redemption for the fallen present. This is of course as it should be, as a part of his task in this work is to advise intending emigrants from the Old World on farming opportunities in the New; it also seems to be his moral one, as he offers to provide his reader with access to the pastoral way of life in which 'every day presents something new ... the spirits are never suffered to flag, and in which industry, skill and care are sure to meet with their due reward.'

In a sense, then, Cobbett's autobiography is a set of symbols, seminal moments, and social markers, which illustrate only those aspects of himself that are relevant to his political purpose. Daniel Green has noted that Cobbett's autobiography is in no sense self-revelation equivalent to the autobiography of Wordsworth or Rousseau.[23] In a private letter of 1800 Cobbett appears to recognize the polemical value of his own self-projection, writing of his forthcoming English newspaper as follows: 'I have no doubt of its success. Much depends upon one's having a tolerable confidence in one's *self*.'[24] Similarly, in a letter to his daughter Anne, in 1819, Cobbett reports that his latest childhood idyll had 'produced a prodigious effect all over the country'.[25] If his self-projection is a polemical tool, then this explains the strange way in which, for all their detail, his autobiographical writings are largely unrevealing; betraying no sense of an inner life, or of a fully-realized individual behind the persona.

Hazlitt defended Cobbett's egoism by pointing out that it was always relevant to the matter in hand.[26] This chapter has expanded on that observation and on this book's previous discussions of Cobbett's developing persona from 'The Soldier's Friend' through 'Peter Porcupine' to 'William Cobbett', whose oppositional character is exemplified by his misremembered autobiography of 1804. I have argued that Cobbett's self-presentation is always a rhetorical matter. This point, along with my developing discussion of the complex language of constitutionalism Cobbett deploys, also reflects interestingly on Hazlitt's judgement on Cobbett: 'in short, wherever power is, there is he against it: he naturally butts at all obstacles, as unicorns are attracted to oak trees, and feels his own strength only by resistance to the opinions and wishes of the rest of the world'. Hazlitt's metaphor of unicorn and oak tree seems peculiarly apt to the use of the ancient constitution and the mythic self-presentation that I have been tracing here. Hazlitt's suggestion that Cobbett *defines* himself through opposition seems supported by the nature of Cobbett's misremembering in his 'Letter to Pitt' of 1804 which identifies a moment of conflict as the impetus to his literary career.

As we turn in Part II to an examination of the Radical writings of Cobbett's maturity I will continue to identify the artifice and rhetorical value of Cobbett's prose style and self-projection, and his apparent reliance on positions of opposition in order to justify and define his own practices. In Part I we have seen Cobbett trying various literary styles of a conservative and oppositional nature in order to find ways of reaching and influencing his changing target audiences, and of establishing himself as a liberated maverick outside conventional party lines. Part II will begin by exploring the conversational and dramatic writings of his early maturity. These texts continue to draw upon and to radicalize the refined and enfranchised literary traditions which we have been discussing so far, but at the same time they draw increasingly upon more popular and populist forms. Simultaneously owing their form to eighteenth-century oppositional journalism, to the Radical style of Paine, and to the novel, the essay and the chapbook, these Radical texts take us from monologue to polyphony, developing an increasingly flexible and transgressive relationship with the political nation and its discursive world.

PART II
Cobbett and his audience

CHAPTER 5

Dialogue and debate

With the birth of the twopenny *Register* of 1816, Cobbett's characteristic urge towards the written reproduction of demotic language is confirmed and extended. Lynne Lemrow has made close observations about Cobbett's style in this period. She identifies as standard the retention of spoken word-order – subject, verb, object – and the breakdown of complex sentences into simpler clauses linked by colons or semicolons. Other common features, though ones which as we know are also characteristic of Cobbett's earlier conservative writings, are 'repetition, anaphora ... parallel structures ... and the rhetorical question ...'[1] By the time of the letters 'To Journeymen and Labourers' and, here, in the 'Letter to Luddites', this increasingly demotic usage is apparent:

FRIENDS AND FELLOW COUNTRYMEN,
At this time, when the cause of freedom is making a progress which is as cheering to the hearts of her friends as it is appalling to those of her enemies, and, when it is become evident that nothing can possibly prevent that progress from terminating in the happiness of our country, which has, for so many years, been a scene of human misery and degradation; when it is become evident that so glorious a termination of our struggles can be now prevented only by our giving way to our passions instead of listening to the voice of reason, only by our committing those acts which admit of no justification either in law or in equity; at such a time, can it be otherwise than painful to reflect, that acts of this description are committed in any part of the kingdom, and particularly in the enlightened, the patriotic, the brave town of Nottingham?[2]

However, as with the letter 'To the Journeymen and Labourers', Cobbett's style also retains refined features – most notably here the choice of sophisticated vocabulary. If from this point onwards Cobbett's texts become increasingly colloquial in order directly to address the working class, it is nevertheless true that the refined audience is still reading. And if the choice of an explicitly working-class audience indirectly speaks to the politically powerful, by ostentatiously excluding them, then so does the choice of an increasingly vernacular style.

This vernacular style owes a great deal to Paine. Extracts from *The Rights of Man* and the *Political Register* of 1817 will establish the similarities (which prompted Olivia Smith to categorize Paine and Cobbett as joint creators of the vernacular style of political debate) and the differences. First, we see Paine's conversational usage which could, with equal justice, be described in the terms outlined by Lynne Lemrow as characteristic of Cobbett's style:

But Mr Burke appears to have no idea of principles, when he is contemplating governments. 'Ten years ago' (says he) 'I could have felicitated France on her having a government, without enquiring what the nature of that government was, or how it was administered.' Is this the language of a rational man? Is it the language of a heart feeling as it ought to feel for the rights and happiness of the human race?

...I know a place in America called Point-no-Point; because as you proceed along the shore, gay and flowery as Mr Burke's language, it continually recedes and presents itself at a distance before you; but when you have got as far as you can go, there is no point at all.[3]

The conversational address to 'you', the homely analogy, and the rhetorical appeals to common sense and reason seem similar to Cobbett's developing style.[4] But Cobbett's increasing tendency to represent oral language in his writings of this period also takes us back to his American practice. We remember his controversial use of colloquialism and his use of the open letter format which allowed the use of personal pronouns: both these features are recaptured in Cobbett's writing after 1816. The difference is that whereas Peter Porcupine's letters were addressed to enemies, and were therefore uniformly prickly, Cobbett's decision to address his friends, and social peers in need of intellectual reassurance, leads to the development of an extremely genial style. After the passage of the Powers of Imprisonment Act and the suspension of habeas corpus in early 1817, Cobbett's *Political Register* – now the *Political Pamphlet* as it only contains a leading essay – begins as follows:

My Good Neighbours,
Yesterday the act passed the Royal Assent! It is now a *law*; and to this law we must now submit! For many, many years, I have been warning my country against the measures, which have finally brought us to this pass;

and, those among you, who have been in the habit of attending the Meetings at Winchester, will remember how the greater part of the farmers and of all those who seemed to be in rather higher life than the rest used to scoff at me, when I foretold to you all what would be the end of the things which I used to complain of.[5]

The abrupt opening, with its failure to explain what act is being referred to, suggests that Cobbett's readers, like Cobbett himself, have been utterly absorbed by political issues. The opening also implies that Cobbett and his readers are engaged in a conversation which has been picked up exactly where it left off the week before. Cobbett speaks of his readers freely as personal acquaintances, whom he might very well have seen at the Winchester Meeting, and as friends who will sympathize with him as the object of scorn, and triumph at his vindication. He dramatizes himself and his reader as possibly rather in awe of those 'farmers' and people of 'rather higher life' who have opposed his views, and by doing so portrays himself as one with the audience he posits in this period. Even the clumsiness of the last clause is endearing, as the broken structure suggests a disrupted and agitated mind.

This is where Cobbett and Paine part company. Paine's 'you' is a kind of political everyman; Cobbett's is a specific character. In America Cobbett's addressee is a specific enemy; here it is a specific friend, one whom he may even have met. In this way Cobbett's writings are more specifically of their time than Paine's – a fact which may account for Paine's greater popularity with political theorists, as his writings seem to speak in a more abstract world of ideas than do those of Cobbett. This was noted by Hazlitt. After acknowledging the similarities between Paine's style and that of Cobbett, he suggested that

> Paine is a much more sententious writer than Cobbett. You cannot open a page in any of his best and earlier works without meeting with some maxim, some antithetical and memorable saying, which is a sort of starting-place for the argument, and the goal to which it returns. There is not a single *bon mot*, a single sentence in Cobbett that has ever been quoted again. If anything is ever quoted from him, it is an epithet of abuse or a nickname.[6]

Hazlitt's point is that Paine, for all his vernacular style, is engaged in producing unified and creative texts which deal with universal issues, whereas Cobbett is engaged in the ephemeral business of day-to-day politics. This difference is signalled if we take another often-quoted extract from *The Rights of Man*:

Not one glance of compassion, not one commiserating reflection, that I can find throughout his book, has [Burke] bestowed on those who lingered out the most wretched of lives, a life without hope, in the most miserable of prisons. It is painful to behold a man employing his talents to corrupt himself. Nature has been kinder to Mr Burke than he is to her. He is not affected by the reality of distress touching his heart, but by the showy resemblance of it striking his imagination. He pities the plumage, but forgets the dying bird. Accustomed to kiss the aristocratical hand that hath purloined him from himself, he degenerates into a composition of art, and the genuine soul of nature forsakes him. His hero or his heroine must be a tragedy-victim expiring in show, and not the real prisoner of misery, sliding into death in the silence of a dungeon.[7]

This passage seems to concern 'real' people, real prisoners in the Bastille, whom Paine claims Burke is neglecting in favour of the dramatic fantasy characters of the French nobility. But even as he makes this assertion, Paine's own writing seems to display the same fault, with his failure to address the real circumstances of his 'prisoner of misery'. That is, Paine's prisoner seems as romantic and notional as Burke's monarch. The picture of the prisoner 'sliding into death in the silence of a dungeon' is, precisely, a picture, a still life. Compare this to Cobbett's address to his 'good neighbours' above, or the following extract from the *Rural Rides*, written five years later:

I was, not long ago, sitting round the fire with as worthy and as industrious a man as all England contains. There was his son, about 19 years of age; two daughters, from 15 to 18; and a little boy sitting on the father's knee. I knew, but not from him, that there was a *mortgage* on his farm. I was anxious to induce him *to sell without delay*. With this view I, in an hypothetical and round-about way, approached *his case* and at last, I came to *final consequences*. The deep and deeper gloom on a countenance, once so cheerful, told me what was passing in his breast, when, turning away my looks in order to seem not to perceive the effect of my words, I saw the eyes of his wife *full of tears*.[8]

It might be argued that to compare Paine and Cobbett in this way is to compare like with unlike. This is largely true of course, but this is also to confirm my suggestion that Cobbett's writing must not be viewed as political philosophy but as polemic aimed at specific readers in specific circumstances.

As polemic, Cobbett's 'realist' style and everyday subject matter are supremely effective. We will see in this chapter how Cobbett's mature Radical texts use and exploit this ephemeral style. We will see that he not only mimics the grammatical simplicity of speech, but incorporates the values and subject matter of ordinary people's conversation within his prose and draws upon the literary culture of the working class. In this way we will see Cobbett's texts as increasingly radical literary constructions and his self-presentation within them as increasingly dramatic.

On 14 December 1816, a month after the success of the letter 'To Journeymen and Labourers' and at the height of Reform fever, Cobbett addressed the leading article of the *Political Register* to his colleague Henry Hunt. He directed it to Hunt's home address, 'Middleton Cottage, near Andover,' and framed it in terms of a private letter:

SIR,
The summer before last, when you came over to Botley and found me transplanting Swedish turnips amidst dust, and under a Sun which scorched the leaves till they resembled fried parsley, you remember how I was fretting and stewing; how many times in an hour I was looking out for a southwestern cloud; how I watched the mercury in the glass, and rapped the glass with my knuckles to try to move it in my favour. But great as my anxiety then was, and ludicrous as were my movements, ten thousand times greater has been that of Corruption's Press for the coming of a PLOT.[9]

The article is written in December and plunges us directly into the warmth of a particularly dry summer. The landscape is, moreover, associated with sensory pleasures like the smell and taste of fried parsley. And the reader – being cast into the third-person role of Henry Hunt – is invited to dramatize himself into that summer sun, watching Cobbett toiling in an agricultural landscape. The emphasis on the narrative 'plot' of Cobbett's agricultural cares makes political ones seem far away and insignificant: we have come upon Cobbett and found him off his guard, in shirt sleeves, and with no thoughts for politics at least for the time being. If Cobbett's intention is to charm and disarm his readers, then the technique is a successful one.

Even as Cobbett explicates the simile between himself and 'Corruption's Press', the pastoral autobiography persists in dominating our attention:

You remember how my wife laughed at me, when, in the evening, some boys having thrown a handful or two of sand over the wall, that made a sort of dropping on the leaves of the laurels, I took it for the beginning of a *shower*, and pulled off my hat and held up my hand to see whether more was not coming, though there was nothing to be seen in the sky but stars shining as bright as silver. Just such has been the conduct of Corruption's sons upon hearing of the *discovery* of Mr. WATSON's and Mr. PRESTON's papers! They sigh for a PLOT. Oh, how they sigh! They are working and slaving and fretting and stewing; they are sweating all over; they are absolutely pining and dying for a Plot!

This is, of course, an epic simile, and follows all the conventions of that technique to create a sense of poetic grandeur. As in the previous extract, Cobbett also uses the long complex sentence to create a sense of sensory reality, where the texture of the sentence – created by the layers and complexity of the information – mirrors the layers and complexity of sensory perception. From Nancy Cobbett's laughter and the pattering of sand on leaves we move to Cobbett's actions and from there, led by his upstretched hand, our attention is drawn to the clear night sky. We journey from hearing through to sight, as in the last extract we moved from sight, through the physical sense of heat, to that of smell with the reference to frying parsley. The stirrings of a revolutionary plot are likened to the mischievous antics of small boys, when the truth is far more serene, like the cloudless sky, and a great deal more beautiful as it is illuminated by the stars. Whether, in this heavily metaphorical poetic prose, the stars represent Cobbett and Hunt, as the illuminators of the people and of the truth, or the people and the truth themselves, is not clear. If it is the former, Cobbett at any rate has forestalled any self-praise by dramatizing the passage ambiguously from the viewpoint of both himself and Henry Hunt. And in so far as 'Hunt's' memories of Cobbett's absurd behaviour draw a parallel between Cobbett and 'Corruption's Press', he also renders those 'villains' and their hopes harmless, ineffectual and – like himself in this story – absurd. That their sighing, working, slaving, fretting, stewing, sweating, pining and dying should, moreover, be not for something useful and nourishing like rain but for discord and revolution, makes their absurdity complete.

Here, the voice of the farmer, in tune with nature – even with the stars – whose only enemy is the weather, and whose motives and desires are self-evident and laudable, is conjured into an epic hero by the use of literary methods in the passage. This is the literary parallel of other ways in which Cobbett uses the image of the farmer, as he identifies with him politically and emulates him even in his dress,[10] perhaps to defuse other more subversive images of Radicalism. These farmer-like qualities are, as Daniel Green notes, a part of Cobbett's 'John Bull' persona,[11] and can be intensely conservative in that they resemble those of 'farmer' George III – they can also be Radical if we remember Cobbett's use of agricultural imagery in the context of American journalism, and the precedent of John Dickinson's republican writings, from Chapter 1.

To see this passage as characterized by differing voices or viewpoints – Cobbett, Hunt, the farmer – who in turn represent different things depending on their context and the perceptions of the reader, also draws our attention to the polyphonic nature of Cobbett's texts, which so far we have only noticed in passing.[12] Olivia Smith has described the way in which Cobbett manipulates 'antagonistic styles' by parroting or reconciling them. Thus she reads the letter 'To the Journeymen and Labourers' with a stress on the various political positions characterized and argued against within it.[13] It is clear that by this kind of incorporation, Cobbett avoids the monologism of the early *Political Register*. By allowing contending voices into his text and by dramatizing himself as only one of these, he invites his reader to make independent judgements about the issues.

But the cards are always stacked: by allowing contending as well as agreeing voices into his text Cobbett may allow ideas to act themselves out dramatically within it, but with clear moral guidelines for the reader to follow. As a method of persuasion the advantage is clear, as the voices contend in a form also reminiscent of a Socratic dialogue, which implies the kind of invitation to judge freely we have just described as a feature of Cobbett's text, while relentlessly pushing the reader's judgement towards one conclusion: '"*Coarse as neck beef!*" will growl out some Englishman, who has filled his bags by oppressions of the poor; or, some other one, who, feeling in his very bones and marrow an instinctive horror of *work*, is desperately bent on getting *a share of the taxes*'.[14] Discussing this passage, Raymond Williams notes the way in which demotic and literary discourses mingle here: he points to Cobbett's 'grafting of colloquial phrases and oral emphases on to the still formal strengths of the consciously public address of his period ...' Williams notes the way in which the 'hard colloquialism' and the 'punching italics' fit into the 'careful formality' of sentence structures and punctuation, and he invites us to ponder the diminished effect if normal sentence order is restored to the beginning of the extract.

Following on from this, I think it is clear that another effect of the inversion is to privilege the dramatic and dialogic over the monologic narrative. If the sentence were ordered normally – 'Some Englishman will growl out "*Coarse as neck beef*!"' – the expression would be instantly contextualized, and the gap between the 'Englishman' and Cobbett as narrator would be instantly apparent. As it is, we are presented with a voice initially out of nowhere, whose value and identity is uncertain until the voice of the literary narrator takes its turn immediately afterwards.

The method is not confined to the period subsequent to 1816, but has been developed during the course of Cobbett's political conversion. In a *Political Register* article of 21 January 1809 Cobbett lists the pensions and sinecures held by Castlereagh's family. After this list, Cobbett goes on: 'There's *loyalty* for you! "Jacobins and Levellers" blush for shame! "Jack Cades" hide your heads! Cease your grumbling, you villainous rebellious ruffians, you bloody-minded dogs, do cease your grumbling and come forth with voluntary sacrifices at this hour of peril!'[15] Here the alien voice occurs at the end of the sentence rather than the beginning, but either position grants it particular force and draws it particularly to our attention as problematical. What is especially interesting about this passage, though, is the way in which the narrator's voice blends into the enemy one. 'There's *loyalty* for you!' is clearly the sarcastic voice of the narrator, but the next two observations addressed to 'Jacobins and Levellers' and 'Jack Cades' seem to hold two simultaneous meanings. One is, again, the narrator, inviting the Radicals – and the reader – to blush for what Cobbett would call the 'brass' and the villainy of the Establishment. The other is also the narrator, but this time adopting the enemy terminology to show up its bankruptcy. This adoption then blends, by the end of the passage, into the undiluted voice of reaction.

This kind of verbal technique was also responsible for Cobbett's imprisonment in 1810, as exactly the same kind of dramatization afforded the authorities an opportunity to prosecute:

Well done, Lord Castlereagh! This is just what it was thought your plan would produce. Well said, Lord Huskisson! It really was not without reason that you dwelt, with so much earnestness, upon the great utility of the *foreign* troops, whom Mr. Wardle appeared to think of no utility at all ... He little imagined, that they might be made the means of compelling Englishmen to submit to that sort of *discipline* which is so conducive to the producing in them a disposition to defend the country, at the risk of their lives ... *Five hundred lashes* each! Aye, that is right! Flog them; flog them; flog them! They deserve it, and a great deal more. They deserve a flogging at every meal-

Dialogue and debate 143

time. 'Lash them daily, lash them duly.' What, shall the rascals dare to *mutiny*, and that, too, when the German Legion is so close at hand! Lash them, lash them, lash them! They *deserve* it. O, yes; they merit a double-tailed cat. Base dogs! What, mutiny for the sake of *the price of a knapsack*! Lash them! flog them! Base rascals![16]

This may merely be sarcasm – of which Cobbett has been described as a master[17] – but if it is, then it is an excellent example of how sarcasm operates by the dialogic representation of discourses that we are invited to dislike, diregard, or despise. Even the sarcasm of ordinary speech works by this method of saying one thing with the explicit intention of meaning another, thereby creating a double perspective on the language being employed. In this passage the language of many voices mingles: Lord Huskisson's, Mr Wardle's, and – we guess – a hundred Establishment voices over the morning paper. But the voice of the narrator seems to break through the customary 'growlings' of reaction, and through the authorial sarcasm, with pained disbelief at the harshness of the penalty: 'What, mutiny for the sake of *the price of a knapsack*!' And the repetitious parroted cries of the punishers betray them increasingly as hysterical and vicious.

If the voices of contending classes are allowed into the text, then we could say that Cobbett's text again differs from those of 'purer' Radicals by mirroring the unreformed world rather than presenting an alternative vision. Cobbett, as we know, also allows problematical issues associated with the working class, like superstition and bigotry, to enter his text. As well as constituting another example of Cobbett's tendency to deal in what *is* rather than what *should be*, this technique suits his polemical purposes also by wooing his audience.[18]

In the Introduction I noted Ian Dyck's suggestion that Cobbett's incorporation of popular sentiments is also a means by which he can make his Radicalism seem safe and familiar to his audience.[19] The irony with this reading – which I accept – is that such a procedure was also used by Burke and the *Anti-Jacobin* to counter Radicalism in the 1790s. Burke's reference to the 'little platoon' of those we love,[20] and the elevation of prejudice into a system,[21] are celebrated; they were echoed by the *Anti-Jacobin* in its opening number as we saw in Chapter 2, when it conceded ironically that it had its 'feelings ... preferences, and ... affections, attaching on particular places, manners, and institutions, and even on particular portions of the human race'. It is the triumph of Cobbett's intellectual impurity and his doomed ancient constitutionalism that these allow him to hijack these discourses of power. Cobbett's dramatization of himself as John Bull stresses his patriotism in a way which, in turn, makes his Radicalism very English, and difficult to dismiss as 'Jacobinism' or as subversive to the interests of the nation.[22]

If polyphony is a feature of Cobbett's prose, as I have attempted to demonstrate here, then one strand in the weave of voices is the discourse of popular superstition spoken by the people he addresses after 1816. That superstition is a feature of the period seems clear. If the English farm worker did not fear agricultural disaster from working on a Sunday like his French equivalent, he did rely on almanacs and fortune-tellers to dictate his decisions, to the extent that such paganism became one of Hannah More's targets.[23] Superstitious dread associated with religion is also in evidence in the popular literature of the period: worshippers at Foleshill Church, for example, became so alarmed by 'Mysterious Knockings' heard in the building that the authorities were obliged to intervene, moving the writer of the broadsheet disapprovingly to point out the greater anxiety which ought to be felt by the flock over the state of their own immortal souls.[24] The passage from *Rural Rides* where Cobbett comes unexpectedly upon a crucifix in Osmond Ricardo's country estate is an example of his use of this kind of quasi-mystic superstition:

there is a SPAN NEW CROSS as large as *life*! Aye, big enough and long enough to crucify a man upon! I had never seen such an one before; and I know not what sort of thought it was that seized me at the moment; but, though my horse is but a clumsy goer, I verily believe I got away from it at a rate of ten or twelve miles an hour.[25]

Another strand in the weave of discourse is the literature of the poor – from chapbook versions of classic texts through fable and history, to the broadsheet account of crimes and executions. Thinking in these terms adds another twist to our interpretation of Cobbett's many self-dramatizations. James Sambrook notes a 'Robinson Crusoe-like' tendency in Cobbett's self-dramatizations, as they often assume that his readers will be 'profoundly interested in his every thought, word and deed'.[26] In the last chapter I quoted the passage from the introduction to *A Journal of a Year's Residence in the United States of America* in which Cobbett describes his father's influence on his childhood love of gardening. In my discussion of the passage I noted its 'mythic' nature, as it presents Cobbett laboriously creating his paradise out of nothing. If we note that his paradise is a homely, cultivated one, however, here too we may begin to see a parallel with Crusoe who similarly builds a civilized world out of the wilderness of his desert island. I have already suggested that many of Cobbett's self-dramatizations are fictional ones, working towards certain rhetorical goals. With his self-identification with Crusoe in these passages, the hero of several chapbook classics, we can begin to see that one recurring method may be to echo the form and content of the chapbook and broadside in order to rework received values and assumptions.[27]

Late in life, Cobbett declared an intention to write his autobiography in full. While it was never written, its projected title interestingly draws attention to its intertextual relationship with chapbook culture. We can see this if we compare that title, 'The progress of a Plough-boy to a Seat in Parliament, as exemplified in the History of the Life of William Cobbett, Member for Oldham,'[28] with the titles of several chapbooks in R. H. Cunningham's nineteenth-century collection:[29] *The Famous History of the Learned Friar Bacon, Giving a Particular Account of his Birth, Parentage, with the Many Wonderful Things he Did in His Lifetime, to the Amazement of all the World.* The history of the *Blind Beggar of Bethnal Green* promises a similarly detailed relation as follows:

Containing his Birth and Parentage; how he went to the Wars and Lost his Sight, and turned Beggar at Bethnal Green; how he got Riches, and educated his Daughter; of her being Courted by a rich, young Knight; how the Blind Beggar dropt Gold with the Knight's Uncle; of the Knight and the Beggar's Daughter being Married; and, lastly, how the famous Pedigree of the Beggar was discovered, and Other Things worthy of Note.

This preoccupation with 'Birth and Parentage' is unsurprising in a hierarchical society; the interest in achievements and the fantasy of extreme social advancement is equally predictable given the rare but not impossible opportunity to rise. Cobbett is, of course, himself an example of this, and the title of his projected autobiography echoes these chapbook biographies. But what is the significance of this self-conscious reference to precedents in popular literature? Ian Dyck has charted Cobbett's determination to win the battle for the pedlar's sack in order to win a working-class audience,[30] but there is more to Cobbett's use of popular literary forms than this. In his radical texts, Cobbett reworks these forms for ideological effect, as we can see by taking a look at the kinds of roles offered to the reader of various types of street literature.

If the Blind Beggar's social rise is dizzying, it is not unusual: in Cunningham's collection we also find the story of King Henry VIII's nocturnal ramblings around London disguised as a commoner and finding true companionship amongst the people.[31] Here the honest cobbler's friendship for Harry Tudor is rewarded by a rise to the rank of courtier. But the fantasy element is strong: Henry is portrayed as a kind of Old King Cole, full of hearty laughter and devoid of class snobbery. The story is one of carnivalesque disruption and fantasy rather than one of possibilities. Real possibilities about final destinations are more in evidence in the popular chapbook literature of crime. In the following letter of confession from a broadsheet the illiteracy emphasizes the authenticity, and the self-dramatization as a heroine from pulp romantic fiction points to the way in which literature can offer ways of creating a persona for the self in unfamiliar and intolerable situations:

Dear William,
The Sad hour is at hand when I must suffer for a crime which I committed in loveing you, I hope god will forgive me, Had my mother given her consent to our union we should have been happy, by her refusal she met the death at my hands and brought me to an untimly end. God bless you and make you happy so prays your dying and affectionate lover
    Mary Jones[32]

That crime broadsheets are a flourishing success throughout the ages says significant things about their readers. For one thing, their popularity indicates their entertainment value. The broadsheet detailing the crime and conviction of William Corder sold a million and a half copies,[33] and comprised a copy of the confession, an account of the execution and a ballad version of events. The visual style and the content of the sheet conformed to strong conventions of crime reporting in the period. The confession described the method of the murder of Maria Marten in entertaining detail; the account of the execution was calculated to chill in an equally entertaining fashion. From a literary point of view, the way in which the concluding ballad reworks the 'factual' matter, to let in superstition and disruption, indicates the close relationship between fact and fiction in these sheets.

Thus, for instance, the prose confession is vague as to the motive for the crime. A quarrel is mentioned, which concerns the burial of a 'child', and the murder is described as an impulsive act which makes subsequent concealment a problem. In the account of the execution, the victim's remorse and the pity he arouses in fellow prisoners is stressed: 'they appeared considerably affected by the wretched appearance which he made, and "God bless you!" "May God receive your soul!" were frequently uttered as he passed along ... Just before he was turned off, he said in a feeble tone, "I am justly sentenced, and may God forgive me".'

The procedure of the ballad is substantially different. Corder's signature to his confession is reproduced in the opening stanza of the ballad as follows:

> Come all you thoughtless young men, a warning take by me,
> And think upon my unhappy fate to be hanged upon a tree;
> My name is William Corder, to you I do declare,
> I courted Maria Marten, most beautiful and fair.

But the remainder of the ballad reworks the crime and the aftermath in ways which depart from the prose section of the broadsheet. Corder in the ballad cruelly premeditates his crime and arrives at the scene equipped for a burial, and supernatural aid comes to Maria Marten's kin:

> Her mother's mind being so disturbed, she dreamt three nights o'er,
> Her daughter she lay murdered beneath the Red-barn floor;
> She sent the father to the barn, when he the ground did thrust,
> And there he found his daughter mingling with the dust.

William Corder is represented in the prose section as not altogether bad; yet in the poem he commits an awful premeditated crime. This implies that there is potential for sin in all. Tract writers and crime reporters with paternalistic aims exploit the crime sheet to suggest that all not only may but probably will err, unless Christian practices are strictly observed and antisocial behaviour shunned. Thus an 'untimely end' on the gallows is repeatedly put down to 'drunkenness, swearing and sabbath-breaking.'[34] In these tracts and reports the implications about the moral make-up of the reader are pretty pessimistic: Henry VIII would be unlikely to choose these men for courtiers because of their superior honesty, integrity and good humour.

This being the case, we can argue that Cobbett's preoccupation with his own biography – which resembles that of a chapbook hero

– creates certain Radical assumptions within and about his readers. Compared to the self-dramatizations offered to the labouring-class reader by much popular literature, Cobbett's self-presentation must be positive, countering as it does these gloomy assumptions about working-class character. In Chapter 7 we shall examine Cobbett's moral writings where these issues are explicit. Here it is only necessary to observe that if – as has been often argued – a part of Cobbett's achievement is to grant the labourer dignity,[35] then it must be achieved in part by offering these positive images of himself.

Such intertextual references to popular culture allow Cobbett to rework images of the working class, then, in the process of dramatizing himself. In the article from 1817 reporting the suspension of habeas corpus, from which I have already quoted, Cobbett urges his readers to read and reread his explanation of what this means and why it has come about. 'When our children's children shall read of this event, they will be all anxiety to know *what was the cause of it.*'[36] Here Cobbett dramatizes his readers and himself as the 'forefathers' of a future generation, implicitly presenting them as potential heroes of a new struggle for freedom; as the authors of a new social constitution in a new England; and creating a Burkean sense of responsibility towards the unborn. Cobbett's integrity is thus bound up with the strengths and the potential of his readers, and in this way he becomes a touchstone, as we noted in the last chapter with the passage from *Rural Rides* which turns Cobbett and the Tilford Oak into fused symbols of continuity.[37]

The passage from *A Year's Residence in the United States of America* where Cobbett describes his childhood gardening experiences, and which I have so far identified as both Crusoe-like and mythic, is actually constructed as a means to gain authority for his observations on farming opportunities in America. While he acknowledges that his full-time career as a journalist makes his farming expertise questionable he asserts that 'one man will gain more knowledge in a year than another will in a life. It is the *taste* for the thing that really gives the knowledge'.[38] Indeed, so confident is Cobbett of his judgements on farming that Part One, Chapter 1 of the work comprises a diary of his experiences in that one year, without amplification or comment. This first chapter of *A Year's Residence* is the supreme example of Cobbett's belief that his every action and experience is of useful interest. On the whole he is right:

July 29. Still the same degree of heat. I measured a water-melon runner, which grew eighteen inches in the last 48 hours. The dews now are equal to showers; I frequently, in the morning, wash hands and face, feet and legs, in the dew on the high grass. The Indian Corn shoots up now so beautifully!
30. Still melting hot.
31. Same weather.[39]

In early June Cobbett's bare style combines interestingly with a more poetical discourse:

9. Rain all day. The wood green, and so beautiful! The leaves look so fresh and delicate! But, the Flowering Locust only begins to show leaf. It will, by and by, make up, by its beauty, for its shyness at present.
10. Fine warm day. The cattle are up to their eyes in grass.[40]

The image of the cattle almost lost in the grass seems to suggest integration and identification, as the cattle are metaphorically swallowed by their own meal. Suggestions of extra spirituality recur as Cobbett finds in the new American world the key to understanding the ancient biblical one. In the hot American climate he learns methods of threshing grain which explain the biblical injunction 'not to *muzzle* the ox as he *treadeth out the grain*,' and which account for Boaz's presence amongst his threshers in the story of Ruth.[41] The implication must be that in this integrated world, with its biblical parallels and stunning natural beauty, we find ourselves nearer to heaven; nearer to God.

Yet this is not Cobbett's final conclusion. In the Preface he declares that however positive his descriptions of America are, he is not campaigning for emigration. 'I myself am bound to England for life'.[42] In Chapter 2 he observes that 'England is my country, and to England I shall return. I like it best, and shall always like it best; but, then, in the word *England*, many things are included besides climate and soil and seasons, and eating and drinking.'[43] This protestation of ultimate attachment to England is repeated again at the conclusion of Part One, and a declaration of his attachment to English governmental institutions is made at the conclusion of Part Three.[44] In the end, Cobbett finds the lushness of America unsatisfying: England signifies more than 'climate and soil and seasons, and eating and drinking.' This seems a rare instance where worldly goods – usually part and parcel of Cobbett's value system[45] – fail to account for all that is necessary for happiness.

James Chandler's reading of this text negotiates this puzzle, however. Chandler depicts Cobbett's text as an anxious response to the surge of emigration to America from postwar Britain. He suggests that Cobbett's tactic of emphasizing the advantages of America while explicitly advising his readers to remain in England can be read as a way of dramatizing the disjunction between the English mythic past and fallen present in response to this increasing emigration. An appropriate response to hardship, his procedures imply, should not be emigration abroad but revolution at home. American hospitality, Cobbett explicitly declares, is only an example of famous old English hospitality. The implication here is that the standard of living achieved in America could be restored to Britain given the political will to do so. America, in other words, is in an important sense merely a rhetorical hook on which to hang a clearer image of what a Radical Britain could be.[46] The diary entries of *A Year's Residence* then, are not as artless as they appear. The appearance of transparent reportage, as the diary format denies artifice, belies the reality of rhetorical design, as all our perceptions are filtered through Cobbett's consciousness for specific purposes.

The diary format of *A Year's Residence* is repeated in *Rural Rides*. Here, however, the text's opacity is obvious and part of its pleasure as Cobbett is the central figure, again a touchstone, holding together the potentially unfocussed picaresque form. *Rural Rides* uses the apparently artless diary form to describe the journeys undertaken, but each entry is characterized by a strong narrative pattern where the day's journey and the experiences it provides give a shape to the political subject matter. On the morning of 31 October 1825, for example, Cobbett reports on the journey from Winchester to Burghclere with his youngest son, Richard, the previous day.[47] 'We had, or I had, resolved not to *breakfast* at Winchester yesterday: and yet we were detained till nearly noon.' The journal entry opens with this observation, and it sets up the issues for the piece as a whole.

The early part of the journal entry is preoccupied with a discussion of what sort of landscape is 'best': most beautiful, most pleasant to live amongst, and most suitable in which to eke out a living. The area 'about Guildford and Godalming, and round the skirts of Hindhead and Blackdown', is for Cobbett the most beautiful. His sense of the beautiful here is purely aesthetic: 'the ground lies in the form that the surface-water in a boiling copper would be in, if you could, by word of command, *make it be still*, the variously-shaped bubbles all sticking up...' For Cobbett, though, 'beauties of *this sort*' are surpassed by Farnham and Kent, where the crops are hops and fruit, the 'fine meadows' give way to 'pretty woods', and the landscape breathes fertility. Yet again, the kind of country best 'to *live on*' is exemplified in the high downs of Hampshire where he is riding in this piece:

And, here is one great pleasure of living in countries of this sort: no sloughs, no ditches, no nasty dirty lanes, and the hedges, where there are any, are more for boundary marks than for fences. Fine for hunting and coursing: no impediments; no gates to open; nothing to impede the dogs, the horses, or the view.

The lack of surface water Cobbett acknowledges to be a potential problem, but he declares that the goodness of the well water makes up for the effort of obtaining it. Here, though, as if nudged by the reference to labour, Cobbett points to the irrelevance of the rather upper-class pleasures he has just been extolling:

As *things now are*, however, these countries have one great draw-back: the poor day-labourers suffer from the want of fuel, and they have nothing but their *bare* pay. For these reasons they are greatly worse off than those of the *woodland countries*; and it is really surprising what a difference there is between the faces that you see here, and the round, red faces that you see in the *wealds* and the *forests*, particularly in *Sussex*, where the labourers *will* have a *meat pudding* of some sort or other; and where they *will* have a *fire* to sit by in the winter.

The reference to food leads Cobbett back to the bare narrative as he records an invitation to lunch refused, and the final decision to ask for bread and cheese at a labourer's cottage, describing the labourer's generosity and his smoking and inefficient hearth. The references to hardship and hunger culminate in a confessional passage which breaks into the chronology of the journal entry. Cobbett describes his and Richard's growing hunger prior to the cheese sandwich, which renders them '*dull*, or rather *glum*. The way seemed long; and when I had to speak in answer to Richard, the speaking was as brief as might be.' At this critical juncture a strap on Richard's portmanteau snaps, and so does Cobbett's patience.

This, which was not the work of more than five minutes, would, had I had *a breakfast*, have been nothing at all, and, indeed, matter of laughter. But, *now*, it was *something*. It was his '*fault*' for capering and jerking about 'so'. I jumped off, saying, '*Here*! I'll carry it *myself*.' And then I began to take off the remaining strap, pulling, with great violence and in great haste. Just at this time, my eyes met his, in which I saw *great surprise*; and, feeling the just rebuke, feeling heartily ashamed of myself, I instantly changed my tone and manner...

If such was the effect on himself, having missed one breakfast but in the confident expectation of obtaining another shortly, Cobbett muses, what must be the effect on him who has no opportunity of ever getting enough to eat? By dramatizing the effects of hunger in this way Cobbett makes his point effectively and goes on to calculate the cost of his sandwich – a mere stopgap snack – as a proportion of a labourer's weekly wage.

Here then is an example of that technique noted by Hazlitt, where Cobbett's best example of an issue is himself.[48] But it is not just that the incident draws attention to the roots of crime in hunger, or the dire inadequacy of current wages and poor relief: it also leads to a subsequent discussion of a *'humanity-meeting'* in aid of black slaves, showing the hypocrisy of caring for people suffering at a convenient distance, while ignoring those nearer at hand. And here we can see the rhetorical benefit of Cobbett's autobiographical method: dramatizing his hunger prompts reader identification; we remember our own, and are compelled to acknowledge the feebleness of any moral superiority we might feel. If we, like Cobbett, cannot go without breakfast without bad temper, then exhortations to the poor to obey the laws of nature and die, or to pull themselves up by the bootstraps, become so much cant. Hunger is no longer an abstraction, embodied by absent black slaves, but is personified in Cobbett's bad temper and the pale faces in the Hampshire countryside that contrast so sharply with the red-faced men of Sussex.

We realize, though, that for this conclusion to be drawn Cobbett's reader must be someone likely to attend such meetings and to have no real experience of hunger. Here, then, Cobbett is prodding the conscience of a middle- or upper-class reader, and not addressing the labourer or journeyman. Along with the suspension of habeas corpus in 1817, which forced Cobbett's second emigration to the United States, came the closure of the loophole which had allowed his *Register* to be sold for twopence. At the same time many of his Radical colleagues felt betrayed by his departure for America. These developments make the nature of Cobbett's real audience and influence from this period on difficult to judge. Many of his most famous and enduring texts were yet to be published; and when they were, they were issued in affordable parts. The working classes continued to read his papers and books, at times widely, as in the build-up to the Reform Act of 1832. But in price his *Political Register* became once more a paper for the better off. For our purposes the real

Dialogue and debate 153

nature of his audience is less important than Cobbett's assumed one: but it is also possible that these contradictions and complications are reflected in Cobbett's increasingly sophisticated exploitation of matters of audience in the 1820s and 1830s.[49]

We can conclude with one preliminary example of this, in the shape of his notorious loathing of tea which found its most comprehensive expression in *Cottage Economy* of 1822. His primary and fairly rational objection to tea is that it is expensive, involves the making of fires even in good weather, and thus wastes money and time. His argument goes further, however, turning tea-drinking into a destructive moral vice:

But is it in the power of any man, any good labourer who has attained the age of fifty, to look back upon the last thirty years of his life, without cursing the day in which tea was introduced into England? Where is there such a man, who cannot trace to this cause a very considerable part of all the mortifications and sufferings of his life? When was he ever too late at his labour; when did he ever meet with a frown, with a turning off, and pauperism on that account, without being able to trace it to the tea-kettle? When reproached with lagging in the morning, the poor wretch tells you that he will make up for it by working during his breakfast time! I have heard this a hundred and a hundred times over. He was up time enough; but the tea-kettle kept him lolling and lounging at home; and now instead of sitting down to a breakfast upon bread, bacon and beer, which is to carry him on to the hour of dinner, he has to force his limbs along under the sweat of feebleness, and at dinner-time to swallow his dry bread, or slake his half-feverish thirst at the pump or the brook. To the wretched tea-kettle he has to return at night, with legs hardly sufficient to maintain him: and thus he makes his miserable progress towards that death which he finds ten or fifteen years sooner than he would have found it had he made his wife brew beer instead of making tea. If he now and then gladdens his heart with the drugs of the public-house, some quarrel, some accident, some illness, is the probable consequence; to the affray abroad succeeds an affray at home; the mischievous example reaches the children, corrupts them or scatters them, and misery for life is the consequence.[50]

It is surely obvious – even from a casual look – that, contrary to most critical conclusions, Cobbett's procedures in this passage are anything but spontaneous. The heavily rhetorical questions at the beginning of the paragraph are calculated to define the reader Cobbett wishes to address – the 'good labourer' who is at the same time 'any man' – and to offer this reader an illusory choice of agreement with, or denial of, his hypothesis. Cobbett slips from this equivocal appeal for the reader's agreement into an assertion of the 'hundred and hundred' examples of tea-related suffering he has come across among his own workforce, in this way answering his own question and shutting down the possibility of alternative explanations for working-class misery. He cleverly assumes that the tea-drinker's bread will be 'dry', as though beer automatically entails bacon and tea automatically rules it out, and follows the labourer's decline into drunkenness and childlessness with methods which seem strongly reminiscent of the evangelical tales of Hannah More which in turn draw on the chapbook and broadside taste for melodrama.[51]

But if Cobbett's attack on tea-drinking is calculated and rhetorical in its methods, how can we account for its apparently irrational and extreme conclusion? Both E. P. Thompson and John Osborne suggest that Cobbett's attacks on tea may be politically motivated.[52] His fellow reformers shared his dislike of tea, though expressing their dislike less shrilly, due to the fact that it was subject to taxation. Indirect taxation was the poor man's burden in the period, on everything from soap and candles to foodstuffs. To reject tea and coffee, then, was a rare opportunity to refuse to pay, and Radicals invented replacement beverages, marketing them as 'Radical Breakfast Powder'.[53] On this basis Cobbett's elaborate rejection of these 'slops' may actually operate as a dramatization of this practical expression of political disagreement with the taxation system being made elsewhere in the political scene.

But there is a problem with this reading, which is that Cobbett urges his reader to turn to home-brewed beer instead. Beer is also subject to taxation in the period, as he acknowledges, so we might feel that our search for political significance is undermined. Specifically, critics of Cobbett would argue that any Radical benefit resulting from his rejection of tea is more than offset by the pointless nostalgia and chauvinism of his preference for beer, which seems always to be associated in Cobbett's prose with the cheese, bread, bacon, and agricultural lifestyle of Merrie England. Cobbett prophesies the end of taxation on malt, adding 'things are, with regard to the labourers, coming back to what they were forty years ago.'[54] Why, critics ask, should such regression be necessarily a good thing?

We can rephrase the question by asking what polemical goal can be served by rejecting one taxed beverage in favour of another – the latter associated with Old England, the former with the foreign and the new. If Cobbett is merely appealing to the xenophobic and self-satisfied attitudes of a populist audience little benefit seems to accrue. Since he is not rejecting taxed beverages altogether like his Radical colleagues, the net financial benefit to such an audience seems nil. If we look at the broader structure of the argument, however, we see that Cobbett's polemical interests are wider than at first seems to be the case.

The piece, which appeared in *Cottage Economy*, begins with an attack on taxation from a national perspective and, significantly, from an upper-class one. 'It appears impossible', Cobbett asserts 'that the landlords should much longer submit to these intolerable burdens [of taxation] on their estates. In short, they must get off the malt tax or lose those estates'. Now we begin to perceive the possibility of a more sophisticated polemical agenda underlying Cobbett's attack, and culminating in the melodrama and pathos of the passage quoted above. Cobbett may not be attempting a general attack on taxation for the sake of the working class and making an unsatisfactory job of it. Instead he may be speaking indirectly to two audiences here – a possibility signalled by the identification of his reader as the 'good labourer' who is also 'any man', which we have already noted. While the chapbook-style melodrama and direct advice about the cost of tea seem aimed at a labouring-class readership, Cobbett may simultaneously and indirectly be appealing to another audience of country gentlemen whose estates are directly hit by the taxation on malt. He seems to be aiming to enlist their support by alerting them to their interest in reducing taxation and, by stressing the benefits of beer over tea, indirectly championing them as malt producers. The moral thrust of the passage is also more likely to appeal to such an audience than to the one it ostensibly targets, as it absurdly stresses violence and social breakdown as the potential consequences of tea-drinking which, as even Cobbett's hostile critics acknowledge, stands for the end of the agrarian order, foreign trade and the social dominance of 'nabobs'. We can draw a parallel here with the hysterical visions of social breakdown which, as we have seen, were envisaged by anti-Jacobin writings of the 1790s. We can note that if Cobbett's procedures are reminiscent of Hannah More then it is also true that her tracts were admired by the panic-stricken upper classes as much or more than by those to whom they were ostensibly addressed. Populism and emotionalism, in other words, are propagandist techniques likely to appeal across social boundaries.

We can see Cobbett's attack on tea answering several purposes then. As well as a commonsensical argument aimed at the poor, pointing out the expense of tea exacerbated by the requirement for fires at all times of year, it also seems framed in a way likely to win more powerful backing for the abolition of tax. More widely, it serves as a symbolic attack on the growing financial and trading economy and all the social change and deprivation which goes with it. If his defence of beer seems as a consequence to be a defence of traditional hierarchical social structures, then this also contributes to the creation of his famous and useful persona as John Bull who, if he is averse to tea on the grounds that it is 'foreign' will presumably object to French Jacobinism on the same grounds. And this persona, as I have already suggested, is another defence against marginalizing accusations of unpatriotic feelings, or alarmingly innovative intentions.

If we look back over this chapter we can see that the techniques which I have identified as Radical are all concerned to involve the reader – and readers of varying status – creating integrations between apparently incompatible ways of thinking, of feeling and of writing. Recurring features have been a conversational tone; polyphony, with the incorporation of contending voices into the text; the absorption of popular prejudice and superstition, with the world view that they imply, to reinforce the values of antiquity and to make Radicalism both unthreatening and English, in a way oddly reminiscent of the reactionary *Anti-Jacobin*; and self-dramatization that emphasizes the subjectivity, drama and dialogue of experience, and invites the reader to create positive self-images in response to the text. The ambiguity of his real audience from the 1820s onwards facilitates this creative invention of and relationship with his implied readers, as we can see from our discussion of Cobbett's strictures on tea.

Techniques and procedures like these are perhaps most apparent in the best-sellers of Cobbett's lifetime. In the next two chapters I will concentrate on *A History of the Protestant Reformation*, *Advice to Young Men* and *The Poor Man's Friend*, to show how Cobbett marries opposing audiences attitudes, themes and literary forms in ways that continue to make Radicalism seem safe and unthreatening, while contriving to make the accepted and traditionally safe seem, on the contrary, challenging and new.

CHAPTER 6

A radical history

Volume I of Cobbett's *A History of the Protestant Reformation in England and Ireland*[1] was first published in parts between 1824 and 1826, and collected into book form in 1826, creating a publishing sensation. Cobbett claimed that only sales of the Bible outstripped those of his book, and George Spater's biography of Cobbett puts the English sales figure by 1828 at 700,000.[2] Cobbett, recurrently seen as a 'John Bull', had taken a history written by a Catholic priest, John Lingard, and had cast it into accessible and popular forms. Characterized by recent critics and biographers as choleric, violent and inaccurate, it conforms to – and seems to exemplify – the stereotyped image of Cobbett from his day to ours. In this vein, for example, Osborne describes Cobbett's judgements in the *History* as 'grotesque'.[3] Other than in these broad terms, however, the text itself has suffered from critical neglect, and the reasons for its phenomenal success have not been satisfactorily addressed.

In view of the text's commercial success, broad stylistic criticisms – that, for example, the *History* is a didactic failure,[4] or that its tone is 'unremittingly shrill'[5] – must be unsatisfactory. For one thing, regardless of its historical accuracy, it is far more entertaining than is usually acknowledged. More importantly, as it will be the aim of this chapter to show, the *History* is a stylistically innovative text, in which Cobbett creates profoundly radical effects by the manipulation of genre, discourse and reader.

Since there has been so little detailed criticism of the *History*, it seems useful to begin by describing its aims and thematic features. We shall see from this description that the text is characterized by a thematic emphasis on opposition, which we shall see again in the formal discussion which will follow on from the description of themes. As these oppositions are repeatedly concerned with upper- and working-class status, rights, and literary forms, it will become clear that the oppositional form highlights inherent class conflicts and moral incongruities in the prevailing historical situation with which Cobbett is concerned. More important for our purposes, the emphasis on both the refined and the vulgar also creates a relationship between the authorial voice and the implied reader which develops those points I have already made regarding the status and involvement of the reader in Cobbett's texts. This developing relationship between author and reader, I will argue, constitutes that aspect of the text which radicalizes historical discourse, a radicalization which I have already identified as my overall concern in the title of this chapter.

We begin, then, with the motives for the work, its goals and its assumptions. On a strictly explicit level the text is a polemic for Catholic Emancipation. Cobbett attempts to rehabilitate the Catholic faith by recognizing its longevity; pointing out that it was the sole Christian faith in England until the Reformation, and that subsequent English histories of that event and the religious practices which preceded it have been written by Protestants.[6]

Almost inevitably the text is also a polemic against certain aspects of the Church of England, and all of Methodism and Utilitarianism. These latter dogmas are seen as linked by the fact that both articulate certain attitudes to the poor. By depicting the monastery as a place of hospitality to the hungry and medicine to the sick, Cobbett creates a vision of an idyllic pre-Reformation system of poor relief; and in opposition to this he sets up a vision of the meanness of Methodist and Utilitarian charity.[7] Chief targets seem to be the *Cheap Repository Tracts* with their easy messages of endurance and resignation, and the population theory of Malthus and his followers. With the rapid approach of the changes in the Poor Laws that were to channel relief through workhouses from 1834, Cobbett's comments upon the issue become increasingly urgent. In 1834 he was to articulate his theory of civil rights for the needy in *A Legacy to Labourers*; here the theory is in its genesis.

The issue for Cobbett is, in the end, not the worthiness of the poor as charitable objects, but their *right* to humane relief. Cobbett is not attempting to establish a Utopian belief in principles of equality – as we have already noted, he is not in any case an egalitarian – but to achieve something more basic and perhaps even more difficult: to combat the assumption that the lower classes have no right at all to consideration as a part of the political nation, nor aptitude for political power. Only by acknowledging their centrality as the producers of national wealth (as in the letter 'To the Journeymen and Labourers') or by stressing their numerical supremacy (as we will see him doing here) can Cobbett establish their right to more than the merest subsistence level of wages or poor relief. And this re-enfranchisement – even rehumanization – can only be achieved by reorientating political and historical discussion to acknowledge and to privilege their experiences and well-being.

If we return to the decisive letter 'To the Journeymen and Labourers' of 1816, we can reach some initial conclusions as to Cobbett's methods which lead us to an appreciation of the thematic impetus to the *History*. In my discussion of the letter of 1816 in Chapter 3, I noted the way in which the piece radicalized the ancient constitutionalism of Burke and Coke, rather than following Radical versions of the myth that laid stress on the 'Norman Yoke'. We saw that by choosing this method, Cobbett took over reactionary discourse and recast it as radical. In this way he could avoid both alienating the conservative lower class, and providing the upper class with the means to brand him as a Jacobin or a traitor.

In Chapter 3 I described the methods by which this radicalization was achieved as consisting of a stress on activity, on real-life actions performed by flesh and blood people to achieve real goals. This stress gained its emphasis by being set in opposition to that laid on passivity, powerlessness and individual insignificance by Coke and Burke. This kind of definition by opposition is clearly related to that description of Cobbett I have quoted from Hazlitt, which depicts him as defining his ideas and his role in positions of antagonism.

In the introductory essay to Volume II of the *History* Cobbett affirms his ideological position and even his flesh and blood reality through the act of remembering his political antagonists. He is about to conclude his introduction, when the date he is writing strikes him: it is the anniversary of his imprisonment of 1810:

Here I had signed my name, and was about to put the date. It was on its way from my mind to my hand, when I stopped my hand all at once and exclaimed: 'Good God! the ninth of July! The anniversary of my sentence of two years' imprisonment in a felon's gaol ... for having expressed my indignation at Englishmen having been flogged, in the heart of England, under a guard of German troops!

From this reminder of the existence of enemies within the government, Cobbett goes on to remember the exultations of 'the

Hampshire parsons' upon his imprisonment, whom he depicts as having 'crowed out aloud, in the fulness of their joy', and from there to a half-oratorical, half-colloquial eulogy to his own political survival: '"What!" exclaimed I again, "and am I, on the anniversary of that very day, putting the finishing hand; yea, sending from under my fingers to the press, the last, the very last words, the completing words, the closing point, of a work, which does the JOB for them and for all their tribe..."' Rhetorical questions, biblical cadences, and oratorical repetition and amplification culminate in the outrageous colloquialism of 'does the JOB'. Already we seem to be in that linguistic territory of mingling and clashing discourse that we have visited before. Cobbett goes on, via a celebration of the success of Volume I of his *History*, to a joyful appreciation of his combined literary and physical powers:

And, then, feeling health and vigour in every vein and in every nerve; seeing, lying before me, manuscript (equal to twenty pages of print) written by me this very day; knowing the effects, which, in the end, that manuscript must have on these parsons, and the great good that it must do to the nation; reflecting, feeling, seeing, knowing, thus, it is, that I, in justice to our pious, sincere, brave, and wise forefathers, and in compassion to my suffering countrymen, and to the children of us all, send this little volume forth to the world.[8]

Now Cobbett defines himself literally through opposition, as he responds with a physical thrill to remembered and anticipated conflict. Here, too, we see other oppositions: one between thought and sense – feeling and seeing, reflecting and knowing; another between the characteristics of past and present – 'pious, sincere, brave...wise forefathers' and his 'suffering countrymen' of the present day. Binary oppositions and contrasts like these we shall see again and again on a thematic and literary level in the work.

But identifications are as important as conflicts: even in the image of contrasting past wealth and present poverty, we are also invited to see an identity of interests between past, present, and future as Cobbett dedicates his book to his forefathers, his countrymen, and his children: 'thus, it is, that I, in justice to our pious, sincere, brave, and wise forefathers, and in compassion to my suffering countrymen, and to the children of us all, send this little volume forth to the world'. Again, the positive corollaries of conflict are brought to our attention.

I have identified a use of thematic opposition in the introduction to

A radical history

Volume II of the work: this is also true of the more influential Volume II.[9] Here too, oppositions and contrasts function as an expression of the work's theoretical framework. We can see this in a passage from early in Volume I:

Will they [the Protestant teachers and historians] tell us that all our fathers, who first built our churches, and whose flesh and bones form the earth for many feet deep in all the churchyards; will they tell us that all these are now howling in the regions of the damned? Nature beats at our bosom, and bids us shudder at the impious, the horrid thought![10]

By referring to the generations long dead as 'our fathers', Cobbett immediately makes their interests seem relevant to us as their 'children', and by establishing this close emotional link with an otherwise remote past he creates a sense of identity between the individual reader, the past and its dead population, and the earth that they form. This kind of identification seems related to the methods of Cobbett's autobiographical writings, where an oak tree can be symbolically representative of a man, and to the introduction to Volume II of the *History* where, as we have already noted, Cobbett's dedication is to people of the past, present and future. In the passage from Volume I that we have been discussing, though, that identity is contrasted with the extreme emotional and psychological alienation of rejecting the past and our forefathers as 'damnable' and 'idolatrous'. Nature rebels at the thought, Cobbett tells us, and a large part of the *History* is concerned with similar emotional unacceptability and conflict.

A key word in the passage just quoted is 'all'. The Catholics were 'all our fathers', they lie in 'all the churchyards' and the Protestant establishment now depicts them as 'all ... howling in the regions of the damned ...' This reminds us again that faith in England before the Reformation was universal and uniform, and it encourages a sense of community between Cobbett and his readers, and amongst the readers themselves. The 'all' is also one half of the key opposition of the text. In this text, the recurring question posed is, if we accept the utilitarian doctrine of the 'greatest happiness of the greatest number', who in fact form this majority? Cobbett answers, they are the very people whom Malthus predicts will starve in the approaching subsistence crisis, and whom Cobbett fears will be sacrificed to the interests of the politically powerful. 'Society', in other words, usually means the vocal propertied few: Cobbett reminds us of the silent masses of the propertyless.[11] The 'all' is continually opposed to the 'few' in the *History*, via a recurring series of binary oppositions in the text: them/us, after/before, starvation/plenty, slavery/freedom.

The first and recurring opposition is that between pre- and post-Reformation England. Before that event, Cobbett repeatedly tells us, 'England was more powerful and more wealthy, and... the people were more free, more moral, better fed, and better clad, than at any time since that event.'[12] The Reformation

> despoiled the working classes of their patrimony; it tore from them that which nature and reason had assigned them; it robbed them of that relief for the necessitous which was theirs by right imprescriptable, and which had been confirmed to them by the law of God and the law of the land. It brought a compulsory, a grudging, an unnatural mode of relief, calculated to make the poor and rich hate each other instead of binding them together as the Catholic mode did, by the bonds of Christian charity.[13]

The source of the difference and the decline, then, is the change in the method of poor relief, which is itself a symptom of a changing attitude towards the labouring class. The thrust of the book is to argue for the rights of the poor to such relief, and to counter Protestant portrayals of the monastery as a parasite on the people by arguing that the tithes granted to an unmarried clergy naturally fed back into the community through monastic 'hospitality' and charity. For Cobbett this method of relief is superior as, he claims, it worked more satisfactorily than the post-Reformation system in which parishes were keen to disclaim responsibility for as many paupers as they possibly could, and where the movement for workhouse conditions which would, in effect, punish poverty was soon to gain a hold.[14] Cobbett argues repeatedly throughout his career that the worker's 'birthright', gained in exchange for obeying the laws of the Parliament he does not elect, and fighting for the property of his social superiors in war, is relief in indigence or old age. Here this idea of the rights of the poor is implicit throughout, as we see in the passage quoted above with its stress on the theft perpetrated by the Reformers, as they 'despoiled... tore from... robbed' the poor of future generations. The Reformation, Cobbett tells us revealingly, 'is not a mere matter of religion, but a matter of rights, liberties, real wealth, happiness, and national greatness.'[15] And the recurring notion woven into the text, that the past has a profound influence on the present, is repeated again as Cobbett traces to the Reformation that present 'state of things which sees but two classes of people in a community, masters and slaves, a very few enjoying the extreme of luxury, and millions doomed to the extreme of misery.'[16]

Here of course we come to that opposition I have noted as central to the text, as the contrast between the few and the many is posited in the context of the new reluctance to grant financial aid to the poor. By a series of examples, Cobbett prods us towards accepting that the political nation and the biological one are two entirely different entities, and that the confusion is proving deadly. Cobbett quotes Hume on the benefits of the Reformation in making men industrious:

> The Catholic institutions 'provided against the pressure of want amongst the people, but prevented the increase of "public riches!"' What, again I ask, is the meaning of the words 'public riches?' What is, or ought to be, the end of all government and of every institution? Why, the happiness of the people. But this man seems, like Adam Smith, and indeed like almost every Scotch writer, to have a notion that there may be great public good though producing individual misery. They seem always to regard the people as so many cattle working for an indescribable something that they call 'the public.'[17]

Equally, though, this distinction between the political and the biological 'people' can exonerate the masses from blame for the actions of the few: thus Cobbett notes Hume's observation that 'the Pope's remonstrances ... [with the English] had "little influence with the nation."' Cobbett is quick to point out the limited applicability of the term 'nation' in this context: 'With the plunderers, he means ...'[18] And in combination with the ignorance as to politics, religion and history endemic among the mass of the people, Cobbett can use this distinction to mourn the intellectual and political disenfranchisement of those he represents. That he identifies with and represents the majority is explicit: 'Now how stand we in this respect compared with our Catholic ancestors? They did not perhaps all vote at elections. But do we? Do a fiftieth part of us?'[19] This political impotence seems to find its intellectual equivalent as he describes the monument to the Fire of London with its accusation of the 'Popish faction' as the arsonists: 'there it now stands, all the world except the mere mob knowing it to contain a most malignant lie.'[20] Cobbett will explicitly address the *History* to the 'good and thoughtless protestant' in the introduction to Volume II of the work, whom he identifies with his past self: 'you cannot be more zealous or more loud upon this score than I was, for many years of my life.'[21] Literally or metaphorically, then, Cobbett identifies at least his former self as a part of the 'mere mob', and designates that ignorant section of Christendom as his target audience.

This stress on the intellectual disenfranchisement of the poor resonates with the polarizing ideology of refinement and vulgarity which discriminates against the poor on the assumption that their 'ignorance' and linguistic incapacity are the result of inherent inferiority rather than educative deprivation. Cobbett's arguments in justification of Catholic Emancipation in the *History* are equally appropriate to this unjust and irrational discrimination against the poor. Emancipation is essential

> when we consider that the principles of the 'Reformation' are put forward as the ground for excluding them from their civil rights, and also as the ground for treating them in a manner the most scornful, despiteful, and cruel; when we consider that it is not in human nature for men to endure such treatment without wishing for, and without seeking, opportunities for taking vengeance; when we consider the present formidable attitude of foreign nations, naturally our foes, and how necessary it is that we should all be cordially united, in order to preserve the independence of our country; and when we consider that such union is utterly impossible as long as one-third part of the people are treated as outcasts ... [22]

Here Cobbett's stress on the danger and senselessness of persecuting such a large section of society identifies the disenfranchised Catholic with the Protestant labourer as both victims of oppression and as potential revolutionaries. Moreover the reason for the persecution of Catholics is as irrational as attitudes towards the poor: 'because, and only because, they have, in spite of two hundred years of persecutions unparalleled, adhered to the religion of their and of our fathers'.

As usual, then, Cobbett's particular arguments have wider significances. Interestingly, however, these two motives for oppression – intellectual inferiority and religious belief – come together later in a problematic passage which discusses the rise of capitalism and its attendant ills as a result of the Reformation. There Cobbett breaks off from a discussion of the rise of the usury in the sixteenth century to make the following observation:

> Jews did it; but then, Jews had no civil rights. They existed only by mere sufferance. They could be shut up, or banished, or even sold at the king's pleasure. They were regarded as a sort of monsters, who professed to be the

lineal descendants and to hold the opinions of those who had murdered the SON OF GOD AND THE SAVIOUR OF MEN. They were not permitted to practice their blasphemies openly. If they had synagogues they were unseen by the people. The horrid wretches themselves were compelled to keep out of public view on Sundays and on saints' days. They were not allowed to pollute with their presence the streets or the roads of a Christian country on days set apart for public devotion. In degraded wretches like these USURY, that is, receiving money for the use of money, was tolerated just for the same cause that incest is tolerated amongst dogs.[23]

At first sight this passage seems to be race hatred of the most crude variety, and an elaboration on Cobbett's habitual designation of capitalism as the 'Jew-system'.[24] Cobbett's observations seem uncomplicatedly anti-Semitic as he uses the Jews apparently as a measure of debasement and corruption, implying that as usurers the Christians are 'no better than' Jews.

But if we examine the passage with more attention, we can see that it is far more complex than this. As we have just seen Cobbett asserting, civil rights must be extended to *all* a country's inhabitants if that country is to be a united and secure one. If Protestants are the descendants of Catholics, then Catholics are the descendants of Jews, and if modern society is guilty of irrational patricide in its persecution of Catholics then the medieval attitudes he is reporting are equally guilty of that crime. Moreover, if Cobbett's standard, Magna Charta, proclaims that 'No Freeman shall be taken, or imprisoned, or be disseised of his Freehold, or Liberties, or Free Customs, or be outlawed, or exiled, or any other wise destroyed ... We will sell to no man, we will not deny or defer to any man, either Justice or Right,'[25] then his description of Jewish disabilities – 'they could be shut up, or banished, or even sold at the king's pleasure,' – cannot be approving. Rather, Cobbett is here reporting what happens to those who are not 'Freemen'. And if that includes the Catholic, and the Protestant agricultural labourer, then Cobbett's representation of medieval anti-Semitism implicitly relates to the anxiety about poverty and the pro-Catholic polemic which permeate the whole of the *History of the Protestant Reformation*.

What is particularly interesting, however, is that Cobbett cannot make this Radical argument quite unambiguously, and that as a result the passage is riven with contradictions. As a counter to the argument I have just traced, Cobbett capitalizes Jewish sins against Christ in a way which implies that he participates in the Christian indignation against Jews, and in the final sentence of the extract the fairly clear separation between the extreme medieval consciousness Cobbett is representing and his own views seems to break down. Does Cobbett endorse this view of Jews as 'dogs' or doesn't he? Is this still the free indirect speech[26] of the fanatical medieval speaker, or is this Cobbett? It is no longer clear here that the comment is the indirect speech of the medieval anti-Semite, as it seems to reveal a degree of analytical thought as to why the Jews deal in usury – because they are 'degraded' – that ill accords with the thoughtless prejudices previously articulated. But on the other hand, it seems to constitute a fair summation of that attitude. If it is such a summation, made by the narrator, there are still problems – where does this narrator stand? The use of the word 'degraded' suggests sympathy with the Jews; the parallel with dogs suggests that his opinion of Jewish intellectual possibilities is extremely limited. Yet the author knows that Jews are human beings and not dogs, so such an exaggeratedly low estimate of Jewish abilities ought to be self-conscious – particularly in the context of the strong parallels being drawn with the disenfranchised classes that Cobbett unequivocally supports. In the end it is impossible to make a definitive judgement about which voice is speaking here – narrator or medieval man – and the resulting ambiguity disguises the Radical implications of the passage.

It is interesting that, as elsewhere, this ambivalence is not unique to Cobbett. In fact Cobbett's anxieties here seem to be very similar to those implicit in Scott's *Ivanhoe* published in 1819 – a text similarly preoccupied with medieval anti-Semitism. Scott represents his Jewish heroine throughout the novel as dramatically superior to her Saxon counterpart, and clearly deserving Ivanhoe's affection, but in the end Ivanhoe unsatisfactorily yet inevitably marries his Saxon princess. These examples of discursive pressure, where it is just not possible to make a completely Radical break with dominant ideological assumptions raise interesting questions too large to be pursued here. Why can Cobbett endorse Catholic Emancipation, when anti-Catholicism has been recently identified as that which *defines* British national identity in this period,[27] yet cannot unambiguously counter less politically-contentious anti-Semitism?[28] Whatever the answer to this question, the rhetorical thrust of the arguments made by both Scott and Cobbett are as follows: that oppression is bad for you; that Jews deal in usury because they have been dehumanized by the oppression of what Scott calls the 'fanaticism and tyranny' of medieval Christian society.[29] This position fails to question whether Jews are really 'degraded', but it does argue for the influence of nurture over nature – an argument that, however ambiguously put, clearly speaks on behalf of other oppressed and marginalized groups, deprived of power on the excuse that they are, similarly, inherently unfit for it.

Cobbett's working-class audience may be ignorant, then – may even be 'degraded' – but in the *History* this is the inevitable result of oppression and of want. Again and again hunger is opposed to happiness and to freedom. Cobbett quotes the utilitarian doctrine: 'What is the object of government? To cause men to live happily.' From this he turns immediately to the second phrase of the equation: 'They cannot be happy without a sufficiency of food and of raiment.' Therefore, he concludes: 'Good government means a state of things in which the main body are well fed and well clothed.' Crime is not crime, he adds, that springs from a lack of necessities.[30]

Neither is freedom a reality in a state of indigence. 'Freedom is not an empty sound; it is not an abstract idea; it is not a thing that nobody can feel. It means, – and it means nothing else, – the full and quiet enjoyment of your own property.' Our forefathers, Cobbett continues, would not let anyone strip them of that right: 'they never suffered anybody to put them to board on cold potatoes and water.'[31] This recurring stress on the contrast between the possibilities of life to one well-fed and to one in a state of starvation is summed up and amplified, close to the end of the text, in a nightmare vision of starvation amongst plenty:

intelligence from the northern counties (1826), published upon the spot, informs us that great numbers of people are nearly starving, and that some are eating horse-flesh and grains, while it is well known that the country abounds in food; and while the clergy have recently put up from the pulpit the rubrical thanksgiving for times of plenty, a law recently passed, mak[es] it felony to take an apple from a tree ...[32]

Such brutal contrasts, along with a laying bare of relationships between past and present, happiness and government, hunger and plenty, are all part of that tradition we have noted in Cobbett of a desire to find and communicate 'truth'. There are recurrent appeals to the truth of the statements made in the *History*, appeals that are necessitated by the fact that Cobbett is turning received wisdom on its head. I have already noted Cobbett's recognition that history is written by the winners. He adds: 'But TRUTH is immortal; and though she may be silenced for a while, there always, at last, comes something to cause her to claim her due and to triumph over falsehood.'[33] For Cobbett, that something is the economic distress that he sees as a direct consequence of the Reformation: distress arising out of deception, that brings with it jails and long hours in factories.

In the face of deception the paramount need is to teach the truth, no matter how gruesome: 'It is surely, then, our duty to teach our children to know the truth... Let them deny, if they can, that this Head of the Church, this maker of it, [Elizabeth I] was a murderer, and wished to be an assassin, in cold blood.'[34] Cobbett is driven, he tells us, by a 'compulsion to look into realities and to discard romance,'[35] one so strong that he freely recants his exaltation of Hampton and Sydney in the letter 'To the Journeymen and Labourers'.[36] Again, as before in his journalism, Cobbett is concerned with sources of facts and information, and this concern leads us to the formal and literary significances of the text.

Thus, discussing the motives behind war with France after the Glorious Revolution, Cobbett describes the discontent of the people as being amongst the many pressures on the new administration. This discontent, he suggests, was due to the authority of oral memory of monastic hospitality:

The confiscation of this [church property] was not yet of so ancient a date as to have been forgotten. Tradition is very long-lived. Many and many then alive knew all the story well. They had heard their grandfathers say that the Catholic Church kept all the poor, that the people were then better off; and they felt, the whole of the people felt, that England had lost by the change.[37]

Cobbett's appeal to oral memory is clearly related to his political and literary agenda in this text. We remember his insistence on the supremacy of the 1760s and 1770s. There are recurring examples of this narrow historical focus throughout his writings: as when, for example, in the *Political Register* of 10 February 1816 he uses 'the memory of the oldest man living'[38] as the yardstick for economic discussion. This kind of narrow view has won him the derision of critics, who prefer the wider historical perspective taken by Radicals of the 'Norman Yoke' variety. But Cobbett's narrowness tells us more about his agenda than merely that he is not a good historian.

Again, as with other examples of Cobbett's intellectual impurity, he is signalling the fact that he is not interested in a broad view. And again, his critics seem to forget that he is not a 'thinker' like Godwin or even Paine: he is primarily a practical politician, working in the present for the present good, for whom seventy years is a long time. Cobbett's stress on oral and living memory seems to emphasize this preoccupation with the political present, and it also privileges this area of debate. That is, he seems by these methods actively to reject academic historical inquiry in favour of lived experience. This is, yet again, perhaps characteristic of the 'John Bull' anti-intellectualism of Cobbett's methods, but it is also a value judgement in favour of 'vulgarity' characterized by Olivia Smith as concerned with concreteness, activity, and an interest in the here and now.[39] Again, we can remember the contrasts I drew between Cobbett's ancient constitutionalism and that of Coke and Burke. And turning back to the passage from the *History* that I have just quoted, we can see that a similar preference is apparent: oral history is true; written history is open to distortion.

The preference for oral history and living memory seems as much part of the privileging of lower-class values and literary conventions here as in the texts discussed in the last chapter. This preference also constitutes a theory of history, which Cobbett would articulate six years later in *Advice to Young Men*:

> We do not want to consume our time over a dozen pages about Edward the Third dancing at a ball, picking up a lady's garter, and making that garter the foundation of an order of knighthood, bearing the motto of 'Honi soit qui mal y pense.' It is not stuff like this; but we want to know what was the state of the people; what were a labourer's wages; what were the prices of the food, and how the labourers were dressed in the reign of that great king. What is a young person to imbibe from a history of England, as it is called, like that of Goldsmith? It is a little romance to amuse children; and the other historians have given us larger romances to amuse lazy persons who are grown up.[40]

This theory, which implicitly acknowledges the kind of class conflicts that we have been examining so far in this chapter, seems to constitute a development of that method we identified in Cobbett's letter 'To the Journeymen and Labourers' of shutting out the refined elite from a discussion that they would usually dominate. But we will see below that this is not a complete account of what is happening in the *History*; and that when other factors are taken into account, the

Radical nature of the text becomes even more immediately apparent, as does its antagonistic relationship with the refined elite.

The first thing to note about the passage just quoted from *Advice to Young Men* is the way in which Cobbett conceives his task as a problem of purpose and content. To write 'true' and 'useful' history, its generic conventions must be discarded: 'romance' is no longer an option. This entails the rejection of certain kinds of subject matter: what Cobbett sees as relevant to history is that which concerns the working class. But in the *History*, written six years before *Advice to Young Men*, this does not mean that kingly conduct cannot be described; only that its impact on the working class should be the rationale behind that description. That is, different aspects of kingly conduct are now of interest. Genre is equally class-based. Cobbett may reject the available 'romances' of monarch-centred history, but he does not replace them with the kind of factual writing he advocates in *Advice to Young Men*. Instead, it is by setting up the rival fantasies of history by the refined elite and history according to the chapbook, and by challenging the assumptions of both, that Cobbett seeks to rework the material. Indeed, in this highly emotional, partisan and iconoclastic polemic in favour of Catholic Emancipation, too dry a reliance on 'facts' would completely undermine the rhetorical purpose of the text.

We can see this if we look back to the popular literature that we examined briefly in the last chapter. Susan Pederson notes in her essay on the chapbook tradition that generalizations about the form are impossible to formulate, as fairy-stories and romances, songsheets and joke-books, almanacs and criminal confessions, and – as a minority – religious tracts and history and biography all come under the broad heading of popular literature.[41] But Pederson identifies some common characteristics: most are 'profoundly irreverent and often amoral'; many rely on fantasy, and are hostile to bourgeois virtues.[42] Bearing this in mind, when we approach popular texts purporting to be 'histories', it becomes clear that the 'story' is always the subversively dominant element at the expense of accuracy. Even in the crime sheets discussed in the last chapter, we can see that fantasy prevailed over 'facts', as Mary Jones cast herself as a gothic mixture of heroine, victim and villain, and William Corder's crime of passion was poetically reworked as the crime of a calculating monster. A similar refusal to be bound by 'facts', and a preference for stories

A radical history 171

cast in the shape of strong literary precedents, is in evidence in the more straightforwardly quasi-historical texts such as *The Famous History of the Learned Friar Bacon, Giving a Particular Account of His Birth, Parentage, with the Many Wonderful Things He Did in His Lifetime, to the Amazement of All the World*.[43] In this historical drama, Bacon is Faustus. As in Dr Faustus, for example, to be a scholar is to be a magician; like Faustus he summons spirits, performs tricks of space and time, and ridicules the proud and the wealthy. Unlike Faustus, however, his powers have no negative side: Bacon is completely in control of his demons and fears nothing from them. In other words, this is Dr Faustus without the moral framework: this is a fantasy of supernatural power unfettered by moral or religious anxieties.

The Comical History of the King and the Cobbler containing *The Entertaining and Merry Tricks and Droll Frolics Played by the Cobbler, How He Got Acquainted with the King, became a Great Man and Lived at Court Ever After*, shares these characteristics. In the previous chapter I noted this text as an example of the fantasy of social advancement: the fantasy element seems strongly signalled by the conclusion of the title 'and lived at Court ever after', with its echo of fairy-tale endings. Like the other texts I have cited, this story is unconstrained by considerations of fact or likelihood. In the context of our present discussion of the *History*, its portrayal of Henry is particularly interesting. It shows how the modern popular estimate of Henry VIII as one of the most interesting and 'human' monarchs was shared by the populace of the eighteenth and nineteenth centuries. Henry laughs, drinks, jokes and plays tricks, whilst also possessing an omniscience which allows him to judge the Cobbler favourably, and to reject judgements based on class and wealth. When we turn to Cobbett's portrayal of Henry in the *History*, the ways in which his picture resembles and varies from this chapbook character tell us interesting things about Cobbett's relationship with his audience and his material.

But before approaching this specific issue, we can make more general points about Cobbett's use of popular precedents in his history. The first, and crucial, observation to be made is that this privileging of what *ought* to be, over what *is*, bears a close relation to the 'grotesque' distortions of the *History*. It is already clear from our discussion of themes that the vision Cobbett presents is the 'true' one, for his rhetorical purposes, in the sense that it accounts for present miseries more satisfactorily than the 'real' history of the Reformation.

The second general point to be made about the relationship of the *History* to popular literature is that Cobbett's own *Political Register* is an example of a popular text, and Cobbett uses the conversational techniques he has developed in the *Register* to address his potentially broader, and ostensibly different, audience in the *History*. In this way the *History* talks across to its readers rather than down – or up – to them, expressing a popular world-view in the vernacular language familiar from the *Political Register*.

We have to be careful here: Cobbett's source for the text, John Lingard, also has a direct and conversational style which in some ways resembles Cobbett's own. Thus, for instance, Lingard notes of a party at Greenwich that 'the reader will not be surprised to learn that Henry's partner was Anne Boleyn.'[44] Cobbett's conversational relationship with his reader, as illustrated in the following passage, could be seen as only an exaggerated version of Lingard's method:

> If you will follow me in this enquiry, I will first show you how this thing called the 'Reformation' began; what it arose out of; and then I will show you its progress, how it marched on, plundering, devastating, inflicting torments on the people, and shedding their innocent blood. I will trace it downward through all its stages, until I show you its natural result... in the present indescribable misery of the labouring classes in England and Ireland...[45]

In a sense, though, Lingard's conjectures as to his readers' responses fall in line with the chapbook tradition of story-telling, a fact which reminds us of Cobbett's definition of refined history as romantic. Lingard assumes our interest in Henry and Anne Boleyn as a romantic hero and heroine; Cobbett's concern for his readers' response in the passage just quoted is that they learn. Where Cobbett exploits the conventions of popular narrative plot, then, his motive seems to be more than one of mere entertainment.

A more basic difference between Lingard and Cobbett emerges in the nature of the reader to whom the texts are respectively addressed. Lingard's third-person reference to 'the reader' suggests a polite and respectful address to one who expects such an approach. Cobbett's attitude is much more relaxed, implying a need to gain the concurrence of a reader used to gossip rather than courtly phrases; a concurrence to be gained by the imitation of dialogue rather than a narrative monologue:

> But, you may say, *why* should anybody, and particularly our countrymen, take such pains to deceive us? Why should they, for so many years, take the

A radical history

trouble to write and publish books of all sizes, from big folios down to halfpenny tracts, in order to make us think ill of this Catholic religion?[46]

The first thing to note, in the light of these observations, is that the individual literary techniques to be deployed are available to all writers; the Radical power of Cobbett's text will consist in the clashing and marrying of these techniques, as with the letter 'To the Journeymen and Labourers'. Cobbett is definitely writing 'history' with all its refined connotations, not a cheap broadsheet; but the incorporation of effects and assumptions associated with the vulgar refocusses the history to point up that opposition between the many and the few which we saw as central to the thematic structure of the text. The quote from the *History* at the opening of this chapter, where Cobbett lays out his intentions for the work as a whole, has echoes of the reactionary horror-rhetoric we discussed in Chapter 2, as it promises plunder, devastation, torments and blood. And if this is an example of the text addressing its vulgar audience with reactionary literary conventions, then it is also crucial to remember that the text is also aimed at the refined elite, who will be similarly incongruously addressed by Radical features and vulgar discourses. The central stylistic feature of the *History* perhaps, is this interchange between refined and vulgar discourse which mirrors the thematic oppositions between the lower and the upper classes.

Effects like the personalizing of the debate in ways reminiscent of Cobbett's scurrilous political journalism remind us that historical kingly conduct is also concerned with political power. Thus, Cobbett dismisses Henry VIII as a 'tyrant', and depicts Thomas Cromwell as a 'ruffian', as though both were present-day borough-mongers.[47] With the popular familiarity exhibited by *The King and the Cobbler*, where the cobbler knows his new acquaintance as 'Harry Tudor', Cobbett refers to the king as 'Old Harry'. Of Thomas Cranmer, however, he writes in a complex style perhaps associated with the fact that he is turning received wisdom on its head. Cranmer's name is

a name which deserves to be held in everlasting execration; a name which we could not pronounce without almost doubting of the justice of God, were it not for our knowledge of the fact, that the cold-blooded, most perfidious, most impious, most blasphemous caitiff, expired at last amidst those flames which he himself had been the chief cause of kindling.[48]

Strong and personal terms like these – even in grammatically complex sentences – bring their object within reach of popular discussion. The result is a subversive one, as Cobbett brings lower-class morality to bear on the activities of Henry VIII, and expresses his moral choices in the language of the *Comical History of the King and the Cobbler*. Faced with Anne Boleyn's pregnancy, Henry's priority is to 'make an honest woman of her'.[49] By casting the need for a legitimate heir in this kind of language, Cobbett reveals the identity of fundamental interests between the upper and lower classes, and the consequent possibility that the actions of one's 'betters' may be a fair topic for inquiry. Given the frequency of unwanted pregnancy as a motive for murder in the crime sheets, there is an almost sinister ring to the use of common phrases in this context. At any rate, the appositeness of language associated with the vulgar to the discussion of kingly conduct is repeatedly demonstrated: as here, with the description of the deteriorating relationship between Henry and Anne Boleyn after the birth of Elizabeth:

This (the birth) did not please the King, who wanted a son, and who was quite monster enough to be displeased with her on this account. The couple jogged on apparently without quarrelling for about three years; a pretty long time, if we duly consider the many obstacles which vice opposes to peace and happiness. The husband, however, had plenty of occupation ... he had, poor man, to labour hard at making a new religion ... Besides which, he had, as we shall see in the next number, some of the best men in his kingdom, and that ever lived in any kingdom or country, to behead, hang, rip up, and cut into quarters. He had, moreover, as we shall see, begun the grand work of confiscation, plunder and devastation. So that he could not have a great deal of time for family squabbles.[50]

This passage begins almost as if over a garden wall, as Cobbett chattily informs us of the shabbiness of Henry's behaviour towards Anne Boleyn. Phrases like 'quite monster enough', 'the couple jogged on', 'a pretty long time' are self-consciously colloquial ones which jar on application to the conduct of a king, yet simultaneously seem peculiarly descriptive of the kind of marriage of convenience that we are hearing described. The sense of inappropriateness increases as Cobbett describes the founding of the Anglican faith in language that likens the task to the building of a pigsty, and executions for treason to an afternoon's butchery. Whatever inappropriateness is evident here, however, is more than matched by that evinced with the sudden switch to the conventionally dignified language of the history book in the penultimate sentence. To describe 'confiscation, plunder and devastation' as a 'grand work', is equally

A radical history 175

inapposite and jarring to the reader's sensibilities. The switch to the discourse of the refined may be connected with the possible intertextual echo here, which would be apparent only to the refined reader, of Marvell's *An Horatian Ode upon Cromwel's Return from Ireland*. In that heavily ironic poem, Marvell uses exactly the same paradox:

> Much to the Man is due.
> Who, from his private Gardens...
> Could by industrious Valour climbe
> To ruine the great Work of Time,
> And cast the Kingdome old
> Into another Mold.[51]

In Cobbett and Marvell, then, we see the yoking together of disparate discourses to undermine received wisdom, and to posit alternative possibilities. The privileging of vulgar discourse and values, in the following passage from the *History*, seems to make possible a meaningful discussion of the 'people's' role in the Reformation; and, at the same time, intertextuality and sophisticated grammatical structures signal the relevance of the passage also to the refined reader. Cobbett relies on grammatical parallels in his ironic assessment of Hume's motives as an historian:

One object always uppermost with Hume is to malign the Catholic religion: it therefore did not occur to him that this sanguinary tyrant was not effectually resisted... because this tyrant had the means of bribing the natural leaders of the people to take part against them, or, at the least, to neutralise those leaders. It did not occur to him to tell us that Henry VIII. found the English as gallant and just a people as his ancestors had found them...[52]

A similar kind of yoking is apparent with Cobbett's imagistic usages in the text. Cobbett appeals to his labouring class readers via clichéd images, fresh, agricultural ones, and ones reminiscent of refined texts. Thus, for instance, we can note how Cobbett describes the developments of Protestantism made by Elizabeth I in familiar imagery: 'she planted, she watered with rivers of blood, and her long reign saw take fast root in the land that tree the fruit of which the unfortunate Irish taste to this hour'.[53] This is standard horror-rhetoric, but is followed closely in the text by an image equally related to the natural world, but new and striking, to describe the growth of understanding. In an examination of 'the poverty and misery' wrought by the Reformation, Cobbett predicts, 'we shall see, clearly as we see the rivulet bubbling out of the bed of the spring, the bread and water of England and the potatoes of Ireland...'[54] The image is a flawed one, as it invites us to see bread, water and potatoes bubbling out of the earth; nonetheless, the image of the bubbling spring is also powerfully related to the idea of seeing previously concealed truths. The implication which makes the image ultimately a strong and appealing one, is that it promises a bubbling up of understanding and knowledge for its readers, whose interpretative and critical faculties have been equally subterranean up until this point.

An equally agricultural image later in the text seems to bring refined imagistic echoes, as Cobbett describes the Irish landlords as 'pastors...total strangers to the flocks, except in the season of shearing'.[55] This is a clever image, as it recalls biblical descriptions of pastors and flocks, where the primary pastor is Christ himself, and from there a whole range of pastoral imagery, from the Church's use of the Shepherd's crook as a symbol of the bishopric, to – for instance – Milton's *Lycidas*, where the seeker after knowledge is dramatized in the role of shepherd, and where the corrupt clergy are depicted as follows:

> Of other care they little reck'ning make,
> Then how to scramble at the shearers feast,
> And shove away the worthy bidden guest.
> Blind mouthes! that scarce themselves know how to hold
> A Sheep-hook, or have learn'd aught els the least
> That to the faithfull Herdman's art belongs![56]

The parallels here seem too obvious to need spelling out; what is interesting about Cobbett's version is the change to the focus of the image. Cobbett is speaking of landlords, not clergy, and this is significant in the context of his recurring depictions of the Reformation as destitute of spiritual and emotional fulfilment. For Cobbett the landlords are the spiritual leaders of the Reformation, and the general image deployed by Milton of clerical excesses, greed and selfishness, is brought down in Cobbett's version of the image to what Marx called the naked cash nexus.[57] Whether or not the Miltonic echo is conscious in Cobbett's image, it seems significant that the range of ideas in Milton's seventeenth-century text should be brought down to the one-dimensional preoccupation with money in Cobbett's nineteenth-century one. That is, as in the earlier reference

A radical history 177

to Marvell, it is to the supremacy of Protestantism associated with the Civil War and the Glorious Revolution as well as the Reformation, that Cobbett traces the attitudes and social system tending to the supremacy of money.[58] Here, then, a reading is available which sees Cobbett reworking accepted, powerful and refined imagery of the Civil War period to elucidate his Radical thesis. Simultaneously, moreover, he appeals to his labouring-class readers familiar with real, not literary, shearing profits, and targets the educated elite with the more specific charges contained in Milton's poem which they alone are likely to recognize. Yet again the emphasis is on the duality of Cobbett's notional reading audience.

A concern with the real experiences of his readers and himself leads Cobbett to the use of himself as example, and the relation of the past to the present. Thus in the course of listing the charges brought against James II, Cobbett repeatedly appeals to the present state of things to undermine the received wisdom that supports the deposition of James by the Glorious Revolution. Cobbett notes that James was as guilty as the politicians of the present day with regard to the suspension of habeas corpus and imprisonment without trial, but he notes with sarcasm that present-day activities are sanctioned by the concurrence of Parliament: 'who is so destitute of discrimination as not to perceive the astonishing difference between a dungeon with consent of Parliament and a dungeon without consent of Parliament!' Here Cobbett seems to be challenging the conventions of historians, as he dwells surprisingly on the idea of the physical dungeon in which offenders are imprisoned, rather than the means and motives of the imprisonment. This seems another example of the vulgarly concrete that we have already noted is a feature of Cobbett's Radical texts. In the same paragraph of the *History*, Cobbett cites himself as another example of present-day misdemeanours: 'coming to our own times, I, for having expressed my indignation at the flogging of English local militia men in the heart of England, under a guard of German troops, was two years imprisoned in a felon's jail...'[59]

This exploitation of his own experiences seems reminiscent of *Rural Rides*, where we noted that Cobbett used himself as a touchstone, and as a unifying image round which to organize his picaresque. In the *History*, we come across passages where the reader is dramatized into the procedures of the text in a way also used in *Rural Rides* and in the *Political Register* letter to Henry Hunt that we discussed in the last chapter. Thus, for example, Cobbett invites his reader to undertake a journey of his own:

> Go to the site of some once opulent convent. Look at the cloister, now become in the hands of a rack-renter the receptacle for dung, fodder and faggot wood; see the hall, where for ages the widow, the orphan, the aged and the stranger found a table ready spread; see a bit of its walls now helping to make a cattle-shed, the rest having been hauled away to build a workhouse; recognise in the side of a barn a part of the once magnificent chapel; and if, chained to the spot by your melancholy musings, you be admonished of the approach of night by the voice of the screech owl issuing from those arches which once at the same hour resounded with the vespers of the monk, and which have for seven hundred years been assailed by storms and tempests in vain, – if thus admonished of the necessity of seeking food, shelter and a bed, lift your eyes and look at the white-washed and dry-rotten shell on the hill, called the 'gentleman's house,' and apprised of the 'board wages' and the 'spring guns,' suddenly turn your head; jog away from the scene of devastation; with 'old English hospitality' in your mind reach the nearest inn, and there, in room half-warmed and half-lighted, and with reception precisely proportioned to the presumed length of your purse, sit down and listen to an account of the hypocritical pretences, the base motives, the tyrannical and bloody means under which, from which, and by which that devastation was effected and that hospitality banished forever from the land.[60]

With the scene at the convent, the effects of the letter to Hunt seem to be reproduced, as the emphasis on physical actions and senses and the skewing of narrative viewpoint combine with heavily metaphorical methods. When the reader lifts his eyes to the hills he does not receive help but is confronted by the blind white walls and morally destitute shell of the 'gentleman's house' with its inhospitable spring guns and ungenerous wages. Here the biblical reference seems aimed at the whole of Cobbett's notional audience, as biblical discourse is the domain of upper and lower classes alike. But the injunction to the reader to undertake certain physical and mental acts is more complex. In so far as the dramatization of the reader in this passage allows him to undertake certain tasks and thoughts, the passage seems yet again to be concerned to empower the rhetorically vulnerable working-class reader. Thus he is not merely granted the physical ability to look up and to turn his head; he is also granted the ability to 'recognise' the remnants of the convent in the architecture of a barn, and to reflect upon the significance of what he sees. As with the letter 'To the Journeymen and Labourers' and the 'Introduction' to Volume II of the *History*, the stress is on the human reality of experience and of possible reform; while the stress on reflection and recognition means that physical realities are not associated with the mob, and the 'mob' itself is reassured of its own reflective powers.

The physical language of the passage also conspires to make of it an extremely well-realized scene: picking out the verbs relating to the reader makes a strong narrative plot: 'Go to... look at... see... recognise... chained to the spot... be admonished... lift your eyes... look... turn your head... jog away... reach the nearest inn... sit down... listen...' With these last three verb groups we come to perhaps the strangest and most vivid aspect of the whole passage, as the reader is not only dramatized as seeing for himself what Cobbett is describing, but he is not released from the fantasy at the close of the passage either. He is to read the *History* sitting in the comfortless inn into which Cobbett has dramatized him. Rather than resting aloof from the text he is reading, the reader is incorporated into it.

While there is yet again another strong intertextual echo in this passage, seemingly aimed at the refined reader, of Crabbe's *The Village* ('Go! if the peaceful cot your praises share,/Go, look within, and ask if peace be there:'[61]) the refusal to leave the reader aloof seems another effect of the strong physical images, and to relate to the means of creating lower-class participation in political discussion that we have already discussed. This method not only invites such participation but actually commands it – literally, as the verbs used are themselves grammatical commands – and metaphorically, as the reader is irresistibly drawn into the text's procedures.

What we are discussing here is, I think, an example of the 'mock-reader' or 'narratee' identified by early reader-response critics. This character is the implied reader of the text whom the author endows with certain characteristics and values, about whom he makes assumptions in order to facilitate his rhetorical purposes, and towards whom he entertains certain persuasive intentions.[62] Thus it is the mock-reader who is confined to the cheerless inn by the passage, and the convention allows us to understand and accept the technique.

In Cobbett's polemical text the mock-reader changes from page to page, with the needs of the argument.[63] Thus, for instance, later in the text, Cobbett will identify his mock-readers in detail as 'my townsmen of Farnham', exhorting them to consider the claims Cobbett is making for the monastery by reference to their living close to Waverley Abbey. Cobbett apostrophizes them as follows:

Come, my townsmen of Farnham; you who as well as I have, when we were boys, climbed the ivy-covered ruins of this venerable abbey (the first of its order in England); you who as well as I have, when looking at those walls which have outlived the memory of the devastators ... you shall be the judge in this matter.[64]

Here the closeness of the relationship Cobbett is trying to create with his reader is clear, as he identifies him with himself, and implies that the intimate knowledge of Waverley Abbey grants him judgemental authority. In the portion of the text that we were discussing before, however, we can see that the dual nature of Cobbett's notional audience complicates the issue at this point. That is, the reader who must visit the ruined convent is not identified so clearly as in the Farnham passage, and may therefore be a representative of either the refined or the vulgar reader, depending on how we read the passage. Where the command form of the verb empowers the vulgar reader – with a reassuring 'you *will* see and understand,' – when applied to the refined reader the relationship changes. Now the second-person verb forms and commands seem accusing, and the exhortation to see and to reflect becomes an exhortation to 'see what you have done'. The forcefulness and immediacy identified here seem in keeping with the techniques that we have noted as features of the *History*: on the one hand revealing thematic contrasts and clashes, and on the other a discourse in which the language of the refined and popular reader mingles in a similarly discordant manner. Colloquialisms with which to discuss kingly conduct, images that recall matter familiar to both the refined and the vulgar reader, and dramatization of the self and of the reader all function to draw the lower-class reader comfortably into the text. At the same time, the intertextual references involve his refined reader, while the other features disrupt that reader's generic expectations and sense of literary decorum.

If we accept the argument put forward in this chapter – that with the *History* Cobbett privileges lower-class values, literary conventions and vernacular speech, while at the same time seeming to acknowledge that the refined elite also number among his audience – then we will be less inclined to see the text as a merely didactic and paternalistic one, which has designs on the way the lower-class reader thinks and on what he believes. Not only is Cobbett, by privileging them, accepting these values, literary precedents and ways of speaking as acceptable for his purposes, but (I will argue here) the significant designs, in this text, are actually upon the consciousness and beliefs of his upper-class reader.

To explicate this assertion, I want to go back to the argumentative aims of the text. At the beginning of the chapter I suggested that as well as a pamphlet in favour of Catholic Emancipation the text was also a polemic against Malthus and Adam Smith, and against the prevailing attitude to poor relief as an act of charity rather than a matter of rights. In this way, while it purports to 'educate' the 'mere mob', the *History* has no desire to change them except in ways calculated to make their demands more vocal and more insistent. All the attitudes and values in need of change, according to the *History*, are those held by the powerful, enfranchised and affluent classes. As I noted at the beginning of this chapter, Cobbett's aim throughout the 1820s and 1830s is to assert the self-evident truth of the right of the poor to their due. But to make this assertion have any power, he must effect a radical change in upper-class perceptions.

The crucial thing to remember about the *History* is that, while it is framed in terms apparently calculated for the benefit of the lower-class reader, the poor are not the only people reading it. In important ways they are ironically incidental, as the real target is the often ostentatiously-excluded refined reader.[65] In a way, the important thing is not *what* is said but *how*. We can now see the function of the way in which Cobbett shuts out the refined reader in pieces like the letter 'To the Journeymen and Labourers,' or here in the *History*. It impresses upon such a reader that debate can occur without him, and points out the self-sufficient moral world of the working class which, as I noted earlier, could afford to reject bourgeois values in its chapbook literature. This qualifies Olivia Smith's judgement that Cobbett 'usually specified the social status of his audience and addressed it accordingly'.[66] By that act he is also saying other things to and about the audiences he is choosing *not* to address. In the *History* we can in fact observe Cobbett undertaking a radical task as, in a total reversal of the norm of moral and educative literature, he writes a 'vulgar' text indirectly to teach the rich about the rights of the poor, rather than a refined one to tell the poor of their own duties. This seems a development of that technique that we noted in *Rural Rides*, of skewing the addressee to challenge easy assumptions about hunger on the part of the middle and upper classes.

This kind of disruption in relation to the notional reader is echoed by the formal characteristics of the text that we have also noted, where intertextual echoes involve the refined reader, while conversational vernacular attracts the vulgar one; where on the one hand the tone of formal history clashes with the irreverent tone and renegade arguments of the content, and on the other the fantastically non-factual form of the chapbook clashes with the content of serious history. This kind of mix and confusion is characteristic of the methods of Cobbett's moral or ethical writings as well as of his history: these will be discussed in the next chapter, where we shall see the same kind of Radical reversal of literary techniques and assumptions about the status of the reader as we have seen in this one.

CHAPTER 7

Tracts and teaching

The conclusion of the previous chapter was that the manipulation of the 'mock-reader' radicalized the methods and assumptions of the *History of the Protestant Reformation in England and Ireland*, and constituted the main literary interest and achievement of the text. In this chapter I want to begin from the issue of mock-reader as I approach Cobbett's teaching texts. While concentrating on *Advice to Young Men* as one of his most enduring successes, and *The Poor Man's Friend* as his personal favourite among his works,[1] this chapter will also touch upon the *Monthly Sermons*, *Cottage Economy* and the *Grammar of the English Language*. It will be my aim to show how the status of the pupil Cobbett imagines he is addressing affects the manner of teaching, and how the choice of mock-pupil affects the political significance of the literary methods of the texts. These contentions will be established by a comparison between *Advice to Young Men* and Hannah More's *Cheap Repository Tracts*, and by a comparison between *Advice to Young Men* and *The Poor Man's Friend*. The chapter will conclude with a discussion of Cobbett's pastoral autobiography, which we will see is crucial to both texts in question and to his rhetorical strategies as a whole.

Critics of Cobbett often note the pre-Victorian prudery of some aspects of his thought, such as his arguments in *Advice to Young Men* against the use of male midwives and his respect for female chastity even to the point of condemning a widow's remarriage. Although he himself deplores the hypocrisy of the growing use of euphemistic language and mock-delicacy coinciding with the increase in prostitution which is a well-documented aspect of the Victorian period, he is – as James Sambrook notes – at times identifiable with the eighteenth-century Mrs Grundy. Discussing the related issue of Cobbett's objection to drink and gambling, Sambrook suggests that 'more than he cared to admit, Cobbett shared the views of the contemporary Evangelicals he despised so much'.[2] John Stevenson notes that Cobbett is in part a forerunner of certain Victorian values: 'hard work, sobriety, domestic bliss, self-help'[3]; while John Osborne argues that its preoccupation with the latter virtue taints *Advice to Young Men* with an anticipation of Samuel Smiles.[4] There do indeed seem to be parallels between *Advice to Young Men* and Hannah More's moral tracts of the 1790s, which in his conservative phase Cobbett had admired.[5] An identification and discussion of these parallels, however, will take us in unexpected directions.

The similarities seem clearest in More's 'Tales for the Common People' – especially in *Tom White the Post Boy*,[6] which will be the focus of our attention here. By a series of short anecdotes and incidents in Tom White's life, basic moral messages are aimed at the labouring class. A brief summary of these anecdotes and their messages seems in order here. Tom White begins as an honest farm labourer, but through wanderlust and a desire for glamour he is led to enlist as a post boy at the Black Bear inn. Encouraged to miss Sunday church services and to break the Sabbath by the customers' habit of travelling on Sundays, and led to swear, drink and gamble by his fellow drivers, Tom temporarily loses his soul, symbolized by a loss of compassion for the horses he drives. This leads inevitably to an accident, through which Tom is redeemed, and after many years as a responsible and honest driver he is rewarded with the offer of a farm-tenancy from his first employer.

This is only the beginning of More's tale, however, establishing Tom as an authoritative voice with the 'common people' she is targeting. By this exciting history he is to carry more weight with sinners as they will acknowledge that he knows about blasphemous fun and has voluntarily rejected it. The moral conclusions drawn are identical to those purveyed by Cobbett, as he too rejects spirits and gambling as pernicious as well as expensive, and uses kindness to animals as a token of a benevolent spirit.[7] In his role as tenant-farmer, Tom advises and aids the poor labourers around him, acting as an intermediary between the upper and lower classes. First, though, he marries, and the similarities are striking between the criteria for choosing a wife that More advances and those advanced by Cobbett. More's definition of a good wife is as follows:

He soon heard of a young woman of excellent character, who had been bred up by the vicar's lady, and still lived in the family as an upper maid. She was prudent, sober, industrious, and religious. Her neat, modest, and plain appearance at church (for she was seldom seen any where else out of her master's family) was an example to all persons in her station, and never failed to recommend her to strangers, even before they had an opportunity of knowing the goodness of her character. It was her character, however, which recommended her to Farmer White. He knew that 'favour is deceitful, and beauty is vain, but a woman that feareth the Lord she shall be praised ...'[8]

Cobbett's advice is given at greater length, but it is prefaced by a summary that indicates the similarity of vision: 'the things which you ought to desire in a wife are: 1. Chastity; 2. Sobriety; 3. Industry; 4. Frugality; 5. Cleanliness; 6. Knowledge of domestic affairs; 7. Good temper; 8. Beauty'.[9] In a manner similar to More's, he goes on to examine each category in turn, explaining the disadvantages of various forms of moral flightiness, laziness, extravagance, physical sloth and irritability. In a manner almost more objective and dry than More's, he suggests that moral character can be indicated by the use of the jaws: 'get to see her at work upon a mutton chop, or a bit of bread and cheese; and if she deal quickly with these, you have a pretty good security for that activity, that stirring industry, without which a wife is a burden instead of being a help'.[10] It is only on the subject of beauty that the moral bases of the two writers' visions disagree; but we will shortly see that this disagreement is central to the differing political and moral effects of the two writers' works.

But at this stage we will restrict our attention to the similarities between *Tom White the Post Boy* and *Advice to Young Men*. In a passage calculated to undermine the holiday traditions of the poor as times of carnivalesque drunkenness, More has Tom explain to one member of his workforce that the money wasted on such debauchery could otherwise buy the family a mutton joint and a quart of ale. The recipient of his advice is impressed, but afraid to break with the tradition of going out to the pub. Tom assures him that homely pleasures are preferable.[11] This emphasis on staying at home is also present in More's *Village Politics*, where Tom Hod is persuaded out of his Jacobin sympathies but is also dissuaded from taking his new-found conservatism to the local pub. Instead he decides to 'mind [his] own business'.[12] Cobbett is equally loud in the praise of domestic comforts and in the condemnation of ale or coffee houses:

Drinking clubs, smoking clubs, singing clubs, clubs of odd fellows, whist clubs, sotting clubs, these are inexcusable, they are censurable, they are at once foolish and wicked even in single men; what must they be, then, in husbands; and how are they to answer, not only to their wives, but to their children, for this profligate abandonment of their homes, this breach of their solemn vow made to the former, this evil example to the latter?[13]

Again there are crucial differences to be assessed later, but the superficial similarities between More and Cobbett are clear. Clearest of all, perhaps, is the assumption that the readers they address stand in need of moral alteration and guidance, and that they themselves are qualified to undertake the task. But here we must turn our attention to those readers whom More and Cobbett seek to teach. By doing so, we will identify the crucial differences between their moral, political and literary purposes.

George Spater, comparing Cobbett's *Advice* to the general run of moral advice in the period, is struck more by dissimilarities than parallels. He stresses its worldly nature and its emphasis on happiness;[14] and it is indeed striking that Christianity is seldom if ever mentioned, and that among the various letters of which the work is composed – to a 'Youth', a 'Young Man', a 'Lover', a 'Husband', a 'Father' and a 'Citizen' – there is not one addressed to a 'Christian'. As is clear from the subject matter and the preoccupations of the last chapter, Cobbett's religious attitudes are inextricably linked with political issues of charity and the poor laws, which are discussed under the heading of citizenship. Unlike Hannah More whose strictures are uniformly and even notoriously aimed at rewards in heaven and quiescence on earth, Cobbett's moral advice aims exclusively to provide as much worldly comfort and contentment as possible. Cobbett had similarly contrasted the 'houses not made with hands' offered by a Dissenting minister encountered on his travels in *Rural Rides*, with the 'snug little cottages' desired by his congregation. Spater's brief comment that Cobbett's *Advice* is an antidote to the 'solemn and otherworldly advice commonly preached to the lower classes' seems to be correct.

But there are two related objections to this assessment. The first and crucial one is that Spater, along with other critics, overlooks the fact that Cobbett's *Advice* is aimed at a different audience; a fact which I have also so far failed to address. Cobbett's *Advice* is addressed specifically in the title and recurrently throughout the book, not to the labouring poor, but 'to young men... in the middle and higher ranks of life'. The second objection to Spater's assessment, which is crucially linked to the first, is that 'solemn and otherworldly advice' was not aimed so much at the poor as at the middle classes. In the

Cheap Repository Tracts at least, More's 'Tales for the Common People' are mainly concerned with earthly conduct, while it is her 'Stories for Persons in the Middle Ranks' which are morbidly religious. What we can conclude from this, which makes the relationship between More and Cobbett particularly interesting, is that Cobbett is aiming methods associated with the 'Tales for the Common People' – that is, worldly and moral advice – at a middle- and upper-class audience used to more religious guidance.

We can show this in several ways. The first evidence for the intended status of the mock-reader of Cobbett's text is in the title where, as I have just noted, he designates his advice as addressed to *Young Men and (Incidentally) to Young Women in the Middle and Higher Ranks of Life*. Much of the advice given is targeted at this audience: Cobbett writes at length about the problems of employing servants, and keeping at least one servant has often been identified as the stamp of gentility among the rising middle class.[15] Theresa McBride has identified the category of people likely to employ one or two servants in the period as including doctors, factory managers, surgeons and bank managers.[16] These, then, as well as the shopkeepers and tradesmen identified by Hannah More as members of the 'middle ranks', are being addressed here. Cobbett writes with even more vigour against the practice of employing a wet nurse, and with this we are entering the sphere of the upper class. E. S. Turner's discussion of this issue suggests that, apart from prostitutes, only women wealthy enough to have a lady's maid and a tenantry to choose a nurse from would be likely to indulge this extravagance.[17]

While these are clear indications, we might still balk at the idea that Cobbett is recommending the mutton-chop test to an upper- and middle-class audience. My answer to this objection is twofold: first, the title tells us to anticipate different mock-readers at different points (men, women, middle and upper class) so we can choose to see the mutton-chop test as aimed at the lower end of the social scale. But my second answer is that it also seems to me to be the point of the text that, in the mix of mock-readers, noblemen really are advised to observe the jaws of their fiancées.

There are other points at which Cobbett's audience broadens to take in the lower-middle class, such as with his condemnation of clubs, and these points support my reading. The range of clubs to which Cobbett refers is broad, from the pub and the oddfellows club to more general terms suggestive of the London gentleman's club.

The very breadth of the range implies a Radical ability to confound class distinctions. If we note that Cobbett abhors the creation of polarized classes of 'masters' and 'slaves' as an aspect of the new economic and social order, we can see that his Radical confounding is not merely confusion. It has become clear throughout this study that the crucial class difference for Cobbett, in the fallen present-day world, is that between the impotent and the powerful, the disenfranchised and the enfranchised, the propertied and the dispossessed. Cobbett perceives his audience as falling into two broad categories: the propertied middle and upper class, and the propertyless labouring or working class. Nice distinctions of rank are, in this context, irrelevant for Cobbett and, as a rule in these texts, for us.

The Radical tangle which ensues in *Advice to Young Men* is, however, not entirely new. Much of the groundwork for *Advice* had appeared in 1821–2 in the *Monthly Religious Tracts*, later renamed *Cobbett's Monthly Sermons*. Sold at threepence for a twenty-six page booklet, the tracts were within reach of most readers, and by their title were identified with the wealth of moral advice on offer to the lower and middle class in the period.

Many of the subjects of *Advice to Young Men* are anticipated – even to the extent that some parts of the *Sermons* seem to be transplanted practically unchanged into the later text – and include the duties of parents, expostulations on drunkenness, on hypocrisy, cruelty, bribery, murder and gambling. But the most interesting feature of the *Monthly Sermons*, which they share with *Advice to Young Men*, is that the audience addressed is often not the usual recipient of this kind of preaching. For example, the sermon on drunkenness is entitled 'The Sin of Drunkenness in Kings, Priests, and People', and the emphasis is in that order. After establishing that 'sin' means a crime against God, and that crimes of this nature are generally perpetrated on an intermediate victim like our neighbour or community, Cobbett turns his attention exclusively to sin among those whose failings directly affect society. With a clear double reference to George IV and Henry VIII,[18] Cobbett declares that kings are ruled by 'inordinate and beastly appetites', warns magistrates of the impairment of judgement effected by alcohol, and asserts that drunken priests alienate and mislead their flocks.[19]

Similarly, public versions of private vices come under attack. If private robberies are capital offences, then we must not forget public ones.[20] Injustices in favour of the rich and against the poor – 'wiping a feather over the backs of the rich, and sending the lash like knives into the backs of the poor' – cannot be tolerated.[21] Murders are equalled for Cobbett by 'those *unseen killings*, which are effected by the unjust and cruel denying of food and raiment to the indigent part of our fellow-creatures...'[22] Cobbett justifies this emphasis by arguing that those who gain most from society owe most to it; and in his sermon on drunkenness he observes only in the final paragraph that it is not '*just*' kings and priests who should be sober, but the people too.[23]

It is the middle and upper classes as much as the poor, then, who are admonished by Cobbett, in the *Sermons*, to refrain from drinking, gambling and foolish marriages, and are enjoined to stay at home in their leisure hours. Similarly, *Advice to Young Men* begins with a stern admonition concerning the sanctity and virtue of useful labour which at first seems – like 'industriousness' – to constitute an appeal to the work-ethic often invoked during the industrial revolution, and usually aimed at 'lazy' workers accustomed to more sporadic agricultural labour.[24] But in fact Cobbett is addressing the potentially 'idle' rich, deprecating the sinecures and office jobs desired by upwardly-mobile middle-class youths, and pointing out the immorality of living on the taxes paid by the indigent labourers.[25] This difference of audience, and the mix of ideas commonly associated with different classes, is crucial to our understanding of the text's political and moral aims.

Thus, returning to the choice of a good wife, we find that Cobbett's advice to the middle-class lover is to emulate as far as possible the ways of the labourer, choosing a 'sober' girl in the country sense of the word, meaning 'steadiness, seriousness, carefulness, scrupulous propriety of conduct...'[26] Noblemen marry for money, labourers for love, and for the former this 'is a disadvantage which, as far as real enjoyment of life is concerned, more than counterbalances all the advantages that they possess over the rest of the community.'[27] Here, of course, is the significance of the final criterion in Cobbett's list of wifely virtues – that of beauty. Cobbett's advice is to follow passion as much as possible, while More stresses utility and virtue at the expense of physical attraction. This is another profoundly political issue, as More's strictures aimed at the poor seem consistent with the line taken by Malthusians who recommended late marriages and 'moral restraint' to keep the population under control.[28] Cobbett, deeply opposed to this attitude to the labouring class, declares that 'the passion that they would restrain, while it is necessary to the existence of mankind, is the greatest of all the compensations for the inevitable cares, troubles, hardships, and sorrows of life...'[29]

Similarly, it is crucial to understand that Cobbett's deprecation of extradomestic pleasures is also aimed at the wealthy as much as at the poor. Again, the difference is political, as More's instruction to the labourer to 'mind his own business' and her rejection of holidays as pagan debauches strike a blow against his few pleasures and moments of independence from his employer, and seek to discourage collective action and mutual support. Susan Pederson argues that the *Cheap Repository Tracts* advocated a revolution in social relationships, encouraging the poor to defer to, and rely upon, the rich rather than each other.[30] In his examination of the Society for the Diffusion of Useful Knowledge, Harold Smith draws a similar distinction between individual 'self-help' of the Samuel Smiles type, effected by private reading and geared to individual advancement, and the kind of 'self-help' favoured by political Radicals.[31] Cobbett's rejection of all clubs for all classes in *Advice to Young Men* reflects his ambivalent position in relation to this issue, as he is isolated in his opposition to political organizations, and favours individual voting and discussion to win hearts and minds.[32] But while Cobbett may reject political organizations, his attitude is continually a collective one, which lays stress on collective 'self-help'; he prefers the model of a community helping itself to established rights rather than one of charity, and lays equal value upon the community and – via the concrete imagery he chooses – upon the individuality of its members. Cobbett's notorious admiration for the bloody sports and holidays of the village bear testimony to the difference of vision between him and Hannah More.[33]

If Cobbett's *Advice* differs from More's 'Tales for Common People', which it seems to resemble, due to its target audience, then it also differs from her 'Stories for Persons in the Middle Ranks'. Most obvious is the complete lack of religious teaching that I have already noted. Equally different is the attitude to citizenship. More's 'Mr Fantom, the newfashioned philosopher' is a disciple of Paine, and his wholesale rejection of the old would be equally repugnant to Cobbett; but for More all middle-class attempts to understand – let alone influence – political realities are presumptuous, ridiculous and socially dangerous. More paints a portrait of good middle-class citizens as follows:

their object was, not to reform parliament, but their own shops; not to correct the abuses of government, but of parish officers; not to cure the excesses of administration, but of their own porters and apprentices; to talk over the news of the day, without aspiring to direct the events of it. They read the newspapers with that anxiety which every honest man feels in the daily history of his country. But as trade, which they did understand, flourished, they were careful not to reprobate those public measures by which it was protected, and which they did *not* understand. In such turbulent times it was a comfort to each to feel he was a tradesman, and not a statesman; that he was not called to responsibility for a trust for which he found he had no talents, while he was at full liberty to employ the talents he really possessed, in fairly amassing a fortune, of which the laws would be the best guardian, and government the best security. Thus a legitimate self-love, regulated by prudence, and restrained by principle, produced peaceable subjects and good citizens ... [34]

This is clearly anathema to all that Cobbett advocates from his period of transition onwards. In the last letter of *Advice*, addressed to a 'Citizen', Cobbett sees social duty, conversely, to include being as well-informed and as vocal in demands for political rights as possible. In the penultimate paragraph of the book Cobbett defines the good citizen, and concludes: 'God has given us a country of which to be proud; and that freedom, greatness and renown which were handed down to us by our wise and brave forefathers, bid us perish to the last man rather than suffer the land of their graves to become a land of slavery, impotence, and dishonour'.[35] Fighting for the rights of the community as a whole, as advocated by Cobbett, is another example of the emphasis on collective self-help that I have just identified as the opposite to the values preached by Hannah More. Again, in her story of 'Mr Fantom', the attempt is to alienate the middle class from the lower class. While her comments elsewhere suggest that the middle and the lower ranks are equally prone to sedition and stand equally in need of wholesome literary fare, and while she deprecates middle-class intellectual aspirations, she nevertheless attempts to instil class snobbery in her middle-class reader. In this way Paine's brand of atheism is dismissed as too vulgar for the middle classes to accept. Paine 'had written only for the vulgar ... had invented nothing – no, not even one idea of original wickedness; but ... had stooped to rake up out of the kennel of infidelity all the loathsome dregs and offal dirt which politer unbelievers had thrown away as too gross and offensive for their better-bred reader'.[36]

More's tactic is continually to fragment all potential political alliances except for one between the giver and receiver of charity and, via education, of correct ideas and patterns of behaviour. Cobbett, conversely, habitually invites numerous alliances. In this text he creates links between the upper and middle classes in a recognition of their legal as well as moral duties towards the poor, and – with values directly opposed to More – between upper, middle and lower, with a recommendation that the two former should emulate the better aspects of labouring-class culture. Thus, as well as admiring the labourer's habit of marrying for love, Cobbett also extols their parental virtues. The pastoral idyll he portrays, however, has additional political significance as it describes what *should be* as much as what *is*, in the ragged world of the poor: 'a labourer's cottage, on a Sunday; the husband or wife having a baby in arms, looking at two or three older ones playing between the flower-borders going from the wicket to the door, is according to my taste the most interesting object that eyes ever beheld'.[37] In characteristic fashion, Cobbett moves from this general image to a particular case, recalling a family in Sussex discovered in just such a posture, and conjecturing upon their probable subsequent emigration to escape from poverty.

These recommendations as to social attitudes, that we have discovered in the works of both More and Cobbett, are further examples of the creation of the mock-reader whereby to influence the real one. If we look at the closing paragraphs of Cobbett's *Advice* from this angle, we can see how the reader is drawn willy-nilly to share the values, views and aspirations of his notional counterpart. After an explanation of his social-contract theory of society, Cobbett exhorts his politically enfranchised reader to support the struggles of the less fortunate: 'here, young man of sense and of spirit, here is the point on which you are to take your stand'.[38] The implication is that only a youth of sense and spirit will do his social duty. But as the reader here is addressed as such a man, his moral response is already decided. Throughout the book Cobbett has specified his reader's status for the sake of argument, and for the sake of reading we have been more or less obliged to take on the personae named. Thus, by turns we have been a youth, a young man, a lover, the husband of a 'good young woman', a dutiful and loving husband, a husband or wife likely to hire a wet-nurse and a male midwife, an impatient reader of Hume, Smollett and Robertson, and a young man immune to the 'barbarous thoughts' of 'Malthus and his tribe'.[39] At this late stage, at least for rhetorical purposes, it is impossible to refuse to become a 'young man of sense and of spirit'. As such, we become Cobbett's allies, and our responses can be confidently predicted and created by him.

After questioning whether the degradations of poverty are just, Cobbett uses the first-person plural pronoun ambiguously, to lead us deeper into collusion with him.[40] Uncharacteristically, for a moment, Cobbett seems to adopt the formal 'we' of the academic text: 'We cannot believe this, and therefore ... we must believe that ... ' This use of 'we' gradually seems to become more personal and less abstract as Cobbett continues 'We all acknowledge that it is our bounden duty to provide ... [for] our children ... ' The introduction of 'all' implies that 'we' now stands for a body of individual people, with individual characteristics. And in the next paragraph, by coming to the question 'how are we to go to work in the performance of [our duty]', Cobbett is using 'we' now to signify him and ourselves: spirited and sensible men. Drawn into the text's procedures in this way, we are unable to resist the penultimate paragraph's summation of our characteristics and our political duties.

At sixpence a part,[41] the *Advice* is obviously aimed at a different audience than the twopenny *Political Pamphlet* (reprinted from the *Political Register*) or the threepenny *Sermons*. But the price difference is not so large as to rule out a potentially broad readership: as with the *History* we seem to be presented with a text conscious of, or at least aiming for, many types of reader, and conscious of the political possibilities presented by that breadth. The choice of the middle and upper classes as the target audience for his moral preaching specifies that they and not the poor are in need of moral reform. *The Poor Man's Friend*, at twopence a part, is more clearly aimed at the poorest readership, but here Cobbett openly declares that he anticipates a more varied audience. At the close of 'Letter II. to the Working Classes of Preston', he describes his mission in the work as follows:

I am extremely anxious to cause this matter [of the poor laws] to be well understood, not only by the working classes, but by the owners of the land and the magistrates. I deem it to be of the greatest possible importance; and, while writing on it, I address myself to you, because I most sincerely declare that I have a greater respect for you than for any other body of persons that I know anything of.[42]

This passage openly describes Cobbett's method of addressing one reader while indirectly addressing another, and explicitly identifies his choice of the working class as his immediate mock-readership as a political act of stating his respect for their intellect and their social status. Earlier, he similarly noted that 'I think it necessary to show, that these poor-laws are the things which men of property, above all others, *ought to wish to see maintained* ...'[43] In other places he addresses this upper-class readership almost directly with the sarcastic claim that his educational efforts towards the poor should please them. The 'loyal and charitable' religious band of evangelicals and diffusers of useful knowledge preach the '*march of mind*' but presumably abhor Cobbett's political rather than moral educational method.[44] In a more stylistic way, Cobbett elsewhere draws the 'man of property' into the fabric of the text, as he assumes his opposition:

if I am told, that the farmers, that the occupiers of houses and land, are *so poor* that they cannot do more for their wretched work-people and neighbours; then, I answer and say, what a selfish, what a dastardly wretch is he, who is not ready to do all he can to change this disgraceful, this horrible state of things![45]

Here we see recurrent features of Cobbett's style, with the cumulative sentence-structure that insistently demands our concurrence and the rhetorical-question grammatical structure which has the same effect. Here, though, Cobbett is responding to one who 'tells' him of middle-class poverty, and that person, designated selfish and dastardly, is clearly the poverty-pleading farmer or householder. The structural parallelism of 'what a selfish, what a dastardly wretch' with 'this disgraceful, this horrible state of things' identifies the sinner with the state of affairs he has produced, while the listening working classes also learn from the exchange, as it provides them with argumentative ammunition and opens their eyes to the excuses of the propertied classes.

The middle and upper class do not necessarily have to be reading for this method to work. Cobbett's choice of explicit and indirect mock-reader is determined by his political aim and by the kind of literature he sees as appropriate to each audience, and the choice sends out messages to his readers, rich or poor. If the middle and upper classes have required a manual on manners, habits and morals, then the poor are given a kind of guidebook to turbulent times: 'I shall endeavour to make this little work *really useful* to the *working classes in all the manufacturing districts*... I shall do everything in my power to guide them safely through the perilous times that are approaching...'[46]

Cobbett offers '*my best advice*... clear notions of their *rights* and *duties*'; but perhaps the most striking feature of *The Poor Man's Friend* is the way in which moral coercion is completely absent. The subtitle of the series promises 'Useful Information and Advice for the Working Classes', which leads us to expect something along the lines of *Advice to Young Men*; but the advice is resolutely confined to political and legal rights, and the discussion of '*duties*' is confined to the last letter of the series, and is different enough to deserve separate examination later in this chapter. This determined refusal to tell the working classes how their lives should be ordered on moral grounds is another reason for the sarcastic pleasure we have seen Cobbett taking in baiting the Society for the Diffusion of Useful Knowledge and the evangelical 'comforters'. Cobbett is not in the business of enlightening or educating the poor in order to adapt them to change, or to improve them as factory workers, as desired by the educational Society.[47] On the contrary, as is often noted by biographers and critics, Cobbett is fiercely opposed to the suggestion that the 'uneducated' labourer is lacking any necessary knowledge. The labourer knows his trade, and Cobbett takes as a slight any suggestion that he might need anything more than this for his moral wellbeing. Thus he repeatedly points out that 'education' literally means 'rearing up' – that French agriculturalists speak of the 'Education du Cochon' – and that physical strength and agility, mental soundness and a knowledge of immediate concerns are enough 'education' for most people.[48] The hostility to formal education seems motivated by a mixture of that 'John Bullish' dislike for effeminacy that critics repeatedly chastise, and a genuine perception that the education offered by the Society for the Diffusion of Useful Knowledge and the moral teaching offered by the evangelicals are calculated more to appease, distract, train and reform the poor than to offer them something of real use in their daily lives.[49] As I noted earlier in this study, Cobbett's strictures in *Cottage Economy* against tea have been widely derided and abhorred; but if we bear in mind that this is the nearest he ever comes to moral preaching to the working classes, then we must see the difference in basic assumptions about the poor evinced by Cobbett and by his opponents. For Cobbett it is the fact that tea changes traditional habits that is loathsome; for Hannah More and her like, traditional habits are precisely what stand in need of reform. Again, in the *Grammar of the English Language*, Cobbett is quick to justify his attempts at education by explaining its purpose:

the good that a knowledge of grammar will bring to his preferred audience of 'soldiers, sailors, apprentices and plough-boys' will be an ability to stand up to and see through their social superiors, along with an ability to express their wants, rights and beliefs in a language of power.[50]

Whatever Cobbett's attitude to his audience of 'poor men', or 'young men in the middle and higher ranks of life', his tactics with which to influence and lead his readership remain the same. As with the closing paragraphs of *Advice*, which we discussed in the last section, in *The Poor Man's Friend* he is quick to make his opinions seem the only possible ones. In a discussion of the recent Preston election at which his mock-readers failed to return him, Cobbett describes the dishonourable conduct of his opponents in a way which assumes that his readers will judge as he does: 'Is there a man, or a boy? no, nor a woman, nor a girl, amongst the radicals of Preston, who would have done such a thing as this!'[51] As with the passage aimed at the farmer or householder which I have just discussed, Cobbett aims cumulative and persuasive sentence structures at the poor man too. A schematic look at the method seems enough. Thus, 'it is very true', one such structure begins,

> that the enormous taxes which we pay on account of loans made to carry on the late unjust wars, on account of a great standing army in time of peace, on account of pensions, sinecures and grants, and on account [the list goes on]... it is very true [the sentence resumes its course] that these enormous taxes... it is very true, that *these enormous taxes*, thus associated, have produced the ruin in trade, manufactures and commerce... this is very true; but, it is not less true, that, be wages or employment as they may, the poor are not to perish with hunger, or with cold...[52]

Again, as elsewhere, rhetorical questions leave the reader no option but to concur: 'What shall we see next? *Workhouses, badges, hundred-houses, select-vestries, tread-mills, gravel-carts and harness*! What shall we see next! And what should we see at last, if this infernal THING could continue for only a few years longer!'[53] The punctuation seems crucial to this passage too, as the question-mark after the first question invites gossipy speculation, put an end to by the italicized reply, and made rhetorical by the repetition of the question ended by an assertive exclamation-mark.

In a discussion of the superior diet enjoyed by imprisoned felons, the use of italics and capitals has a similar effect of haranguing the reader – as though Cobbett is attempting to import the rhythms of the sermon or political address into the written medium. The implied orality seems specifically aimed to appeal to the predominantly oral culture of the poor: 'Why, if they be CONVICTED FELONS, they are, say the Berkshire gaol-regulations, " to have ONLY BREAD and water, *with vegetables*, occasionally, from the garden ... on Sundays, SOME MEAT AND BROTH"!'[54] As with the farmer or householder, the speech of the poor is also anticipated: 'if you, in Lancashire, were to hear this said of the state of Hampshire, what would you say? Say! Why, you would say, to be sure, "Where is the LAW; where are the constables, the justices, the juries, the judges, the sheriffs, and the hangmen?"'[55]

The appeal to the emotions that we noted in Cobbett's apostrophe to 'young men of sense and spirit', is also echoed in an appeal to the heart that follows on from a legalistic discussion of the poor-law. The intended reader of this appeal seems to be at once the suffering poor man and his wealthy oppressor:

The very nature of man makes him shudder at the thought. There wants no authorities; no appeals to law books; no arguments; no questions of right or wrong: that same human nature that tells me that I am not to cut my neighbour's throat, and drink his blood, tells me that I am not to make him die at my feet by keeping him from food or raiment of which I have more than I want for my own preservation.[56]

This of course reminds us of the passage from the *History* where Cobbett asserts that the depiction of our forefathers as damned blasphemers pains us. As a rule in *The Poor Man's Friend*, as I have already noted, explicit instruction in moral feeling and behaviour is lacking, Cobbett only indirectly demanding that his readers agree on certain key issues by assuming that they already do so. When he does openly approach the 'duties' of the poor in this text, in the last letter of the series, his method changes to show interesting parallels to and contrasts with the methods of *Advice* and the most influential numbers of the *Political Register*.

Letter I and Letter V of *The Poor Man's Friend* differ from those that come between in that, in these two, Cobbett addresses the people of Preston more directly as prospective voters. As a result, some later editions of the work omitted these sections as irrelevant to the main thrust of the book, which was to explain the philosophical and legal basis of the poor-law.[57] For our purposes, however, Letter V is particularly interesting. This Letter differs from those which precede it in its circuitous argumentative route and in the couching of the arguments proffered in a framework of autobiographical writing. The previous letters have come swiftly and bluntly to the point, but this begins with an anecdote reminiscent of the letter to Hunt in the *Political Register* discussed in Chapter 5:

> Walking out in my gardens this morning, and seeing, among my brocoli [sic] plants, the devastations of the devils of caterpillars, put me in mind of what I told you about STANLEY and WOOD... From the moment that Stanley became a placeman, he *ceased to be a Member of Parliament*. You, therefore, have, now, but one Member of Parliament... You must have two indeed, before next spring, and now we shall see who is to be one of these two, I WILLIAM COBBETT, OR STANLEY![58]

The autobiography is motivated in part by the fact that the letter is a manifesto, an advertisement for Cobbett. But as it is in this letter alone that there is any attempt to discuss the 'duties', moral or otherwise, of the poor, the autobiographical method seems to have an added significance. Cobbett first identifies his own duty to his readers: 'a literary duty to perform now immediately, and that is, writing and sending to you, the Fifth and last Number of the POOR MAN'S FRIEND.'[59] A paragraph later, he identifies the 'ONE GREAT DUTY' of his readers, which is 'to vote at the next and at every election, according to the dictates of your own consciences...' To reinforce the solemnity of this duty, which at first sight lacks moral weight, Cobbett invokes the Apostle: 'What advantageth it a man, if he gain the whole world, and lose his own soul?' He adds his own message to the biblical one: 'And if a man violate his oath, he is guilty of a mockery of God; and in this particular case, of treason against his neighbour'.[60] This is interesting, as he seems to use the potential superstition of the people he addresses to imply that dire and supernatural punishments will follow any failure to live up to his expectations of them, rather than attempting to build up a sense of rationality, as Paine for instance would attempt to do in this context. Cobbett, in other words, while he is at pains to provide the labourer with facts, is ready to employ the strategy of appealing to his readers' emotions (as indeed we have already frequently seen) rather than to their intellect alone. The passage is of particular discursive interest as it takes an image common to both popular and elite writings and reworks it with his customary stress on the realities of poverty. The image of the caterpillar is common to both the plebeian millennial writings of Richard Brothers, and to *Richard II*, where Shakespeare refers to the 'caterpillars of the Commonwealth'.[61] Cobbett reworks the image by concentrating on the victim of the caterpillars, returning to the image of the blighted broccoli, drawing out the comparison between parasites and 'tax-eaters', and challenging his readers as follows:

> Now, the thing for you to consider is, whether you have the power of assisting in rescuing your country from these insatiable devourers; whether YOU have it in YOUR POWER to do anything that shall prevent, or tend to prevent, you and your wives and children ... from continuing to resemble so nearly these devastated leaves of my brocoli ... [62]

This image, at once challenging and comic, works on more than one level to achieve its goal. By beginning with a non-metaphoric description of a real garden, Cobbett turns his enemies into real garden caterpillars. As such, they are reassuringly feeble enemies with which to present the poor reader. The comparison between the labourer and his family and the broccoli is funny and appealing, while at the same time deeply offensive to their dignity. For reasons of self-respect as well as physical survival, the labourer cannot long accept a self-dramatization as a vegetable.

Having thus created a degree of political will, in his mock-reader at least, Cobbett goes deeper into the issues on which he intends to take his electoral stand. The preoccupations are familiar from the whole canon of his writing: he will accept no money from the taxes, will bribe no voters, will take no subscription. He is used to living frugally, rising early and working hard. In almost the same breath, he asserts the worldly credentials he might have boasted had he played along with the government earlier in his career. 'I might have been a lord by this time',[63] he muses, but declares that such an eventuality would have robbed him of his special status: 'the name of William Cobbett would have been sunk; I should have been a poor thing compared to what I am, and have been, like CANNING, forgotten before I was rotten'. Again, serious issues are rendered in a faintly comic way, here the multisyllabic rhyme of 'forgotten/rotten' recalling the music hall or the ballad. And then, as a suddenly serious coda to this bantering self-assessment, Cobbett sums up his career and achievements with the tone of a Horatian ode or a Shakespearian sonnet:

> Now I shall be remembered for many an age to come; I shall give delight and information to generations not yet born; and, which is a great deal more important in my eyes, shall end my days with knowing that I have been a

great benefactor to my country; and that if I should not live to see a restoration of liberty and happiness completed, I have sown the seeds, widely and thickly sown the seeds of such restoration.[64]

Cobbett's eternal summer shall not fade, then. Like Horace, he has

> achieved a monument more lasting
> than bronze, and loftier than the pyramids of kings,
> which neither gnawing rain nor blustering wind
> may destroy, nor innumerable series of years,
> nor the passage of ages.[65]

This kind of ritualized self-celebration seems to lie behind Cobbett's poetic vision in the first two lines of the passage quoted here. The remainder of the passage is notable for the rare acknowledgement not only that his aims may not be realized in his lifetime, but that he is mortal at all. James Sambrook has noted the curious way in which the autobiographical anecdotes in *Advice* are entirely free of a consciousness of death: 'It is characteristic of Cobbett that he should still enjoy...childhood experience, unclouded by the sense of mortality and mutability with which many a man would have recalled an event in his own life sixty years earlier'.[66] Here, when Cobbett does acknowledge mortality, the acknowledgement is counterbalanced by a declaration of other kinds of immortality: the immortality of fame, of his achievements, and, via his image of himself as a sower, of the immortality of the agricultural landscape which he celebrates.

At this solemn point in his letter, Cobbett's focus changes: 'so much for myself and *my* duty: now for you and *your* duty'.[67] Only at this point, when he has pledged his life and immortality to the aid of his audience, does he bring himself to descant on their moral and political duties. Even then, it is only after a review of the state of the poor and a recapitulation of his arguments through the preceding numbers of *The Poor Man's Friend* that Cobbett can bring himself to address his reader with an extended moral imperative: 'But all depends upon YOU, the whole country will be looking to you: stand you by your duty; take your own parts; resent your own wrongs; and, there is not a man in England that does not think that I shall stand firmly by you'.[68] Now Cobbett is again a moral touchstone: if he stands by them, then that is an indication of their moral valour.

I have already noted that Letter V recalls the *Political Register* article to Hunt that we discussed in Chapter 5. The agricultural imagery in both provides a conversational introduction which leads the reader into the political debate. In both, this imagery also implies things about the status of the reader; not that he is necessarily an agricultural labourer – which would clash with the explicit target of *The Poor Man's Friend*, who is a cotton weaver – but that his interest in the pastoral is likely to be a workmanlike one. In contrast, Cobbett's autobiographical pastoral in *Advice* more closely resembles the pastoral idyll of the poet than the muddy turnip or broccoli patch of the farmer or peasant. Describing the landscape of New Brunswick, Cobbett stresses the aesthetic rather than practical values of the scenery:

some of these spots far surpass in rural beauty any other that my eyes ever beheld; the creeks abounding towards their sources in waterfalls of endless variety, as well in form as in magnitude, and always teeming with fish, while waterfowl enliven their surface, and while wild-pigeons, of the gayest plumage, flutter, in thousands upon thousands, amongst the branches of the beautiful trees, which sometimes for miles together form an arch over the creeks.[69]

Two paragraphs later Cobbett asserts that 'if nature, in her very best humour, had made a spot for the express purpose of captivating me, she could not have exceeded the efforts which she had here made'.[70] Thus he establishes a vision of a fairy-tale landscape, in which to play out a fairy-tale version of an autobiographical moment. Lost in these beautiful woods, he comes across a 'large and well built log dwelling house' whose occupants soon become his firm friends and whose daughter almost wins him away from his betrothed. Cobbett notes the romantic nature of the story as he describes his arrival, cold and sick and afraid, at the door of the house: 'no hero of eastern romance ever experienced a more enchanting change'.[71] To render a potentially shameful anecdote in these terms is of course a way of denying responsibility for the conduct thus described – if Cobbett is under an 'enchantment' then he cannot be blamed for the near betrayal.

These more or less literary effects, of self-dramatization and the rendering of reminiscence as a romantic tale, perhaps also account for the popularity of *Advice* with literary critics and biographers. Many note the fictionality of the *Advice* as, for instance, it paints a picture of mythic happiness in the Cobbett household at a time when Cobbett's marriage and his relationship with his children was disintegrating, and he himself falling into a paranoid madness similar to that of Rousseau.[72] Most critics also note that this picture is created for rhetorical purposes, and thus achieve that recognition of literary distance between author and persona which I have suggested is often lacking in criticism of his more directly political prose.

But there is more to say about the fictionalized autobiography of *Advice* than merely that its presentation of self is dramatized. In the context of the *Advice* as a moral tract, we can see Cobbett perhaps learning from Hannah More and, consciously or unconsciously, exploiting the accidental similarities between himself and her characters, to turn her lessons back on the class from which they emanate. We can see this by merely looking back to the story of *Tom White the Post Boy* which I discussed earlier. Tom White, like Cobbett, is born an honest farm worker. Like Cobbett, he is restless and filled with longings for travel: like Cobbett he 'enlists', though as a post boy rather than as a soldier. The two ways of life are similar, however, as both throw the lads among bad company and expose them to bad habits. Where the two stories differ is in the response of each character. Tom White is seduced by the pleasures of sin, and only in maturity does he gain moral authority with his neighbours. Cobbett, conversely, learns grammar while his companions drink and gamble,[73] and – with an almost unprecedented promotion – rises to the rank of sergeant-major.[74] The paths of the two characters rejoin, however, as both become farmers in their own right, treat their labourers well, and take it upon themselves to offer moral and practical advice. Again, it is only in the moral component of the message that their advice differs.

Being, at an age *under twenty years*, raised from corporal to sergeant-major *at once*, over the heads of thirty sergeants, I naturally should have been an object of envy and hatred; but this habit of early rising and of rigid adherence to the precepts which I had given you really subdued these passions, because every one felt that what I did he had never done, and never could do... long before any other man was dressed for the parade, my work for the morning was all done, and I myself was on the parade, walking, in fine weather for an hour perhaps... When the regiment or part of it went out to exercise in the morning... and the matter was left to me, I always had it on the ground in such time as that the bayonets glistened in the *rising sun*, a sight which gave me delight of which I often think, but which I should in vain endeavour to describe... When I was commander, the men had a long day of leisure before them: they could ramble into the town or into the woods; go to get raspberries, to catch birds, to catch fish, or to pursue any other recreation, and such of them as chose, and were qualified, to work at their trades. So that here, arising solely from the early habits of one very young man, were pleasant and happy days given to hundreds.[75]

It is clear, I think, that Cobbett's attitude towards his soldiers resembles that of Tom White towards his neighbours as far as the paternalism of his views is concerned. But the ultimate good gained by Cobbett's paternalism is of a less practical nature than Tom White's. Granting his soldiers a choice of occupation, with a glorious disregard for the work ethic, Cobbett paints an image of pastoral bliss. His men 'ramble' whither they please, picking raspberries and hunting and fishing in the woods, like small boys or noble savages, only pursuing their 'trades' if they choose to do so. And if they are enabled to undertake these pastoral, Cobbett-like activities because of Cobbett's own 'early habits', then it seems to me that he is projecting himself onto the regiment, and drawing the regiment to himself, in a way reminiscent of his relationship with England. This is a process whereby both partners – there Cobbett and England, here Cobbett and his men – grow in stature in each other's reflected glory.

A different set of assumptions altogether underlie the stories by Cobbett and by More. Sambrook has noted that Cobbett sees the child, like Rousseau whom he quotes, as an innocent being; Hannah More in contrast stresses that the child is innately corrupt.[76] This seems to me to relate to the parallel issue that More sees Tom White's corruption by his fellows as inevitable, redeemable only by religion and a sense of personal weakness, whereas Cobbett stresses his own resistance to the temptations of the senses, and by doing so avers the possible moral strength and self-determination of youth and secularity. Again, the idea of a self-sufficient and morally admirable working class seems related to both these issues, as these qualities are precisely those that More's working class lacks. Choices cannot be offered to the poor in the scheme of things painted by More: paternalistic restraint is necessary, both literally – with regard to the corrupt and erring child – and socially, as the working classes are viewed as the helpless infants of the social family.

It is significant that Cobbett stresses his own youthful rectitude, and the moral superiority of the labouring class. Recognizing the power of the *Tom White* method of dramatizing moral lessons, he stresses the aspects of his own life that conform to the Dick Whittington formula that *Tom White* exploits, while changing the moral lessons to be drawn, and inverting the nature of the audience to be addressed. In an odd way, then, in the *Advice* we see autobiography propelled by the needs of fiction, not merely in the sense that Cobbett romanticizes his memories for the purpose of self-aggrandizement, but also in the sense that his life-story becomes a peg on which to hang a rhetorical device. In this second sense the method is the reverse of self-aggrandizement.

But the vexed issue of the status of the self is still important even in this sense. We noticed earlier that Tom White's early errors and redemption earn him moral authority with his readers, which in turn grants him the political authority to speak and be heard on political issues. This literary device seems to find its roots in the chapbook confession literature that we discussed in Chapter 5, where the felon's confession incorporates a warning to others not to make the same mistakes. Cobbett's use of the method of positive self-portrayal in *Advice* must be seen as serving the same literary purpose to achieve the same kind of authority, but equally to create the kinds of positive self-images that I suggested in Chapter 5 were a by-product of his egoism, for the benefit of the working class. And we have seen how he attempts explicitly to gain authority with and for his working-class reader in *The Poor Man's Friend* by portraying himself as supremely dedicated to their cause. It has been the aim of this chapter to suggest that the creation of the mock-reader of the text furthers this process by making suggestions about the moral and political needs of the respective social classes Cobbett chooses to address. In this sense, of course, the actual participation of the kinds of reader he suggests are reading is as irrelevant as the truth or otherwise of his self-presentation. We return to the point from which we began, as we are obliged to recognize the rhetorical strategies operating in Cobbett's often apparently artless text.

CHAPTER 8

Constituting the nation

If Part I of this study was mainly concerned to identify and interpret Cobbett's rhetorical pragmatism and politically-motivated self-presentation, Part II has explored the polyphonic nature of his mature Radical style. We have noted the recurring incorporation of conflicting political voices within his texts in a dialogue which is conceived in relation to a clearly-realized range of similarly polarized readers.

In previous chapters I have explored the enabling nature of this polyphony and manipulation of mock-readers for a linguistically insecure working-class audience, and the potentially alienating nature of the same tactics for readers used to literary dominance. Most of all I have stressed the radically enabling *and* alienating effects of addressing such polarized readerships simultaneously. In *Advice to Young Men* and in various other moral tracts, we have seen how Cobbett confounds class difference by stressing the shared values and needs of audiences widely separated by wealth and position. In his influential *History of the Protestant Reformation in England and Ireland* we have seen the same tactic as a means of dramatizing the riven social realities of the nineteenth century where the 'few' stand for the 'all', where the biological nation is detached from the political one.

It is with this tension between different senses of nationhood – of obvious and urgent relevance to Cobbett as politician and Radical leader – that I shall conclude. As with Chapter 4, which ended Part I, this chapter will move away from detailed chronological study towards a broader assessment of the aims and effects of Cobbett's polyphonic style, arguing that this literary practice reconstitutes and redefines Cobbett's 'Old England' in ways which both reflect and attempt to resolve the anxieties of political and discursive disenfranchisement which have dominated this study.

At the start of that section of *Rural Rides* in which Cobbett describes his journey from Dover to London he makes the following observation:

> I have often mentioned, in describing the parts of the country over which I have travelled; I have often mentioned the *chalk-ridge* and also the *sand-ridge*, which I have traced, running parallel with each other from about Farnham, in Surrey, to Sevenoaks, in Kent. The reader must remember how particular I have been to observe that, in going up from Chilworth and Albury, through Dorking, Reigate, Godstone, and so on, the two chains, or ridges, approach so near to each other, that, in many places, you actually have a chalk-bank to your right and a sand-bank to your left, at not more than forty yards from each other. In some places, these chains of hills run off from each other to a great distance, even to a distance of twenty miles. They then approach again towards each other, and so they go on. I was always desirous to ascertain whether these chains, or ridges, continued on thus *to the sea*. I have now found that they do. And, if you go out into the channel, at Folkestone, there you will see a sand-cliff and a chalk-cliff. Folkestone stands upon the sand, in a little dell about seven hundred or eight hundred yards from the very termination of the ridge. All the way along, the chalk-ridge is the most lofty, until you come to Leith Hill and Hindhead; and here, at Folkestone, the sand-ridge tapers off in a sort of flat towards the sea... Every where, the soil is the same upon the top of the high part of this ridge. I have now found it to be the same, on the edge of the sea, that I found it on the North East corner of Hampshire.[1]

Daniel Green quotes the beginning of this passage as evidence that the Surrey landscape is a familiar part of Cobbett's 'inheritance'.[2] But as the passage proceeds it becomes clear that Cobbett is not just claiming familiarity with Surrey. He traces the geographical contours of England with as much familiarity as if he were describing the features of his own village. He later adds triumphantly that he has now identified the same chalk-ridge in Coombe, Ashmansworth, Highclere, Kingsclere, Ropley, Dippinghall, Merrow, Reigate, Westerham, Godstone, Sevenoaks and Hollingbourne, as well as at Folkestone.[3] Jonathan Bate suggests that this kind of recitation of place names is usually the act of an outsider to the places described, since locals have no need to indulge in this kind of self-validating activity.[4] However, as a traveller who seems in these passages to attempt to create a sense of locality for a whole nation, Cobbett's recitation in this case actually acts as a way of linking these disparate places together as they coincide with what he wants to present as a part of the geological skeleton of southern Britain. Thus far, we seem to be in the same territory as the Tilford oak, which acts as a similar symbol of endurance and community in the English organic state.

It is interesting, however, to look at this passage through the focus of Linda Colley's observations about the nature of British national identity. Her observation that Britishness is inextricably linked with island status draws attention to the way that Cobbett's geological observations reflect – and reinforce – an assumption that England is a physical, not merely a political, entity as he maps the nature and boundaries of southern Britain with reassuring precision. Whatever we think of what goes on within Britain, its boundaries, at least, remain certain. This confident creation of England and Englishness is reinforced as Cobbett's chalk and sand ridges halt abruptly at the coast which faces out towards France. As Colley adds, British national identity may be predicated upon island status, but it is reinforced historically by British self-perception as being *different* as well as separate from the continent (and particularly from France).

Colley makes this point, however, as a way of accounting for the existence of a British national identity in a region actually characterized by extreme diversity of culture. Her observation that 'men and women decide who they are by reference to who and what they are not', and her suggestion that national identity may be merely a desperate alliance in the face of Otherness,[5] might lead us to question the confidence of geographical separateness and internal cohesion asserted by Cobbett's geological observations. And by looking at Cobbett's broader project in *Rural Rides* as a whole it does become clear that his apparently coherent physical nation in this text is achieved by exclusion and omission in just the way Colley describes. His unifying travels in fact never take him further north than Oxfordshire, and (as the title indicates) never take him into the city. Cobbett's England, as has often been noted, is a partial vision which excludes the northern and urban and thus, by implication, the industrial revolution.

The recognition of this partiality qualifies the inclusive organicism of Cobbett's many constructions of Old England which we have encountered throughout this study and discussed at length in Chapter 4. But the tension implied by Cobbett's unified yet partial conception of Britain in some sense reflects the similar tensions and contradictions we have explored within the polarized *social* landscapes he represents in his political writings, where he mourns what he sees as the accelerating movement from the complex and binding hierarchies of feudalism to the stark polarizations of capital and labour – or, as he calls them, masters and slaves.[6] This chapter will explore the ways in which this vexed perception of the period constrains the form and content of his radical rhetoric, and will place that rhetoric among a range of Radical writings from the postwar period.

As a rhetorical response to social polarization, the apparent failures and omissions of Cobbett's national images look representative rather than idiosyncratic. John Williams, for example, traces the traditional use of landscape in seventeenth- and eighteenth-century pastoral poetry as the symbol of a *political* as well as geographical 'prospect', where the harmony or disharmony of the viewed landscape symbolizes the harmony or disharmony of the state and he points out that this could make the real landscape 'secondary or even embarrassing' to its literary counterpart, and that as a result pastoral landscapes tend to be either places of idyllic labour, or else empty. He also suggests that this disjunction between the ideal and the real becomes an increasingly urgent one as the eighteenth century draws to a close, and that Wordsworth is particularly exercised by this problem.[7] If these tensions in the representation of the physical and social landscape parallel those we encounter in Cobbett's writing, and this tension is one grounded in social tensions and anxieties, then in Cobbett's political prose, as in the poetry discussed by Williams, solutions are likely to be temporarily and unsatisfactorily achieved by exclusion and omission. If pastoral landscapes are empty, then so is Cobbett's image of national unity with which this chapter began. When landscapes are populated in *Rural Rides* the emphasis tends to be on disharmony and on division.

While this is not surprising in a work of social criticism, the contrast between social fragmentation and geographical coherence stresses the special problems attached to a Radical idea of the nation. It is interesting, I think, that Cobbett's political travel narrative expresses its social unease by creating a sense of invasion by hostile races, classes and values which are not merely 'foreign' and 'other' in a way which would somehow provide internal national cohesion in the way described by Colley, but instead constitute an invasion *from within*. So, for instance, while he depicts Cheltenham as a place full of 'sooty-necked Jews ... East India plunderers, [and] West India floggers', he also notes disapprovingly its population of 'English tax gorgers ... gluttonous drunkards and debauchees of all descriptions'.[8]

Describing his journey from Tenterden to Folkestone, Cobbett tells the following anecdote:

> In quitting FRANT I descended into a country *more woody* than that behind me. I asked a man whose fine woods these were that I pointed to, and I fairly gave *a start*, when he said, the MARQUIS CAMDEN's! Milton talks of the *Leviathan* in a way to make one draw in one's shoulders with fear; and I appeal to anyone, who has been at sea when a whale has come near the ship, whether he has not, at the first sight of the monster, made a sort of involuntary movement, as if to *get out of the way*. Such was the movement that I now made.

Cobbett goes on to note that the Marquis 'spreads his length and breadth over more, they say, than *ten or twelve thousand acres of land*... But, indeed, what estates might he not purchase?'[9] In this passage it is almost as though Cobbett is moving behind enemy lines in a war zone. There is a recurring sense in *Rural Rides*, then, that England is in some sense an *occupied* territory.

Cobbett's rejection of Norman Yoke Radicalism, however, initially seems to make this image a vexed one. Unlike Paine, for instance, who presents the aristocracy as foreign bandits, Cobbett represents them as potential allies. He asserts repeatedly that if only aristocrats would follow his political advice and vote for Reform their estates would be saved from the bankruptcy likely to result from Government policies, or from starving and violent mobs. Cobbett is willing to accept the aristocracy, in other words, as a legitimate part of the nation, unlike Norman Yoke Radicals. But he represents this willingness as continually obstructed by the treacherous nature of these English aristocrats who are bent on destroying their nation and their own estates along with them. As another rhetorical opposition between unity and division – between the possibility of social harmony and the reality of social conflict – this portrayal of class relationships again returns us to the simultaneously unified yet partial image of Britain with which this chapter began. And as with the partiality of that image, Cobbett's willingness to embrace the existing political nation is another site of apparent political weakness, allied to his constitutional nostalgia which similarly values the hierarchic organic nation of the (mythical) past.

The apparent idiosyncrasy of this view is qualified, however, if we compare it with the Radical myth of Peterloo. Radical accounts of that event stress the peacefulness of the gathering and depict the attack by the yeomanry cavalry as an unprovoked massacre. The ruling class, in other words, is represented as mowing down the working classes as they peacefully and even politely request an extension of the franchise. Here too, then, the rhetorical thrust of the myth is to draw a contrast between the conciliatory desires of the poor and the brutality of the rich.

Both Cobbett's rhetoric of frustrated conciliation with the upper classes and the Radical myth of Peterloo draw on a powerful strand of popular political imagery in the period, expressed mainly through the petition to Parliament, which imagines that the rich must be unaware of the poor's suffering, and believes that if only they (and particularly the king) can be informed of popular distress, something will be done. Michael Scrivener relates this popular belief in paternalism[10] to Hone and Cruikshank's Radical cartoon of 1819, *The Political House that Jack Built*. He identifies in the pamphlet what he calls an 'unconscious' argument that 'the Nation should be maternal and nurturing, but instead it is both self-indulgent and aggressive'.[11] Scrivener identifies this tension in the illustrations by Cruikshank where mothers lie bayoneted by the yeomanry cavalry and where maternal images of Britannia attempt to protect English liberties against the marauding authorities.

But the same tension is also apparent in Hone's accompanying text I think. Like Cobbett, Hone posits the idea of a nation which is internally riven, but he also posits, through his juxtaposition of images and the use of rhyme, the possibility (or perhaps the reality) of organic interrelationships between apparently polarized classes. Internal division is the explicit message, as Hone catalogues the social injustices of a nation which contains at one extreme, the 'dandy of sixty...all shaven and shorn', and at the other the 'people all tattered and torn'. But formally the message is national unity. The way his images of the polarized classes rhyme with each other in this cartoon might be an image of their mutual dependence or equivalence as inhabitants of the house, and the verse form itself is based on the building up of a sense of interrelationship and dependence between different parts of society. The cartoon begins with the line 'This is the house that Jack Built', with a pictorial representation of a classical building festooned with banners symbolizing the 'king, lords and commons'. The second verse adds to this, under a picture of a safe containing Magna Charta, the Bill of Rights and habeas corpus: 'This is the wealth that lay in the house that Jack Built'. The third shows a motley crowd of noblemen with the caption 'These are the Vermin that Plunder the Wealth that Lay in the house that Jack Built.' By the time we get to the introduction of 'the people', they inhabit a complex web of such consequential relationships:

> These are THE PEOPLE
>   all tatter'd and torn,
> Who curse the day
>   wherein they were born,
> On account of Taxation
>   too great to be borne,
> And pray for relief,
>   from night to morn;
> Who, in vain, Petition
>   in every form,
> Who, peaceably Meeting
>   to ask for Reform,
> Were sabred by Yeomanry Cavalry,
>   who,
> Were thank'd by THE MAN,
>   all shaven and shorn,
> All cover'd with Orders –
>   and all forlorn;
> THE DANDY OF SIXTY,
>   who bows with a grace
> And has *taste* in wigs, collars,
>   cuirasses and lace;
> Who, to tricksters and fools,
>   leaves the State and its treasure,
> And when Britain's in tears,
>   sails about at his pleasure;
> Who spurn'd from his presence
>   the Friends of his youth,
> And now has not one
>   who will tell him the truth;
> Who took to his counsels,
>   in evil hour,
> The Friends to the Reasons
>   of lawless Power,
> That back the Public Informer,
>   who
> Would put down the *Thing*,
>   that, in spite of new Acts,
> And attempts to restrain it,
>   by Soldiers or Tax,
> Will *poison* the Vermin,

> that plunder the Wealth,
> That lay in the House,
> that Jack Built.[12]

In this cartoon these cumulative verses create not only a cumulatively angry effect, but also a relentless and repeated driving home of the equivalence and interdependence of the various parts. And if this relationship is one based primarily on exploitation, we might see the stress on mutual dependence not only as a reflection of the popular belief in paternalism, but also as a formal parallel to the argument made by Cobbett in his letter 'To the Journeymen and Labourers', and repeated by Radicals throughout the postwar period and beyond, that the poor whom the rich despise actually create and sustain the rich in their privileged lifestyles. Hone's pamphlet and Cobbett's images of national unity are ways of asserting the consequent right of the working classes to membership of the political nation – a physical and social place in which all its inhabitants have an equal stake. The simultaneous emphasis on division and conflict evident in the work of both writers is rooted in their Radical perceptions of the social injustice which prevents the establishment of this kind of nation.[13]

I have so far related the apparently placatory agenda in Cobbett and Hone's writing to popular political discourse and have suggested that this is an attitude likely to be shared by their readers and therefore rhetorically effective. We can see, though, that this may be a manoeuvre that also negotiates rhetorical *problems* as well as rhetorical *strengths*. We have noted throughout this study that if the political nation is the enfranchised one then it holds the monopoly on political discourse. The disenfranchised effectively have no discursive space within which to make their political claims or within which to address each other. Olivia Smith, and more recently Jon Klancher, have explored the ways in which Radicals create new notional audiences, and attempt to create a discursive space in which to address them.[14] The idea of nation is central here, as creating a convincing – and powerful – new constituency of the disenfranchised seems likely to involve finding a discourse and a notional image of that audience which is in some way unifying and *national* in a society economically and culturally diverse. Linda Colley points out that a sense of national identity can be an empowering and potentially democratic phenomenon, and that the ruling class in the Romantic period were extremely reluctant to encourage mass demonstrations, even for patriotic purposes, for fear of unifying the country in less desirable ways.[15] It is interesting that the first of Cobbett's cheap papers in 1816 was the open letter addressed 'To the Journeymen and Labourers of England, Wales, Scotland and Ireland'. If, as we have seen, Cobbett's cheap papers galvanize a national audience of the disenfranchised, they do so by attempting to create a sense of national community similar to that with which I began this chapter. He addresses his readers as 'Friends and Fellow Countrymen', as 'Beloved Countrymen' and, maybe most convincingly for this argument, he addresses them as 'My Good Neighbours'.

But as we have also seen, the attempt to address the linguistically disenfranchised may end in finding common ground through the national language and discourse of the very centre which they oppose. We have already explored the writings of the early nineteenth century from this perspective, and the same problems continue to vex the postwar period. John Lucas points to John Clare as an example of the way in which regional dialects are invalidated by the tyranny of the centre,[16] while reading the Radical press of the late 1810s in this context one finds some Radical papers like the *Gorgon* and the *Medusa* preaching atheism and Republicanism in a Godwinian style which is, perhaps, an appropriate register to their intellectual content, but which seems a wildly inappropriate one to their target audience. Wooler's weekly *Black Dwarf*, which followed Cobbett's example in publishing cheaply through the late 1810s and which was more successful than Cobbett's paper in urban areas, is extremely allusive and 'Literary'. The prospectus to its opening number began as follows:

It may be required of us to declare whether the Black Dwarf emanates from the celestial regions, or from the shades of evil – whether he be an European sage, or an Indian savage – whether he is subject to the vicissitudes of mortality, or a phantom of the imagination – in what shape he appears, by what authority he presumes to write – what object he has in view, and whether his designs are wicked or charitable. In answer to all these probable topics of enquiry, our simple reply is, that we are not at liberty to unfold all the secrets of his prison-house, to ears of flesh and blood. We have, besides, no wish to perplex the mind, or draw too largely upon the faith of the enquirer. Were we to state what he is, the infallibility of the pope, the miracles of Mahomet, and all the wonders that wanton fancy ever drew, would appear probable and consistent to the story we should unfold. But these disclosures we must reserve, until better times ensure the civil treatment of so singular a stranger.

While this is funny and sophisticated, it is also clear that Wooler's Radical tactic here is to appropriate and to subvert the language of refinement rather than to create a new Radical discourse *representative* of its readers.

It is interesting to look at Shelley's *Mask of Anarchy* from this perspective. It is a critical commonplace that the poem draws on various discourses likely to appeal to a working-class readership – Richard Cronin recently observed that the text relies on Shelley's 'suppression of his own voice in search of the anonymous authority of the broadsheet balladeer',[17] while David Punter calls it a 'collage of discourses' and identifies the voice of England at the end of the poem as the 'straight-forward but clumsy accents of a stump orator'.[18] The instability of Shelley's Radical discourse in this poem, however – as he runs through a variety of different Radical languages – suggests an uncertainty about how to address his audience which relates to the discursive anxieties we have been tracing throughout this study. Timothy Webb compares the opening of the poem with its 'poignantly awkward rhythms' to the traditional folksong,[19] and this observation is supported by the street-ballad allegory of the opening. The poem then slips into the language of Revelation which identifies it with the apocalyptic discourse of Dissent and ultra-Radicalism, and culminates in the constitutional language of the stump orator. This spokeswoman for England is female and, as Michael Scrivener points out, a maternally protective figure. As such, she is interestingly reminiscent of Hone's and Cobbett's conciliatory and inclusive national images.[20] Like other Radicals in the period, this orator seems to be conscious of the pervasive problems of discourse. Her rhetoric is one which tries to identify the people she addresses *literally* with constitutional imagery as she asks

> 'What is Freedom? – ye can tell
> That which slavery is, too well –
> For its very name has grown
> To an echo of your own',

and goes on to assert that slavery 'is' the life led by the English poor. This seems to be an attempt to claim this language as an authentic expression of working-class experience,[21] but the attempt is vexed by the contested nature of constitutionalism – a vexation perhaps signalled by the anxious collage of discourses Shelley has previously deployed.

Criticism of this poem tends to mention Shelley's ambivalent feelings about the Reform movement as he shares the analysis of the problem made by Radicals like Cobbett but is alienated from the working class and from the possibility of violence.[22] This ambivalence seems present in the poem when it oscillates between assertions that the poor are kept alive only for the benefit of the rich and between images of tyrannical aristocrats on the one hand, and on the other the representation of Reform, or 'Freedom' as a force for peace which subdues the desire for revenge, ending with an ambivalently violent image of non-violence.[23] But in the context I have been delineating, this is not just a personal ideological ambivalence. When the spirit of England says that

> 'Thou art Peace – never by thee
> Would blood and treasure wasted be
> As tyrants wasted them, when all
> Leagued to quench thy flame in Gaul',

she seems to be drawing on the same idea that I identified in Hone and Cobbett: the Radical myth of willingness on the part of the oppressed to accept their oppressors, in contrast to the divisive actions of the rich. Ambivalence towards separatism and violence on the one hand, and the attempt (or the need) to reach some kind of accommodation with the enfranchised political nation on the other, is not just the anxiety of the aristocratic democrat, in other words, but is a problem which exercises the mainstream Radical movement itself.

The preoccupations and conclusions of the last few chapters of this study offer immediate answers as to how Cobbett seeks to deal with this tension. His polyphonic style, while it makes its own conclusions and preferences clear, seems like a dramatization of an *inclusive* nation characterized by many different voices. Other successful texts of the postwar period seem to adopt similar tactics, even if their tone is different. Thus the extract from the prospectus to the *Black Dwarf* which I have already quoted is characterized by a similarly *dialogic* creation of two simultaneous perspectives on its own language use. The first perspective is a genuine exuberant pleasure in its own playful literary allusiveness. The second, simultaneous and dialogic perspective exists in the extent to which the extract is also a parody of the literary, implicitly anticipating its non-literary readership's amused derision at its extremism and hyperbole. In other words, it appropriates refined language, and allows its marginalized readership genuinely to enjoy it, but it does so with a dialogic awareness of its reception by the margins, thus including the centre but, by putting its language in notional quotation marks, denying its automatic authority.[24]

A large factor in Cobbett's contemporary success is that he similarly refuses to exclude the centre entirely from his work. What he succeeds in doing in his best writing, as we have seen, is to skew the emphasis so that instead of the disenfranchised eavesdropping on enfranchised political discussion, the enfranchised find themselves eavesdropping on the poor. As I suggested earlier, Cobbett continually stresses the rights of the working class to membership of the political nation and he makes this a reality by holding hostile readerships together in his texts. That is, his texts are *constitutive* of a Radical nation;[25] within them, if anywhere, the polarized classes meet both as readers and as interests, and it is in this sense that Olivia Smith is right to recognize Cobbett's project as a 'healing' one. Linda Colley suggests that if a sense of national identity is achieved in the period it is largely through the establishment of a national media,[26] and Cobbett's cheap *Political Register* is certainly the largest and most national paper of the time. If his texts are constitutive of an inclusive but self-assertive Radical nation, it is not an idealized one where bigotry, populism and the cult of personality hold no sway. But nor is it merely a pessimistic vision of irreconcilable class conflict and oppression. Rather, Cobbett's Radical nation resembles England as he represents it in the passage with which I began this chapter. His representation of the classes oscillates between a sense of contiguity and conflict in the same way that his two geological ridges approach and recede from each other. But like the two ridges, which may diverge but which are always clearly discernible running throughout the breadth of the country, the polarized classes are always contained within Cobbett's national radical text.

Notes

INTRODUCTION: CHANGE AND CONTINUITY

1 William Cobbett, *Advice to Young Men and (Incidentally) to Young Women in the Middle and Higher Ranks of Life*... (London, 1829–30), para. 4.
2 William Hazlitt, 'Character of Cobbett', in *The Complete Works of William Hazlitt*, ed. by P. P. Howe, 21 vols. (London, 1931), VIII, pp. 52–3.
3 In this study, 'Radical' will refer to the efforts to secure a Reform in Parliament, while 'radical' will denote the more general attempt to counter prevailing attitudes and assumptions inimical to working-class political involvement.
4 Daniel Green, *Great Cobbett, the Noblest Agitator* (London, 1983), p. 246.
5 According to Karl W. Schweizer and John W. Osborne, *Cobbett in His Times* (Leicester, 1990), p. 174.
6 Robert Altick, *The English Common Reader* (London, 1957), pp. 329 and 392.
7 Hazlitt, 'Character of Cobbett', p. 50.
8 Cobbett's grand gesture was a flop, and the bones remained in a suitcase in his possession until they were eventually lost.
9 Leigh Hunt, *White Hat*, 13 November 1819, quoted in W. H. Wickwar, *The Struggle for the Freedom of the Press, 1819–1832* (London, 1928), pp. 52–3.
10 J. C. Belchem, 'Henry Hunt and the Evolution of the Mass Platform', *English Historical Review*, 93 (1978), 739–73, especially 741 and 746.
11 J. R. Dinwiddy, *From Luddism to the First Reform Bill: Reform in England 1810–1832* (Oxford, 1986), p. 28.
12 E. P. Thompson, *The Making of the English Working Class* (Harmondsworth, 1968), pp. 822–4.
13 *The History of the Times: the 'Thunderer' in the Making 1785–1841* (London, 1935), p. 252.
14 William Cobbett, *Weekly Political Register*, 18, 14 July 1810, col. 20.
15 Ibid., 18, 1 September 1810, cols. 258–9.
16 Ibid., col. 262.
17 Ibid., 20, 3 August 1811, cols. 130–1.

18 Ibid., 21, 18 April 1812, cols. 497–8.
19 Noel O'Sullivan, *Conservatism* (London, 1976), pp. 83–4.
20 Crane Brinton, *English Political Thought in the Nineteenth Century* (New York, 1962), pp. 61–2.
21 Raymond Williams, *Cobbett* (Oxford, 1983).
22 J. L. Hammond, *The Last Hundred Days of English Freedom* (London, 1921), p. 5.
23 Thompson, *English Working Class*, pp. 823–4.
24 Joel Wiener, review article on James Sambrook, *William Cobbett*, in *Victorian Periodical Newsletter*, 8 (1975), 135–7, especially 137.
25 Martin Wiener, 'The Changing Image of William Cobbett', *Journal of British Studies*, 13 (1974).
26 Cobbett, *Political Register*, 5, 16 June 1804, col. 935.
27 Ibid., 19, 23 February 1811, col. 452.
28 For the Roman/Saxon conflict see Samuel Kliger, *The Goths in England: a Study in Seventeenth and Eighteenth Century Thought* (Cambridge: Mass., 1952), p. 2.
29 Marilyn Butler, *Burke, Paine, Godwin and the Revolution Controversy* (Cambridge, 1984), p. 259. Cobbett has received literary-critical attention now and then, but of a problematic and often limited kind. On the one hand, as is noted by Gerald Duff in his own partly literary account, *William Cobbett and the Politics of Earth* (Salzburg, 1972) pp. 118–19, it has often failed to make the link between literary practice and political purpose – an extreme example is Edmund Blunden's observation in *Votive Tablet: Studies Chiefly Appreciative of English Authors and Books*, (London, 1931) that Cobbett's digressive style in *Rural Rides* is a response to 'the horns of elf-land faintly blowing'. Many other 'literary' accounts of Cobbett merely trace intertextual relationships between Cobbett and 'literary' figures, e.g. T. A. Birrell, '*The Political Register*: Cobbett and English Literature', *English Studies*, supp. (1964), pp. 214–19. Recent readings of Cobbett have acknowledged the literary status of his own texts, but none give his style the sustained attention Butler requires. Both James Sambrook's literary biography, *William Cobbett* (London, 1973) and his article 'Cobbett and the French Revolution', *The Yearbook of English Studies*, 19 (1989) are mainly biographical. Gerald Duff's examination of Cobbett is mainly concerned with ideological themes, but he does comment usefully on the 'revelationary' nature of Cobbett's prose where the recurring stylistic feature is the declamatory announcement of truths already realized, p. 122. Daniel Green's excellent biography, *Great Cobbett: the Noblest Agitator* (London, 1983) makes many extremely perceptive observations in passing concerning Cobbett's style and briefly assesses his stylistic skills, pp. 447–9. A more general and theorized discussion of issues related to my own can be found in Jon Klancher's *The Making of English Reading Audiences 1790–1832* (Madison, 1987), and in Kevin Gilmartin's '"Victims of Argument, Slaves of Fact": Hunt, Hazlitt, Cobbett and

the Literature of Opposition', *The Wordsworth Circle* (1990), 90–6, both of whom, however, are only concerned with Cobbett among others. My own approach most nearly resembles that of Lynne Lemrow, in her article 'William Cobbett's Journalism for the Lower Orders', *Victorian Periodical Review*, 15 (1982), which attempts to identify the basic linguistic and stylistic features of his rhetoric, and Olivia Smith's *The Politics of Language 1791–1819* (Oxford, 1984) which examines the political meaning of literary practice. Most recently, Ian Dyck's *William Cobbett and Rural Popular Culture* (Cambridge, 1992) makes many points related to my own. However the brevity of Lemrow's study, Smith's concentration on Cobbett as grammarian, and Dyck's mainly social-historical approach all leave the gap essentially unfilled.

30 Gareth Steadman Jones, 'Rethinking Chartism', in *Languages of Class: Studies in English Working Class History 1832–1982* (Cambridge, 1983), pp. 90–6.
31 As Daniel Green briefly notes, *Great Cobbett*, p. 11.
32 By 'discourse' I am designating a coherent language use which may imply a whole web of values and attitudes.
33 E. A. Wrigley, *Continuity, Chance and Change: the Character of the Industrial Revolution in England* (Cambridge, 1988), p. 9.
34 According to Michael Foot in the introduction to his edition of Jonathan Swift's *Gulliver's Travels* (Harmondsworth, 1967), p. 7.
35 Olivia Smith, *Politics of Language*, p. 3.
36 All of the following summary of Smith's arguments about ideas of refinement and vulgarity come from Chapter 1 of her study unless otherwise indicated.
37 Cobbett, *Political Register*, 11, 24 January 1807, cols. 117–18.
38 Ibid., 11, 13 June 1807, cols 1047–8. Smith *Politics of Language*, makes reference to this extract, p. 235.
39 Smith, *Politics of Language*, discusses this at length in Chapter 3 – see especially pp. 81–4 and 96–109.
40 Ibid., Chapter 3, especially pp. 128–50 and 171–201.
41 Ibid., Chapter 2, especially pp. 35–57.
42 Ibid., pp. 1–2.
43 Ian Jack, *English Literature 1815–1832* (London, 1963), p. 19.
44 William Hazlitt, 'The Spirit of the Age' in *The Complete Works of William Hazlitt*, ed. by P. P. Howe, 21 vols. (London, 1931), XI, pp. 177–8. Hazlitt is disingenuous here, in that Hunt did more to invite prosecution than he allows.
45 Smith, *Politics of Language*, p. 30.
46 Daniel Cottom, 'Taste and the Civilized Imagination', *The Journal of Aesthetics and Art Criticism*, 39 (1981) p. 367.
47 Ibid., p. 378.
48 In a letter to Thomas Love Peacock, 20/21 June 1819, *The Letters of Percy Bysshe Shelley*, ed. by Frederick L. Jones, 2 vols. (Oxford, 1964), II, *Shelley in Italy*, p. 99.

49 Malcolm Kelsall, *Byron's Politics* (Brighton, 1987), p. 193.
50 In a letter to John Cam Hobhouse, 29 March 1820, *Byron's Letters and Journals*, ed. by Leslie A. Marchand, 9 vols. (London, 1977), VII, *Between Two Worlds*, p. 63.
51 As Marjorie Levinson persuasively argues, *Keats's Life of Allegory: the Origins of a Style* (Oxford, 1988), Introduction, especially pp. 11–15.
52 To C. W. Dilke, 4 March 1820, in *The Letters of John Keats 1814–1821*, ed. by Hyder Edward Rollins, 2 vols. (Cambridge, 1958), II, p. 272.
53 Green, *Great Cobbett*, p. 277.
54 Karl Marx and Friedrich Engels, *Manifesto of the Communist Party*, trans. S. Moore, 2nd edition (Moscow, 1977), p. 61.
55 Christopher Hill, *Puritanism and Revolution: Studies in the Interpretation of the English Revolution of the Seventeenth-century* (Harmondsworth, 1986), Chapter 3. Raymond Williams, *The Country and the City* (London, 1985), p. 10.
56 Raymond Williams, *Country and the City*, pp. 9–11.
57 Cobbett, *Political Register*, 6, 27 October 1804, cols. 617–18.
58 Bolingbroke, *The Craftsman: Being a Critique of the Times by Caleb D'Anvers of Grey's-Inn Esq.*, 2 August 1729, in *Lord Bolingbroke: Contributions to the Craftsman*, ed. by Simon Varey (Oxford, 1982), p. 96.
59 Ibid., 7 September 1728, p. 54.
60 Cobbett, *Political Register*, 10, 9 August 1806, col. 193.
61 J. G. A. Pocock, *The Ancient Constitution and the Feudal Law: A Study of English Historical Thought in the Seventeenth Century. A Reissue with a Retrospect* (Cambridge, 1987), Chapters 2, 3, and Chapter 3 of the *Retrospect*.
62 Edmund Burke, *Reflections on the Revolution in France*, ed. by Conor Cruise O'Brien (Harmondsworth, 1970), pp. 100–4.
63 J. G. A. Pocock, 'Radical Criticisms of the Whig Order in the Age between Revolutions', in *The Origins of Anglo-American Radicalism*, ed. by M. Jacob and J. Jacob (London, 1984).
64 Ibid., pp. 50–3.
65 Janice Lee, 'Political Antiquarianism Unmasked: the Conservative Attack on the Myth of the Ancient Constitution', *Bulletin of the Institute for Historical Research*, 55 (1982), 166–79.
66 J. A. Epstein, 'The Constitutional Idiom: Radical Reasoning, Rhetoric and Action in Early Nineteenth-century England', *Journal of Social History*, 23 (1990), 553–74.
67 Ian Dyck, 'Debts and Liabilities: William Cobbett and Thomas Paine', in *Citizen of the World: Essays on Thomas Paine*, ed. by Ian Dyck (London, 1987), pp. 95–100. He makes the same argument throughout *William Cobbett and Rural Popular Culture* (Cambridge, 1992) where he stresses that Cobbett shares the values and aspirations of an inherently conservative rural labouring-class culture, see especially pp. 39–40.
68 Wrigley, *Continuity*, pp. 3–9. Raymond Williams, *Cobbett*, similarly stresses that the period's changes do not break into a serene period of agricultural harmony, but that the agricultural economic system had

been riven by changes for many years. Williams uses Cobbett himself to argue along lines similar to Wrigley's, pp. 59–63.
69 Eric Hobsbawm, *The Age of Revolution: Europe 1798–1848* (London, 1977), pp. 36–7. David Miller, *Philosophy and Ideology in Hume's Political Thought* (Oxford, 1981), p. 141.
70 For a discussion of the discursive significances of the Gothic see Robert Miles, *Gothic Writing 1750–1820: a Genealogy* (London, 1993).
71 Lois Whitney, *Primitivism and the Idea of Progress in English Popular Literature of the Eighteenth Century* (Baltimore, 1934), pp. 22–6.
72 Ian McCalman, *Radical Underworld: Prophets, Revolutionaries and Pornographers in London, 1795–1840* (Cambridge, 1988), p. 85.
73 Ibid., p. 237.
74 William Cobbett, *Remarks of the Pamphlets Lately Published Against Peter Porcupine*, reproduced in *The Life and Adventures of Peter Porcupine, with other Records of His Early Career in England and America*, ed. by G. D. H. Cole (London, 1927), p. 105.
75 Again this suggests a possible relationship between Cobbett and figures like Keats and Leigh Hunt who are similarly caught between classes and similarly discomfiting to contemporary and subsequent criticism.
76 McCalman, *Radical Underworld*, pp. 46–7. He makes the link between blasphemy and populism, pp. 139–49.
77 Klancher notes Cobbett's transgression of class audiences, *English Reading Audiences*, p. 121.
78 Smith, *Politics of Language*, pp. 227–51.

1 EARLY WRITINGS 1792–1800

1 Ian Dyck, *William Cobbett and Rural Popular Culture*, (Cambridge, 1992), pp. 30–2. This will be discussed at more length in Chapter 3.
2 In William Cobbett, *Weekly Political Register*, 23 June 1832.
3 William Hazlitt, 'Character of Cobbett', in *The Complete Works of William Hazlitt*, ed. by P. P. Howe, 21 vols. (London, 1931), VIII, p. 54.
4 Daniel Green, *Great Cobbett: The Noblest Agitator* (London, 1983), p. 116.
5 William Cobbett, *The Soldier's Friend* (London, 1792), pp. 19–20.
6 Ibid., p. 8.
7 Ibid., p. 21.
8 Frances Canavan, *Edmund Burke: Prescription and Providence* (Durham, NC, 1987), p. 88.
9 Richard Price, *A Discourse on the Love of Our Country* (London, 1790), reproduced in *Burke, Paine, Godwin and the Revolution Controversy*, ed. by Marilyn Butler (Cambridge, 1984), pp. 23–32.
10 Thomas Paine, *The Rights of Man*, ed. by Eric Foner (Harmondsworth, 1985), p. 51.
11 V. L. Parrington, *Main Currents in American Thought* (New York, 1930), pp. 274–8.
12 J. G. A. Pocock, 'Radical Criticisms of the Whig Order in the Age

between Revolutions', in *The Origins of Anglo-American Radicalism*, ed. by M. Jacob and J. Jacob (London, 1984), p. 44 also notes this American preoccupation with British Governmental models.
13 John C. Miller, *The Federalist Era 1789–1801* (London, 1960), Chapter 9.
14 William Cobbett, *A Bone to Gnaw for the Democrats; or, Observations on a Pamphlet entitled 'The Political Progress of Britain...'* (Philadelphia, 1795), in *Porcupine's Works*, ed. by William Cobbett, 12 vols. (London, 1801), II, p. 21.
15 *Columbian Centinel*, 16 January 1796.
16 Edmund Burke, *Reflections on the Revolution in France*, ed. by Conor Cruise O'Brien (Harmondsworth, 1970), p. 106.
17 Ibid., p. 120.
18 Ibid., p. 181.
19 *National Gazette*, 5 June 1793, quoted in F. L. Mott, *American Journalism: a History 1690–1960*, 3rd edition (New York, 1962), p. 125.
20 Linda K. Kerber, *Federalists in Dissent: Imagery and Ideology in Jeffersonian America* (London, 1970), pp. 16–22.
21 John Tebbel, *The Compact History of the American Newspaper* (New York, 1963), pp. 1–25.
22 Pat Rogers, *An Introduction to Pope* (London, 1975), p. 5.
23 John Wilkes, *The North Briton* (London, 1763), 5 March 1763, pp. 174–5.
24 Junius, *Public Advertiser*, reproduced in Claude-Jean Bertrand, *The British Press: an Historical Survey* (Paris, 1969), p. 84.
25 Tebbel, *Compact History*, p. 68.
26 Cobbett, *A Bone to Gnaw for the Democrats* (Philadelphia, 1795), p. 38.
27 Ibid., p. 62.
28 Ibid., in *Porcupine's Works*, p. 61.
29 See R. B. Rose, 'The Priestley Riots of 1791', *Past and Present*, 18 (1960), 68–88; F. W. Gibbs, *Joseph Priestley: Adventurer in Science and Champion of Truth* (London, 1965); Jack Lindsay (ed.) *Autobiography of Joseph Priestley* (Bath, 1970).
30 Cobbett, *Observations on the Emigration of Dr Priestley*, in *Porcupine's Works*, I, p. 151.
31 Quoted in Green, *Great Cobbett*, p. 161.
32 Cobbett, *Observations*, in *Porcupine's Works*, I, p. 177.
33 Ibid., pp. 161–2.
34 Ibid., p. 178.
35 Ibid., pp. 191–2.
36 James Callender, *The Political Progress of Britain: or, an Impartial History of Abuses in the Government of the British Empire*, 3rd edition (Philadelphia, 1795), p. 28.
37 Cobbett, *A Bone to Gnaw for the Democrats*, p. 3.
38 Ibid., p. 6.
39 Ibid., p. 7.
40 Olivia Smith, *The Politics of Language 1791–1819* (Oxford, 1984), p. 234.
41 Cobbett, *A Bone to Gnaw for the Democrats*, p. 14.

42 Ibid., p. 30.
43 Cobbett, *Remarks of the Pamphlets Lately Published Against Peter Porcupine*, discussed in Green, *Great Cobbett*, p. 150.
44 Cobbett, *A Bone to Gnaw for the Democrats*, p. 22.
45 Cobbett, *Observations*, pp. 197–8.
46 Ibid., pp. 187–8.
47 Ibid., p. 187.
48 Cobbett, *A Bone to Gnaw for the Democrats*, pp. 46–7.
49 William Cobbett, *Rural Rides* from articles in the *Political Register* 1822–6 (London, 1830), p. 261.
50 William Cobbett, *A Kick for a Bite; or, Review upon Review ... in a Letter to the Editor, or Editors, of the American Monthly Review* (Philadelphia, 1795), 'Advertisement', p. 3.
51 Ibid., p. 5.
52 Ibid., p. 10.
53 As is noted by George Spater, *William Cobbett: the Poor Man's Friend*, 2 vols. (Cambridge, 1982), p. 3.
54 William Cobbett, 'Letter I to the Rt Honourable William Pitt', in *Political Register*, 6, 29 September 1804, col. 453.
55 Cobbett, *A Kick for a Bite*, p. 6.
56 Ibid., p. 12.
57 Ibid.
58 Ibid., p. 13.
59 Ibid., pp. 18–19.
60 Tebbel, *Compact History*, pp. 44–7.
61 G. A. Cranfield, *The Press and Society: from Caxton to Northcliffe* (London, 1978), p. 13.
62 Ibid., p. 15.
63 Ibid., pp. 17–18, 25–6.
64 James Quicksilver, *The Blue Shop; or, Impartial and Humorous Observations on the Life and Adventures of Peter Porcupine* (Philadelphia, 1796), p. 9.
65 John Dickinson, *Letters from a Farmer in Pennsylvania to the Inhabitants of the British Colonies*, ed. by R. T. H. Halsey (New York, 1903), p. 5.
66 William Cobbett, *The Life and Adventures of Peter Porcupine*, in *The Life and Adventures of Peter Porcupine with other Records of His Early Career in England and America*, ed. by G. D. H. Cole (London, 1927), pp. 33–4.
67 William Cobbett, *Porcupine's Gazette*, 4 March 1797, in *Porcupine's Works*, V, pp. 3–4.
68 Ibid., p. 210.

2 A VERSION OF REACTION

1 Asa Briggs, *William Cobbett* (London, 1967), p. 26.
2 J. T. Boulton, *The Language of Politics in the Age of Wilkes and Burke* (London, 1963), p. 34.
3 Ibid., pp. 35–6.

4 Ibid., p. 109.
5 Olivia Smith, *The Politics of Language 1791–1819* (Oxford, 1984), pp. 42–4.
6 In Marilyn Butler (ed.), *Burke, Paine, Godwin and the Revolution Controversy*, (Cambridge, 1984), pp. 215–16.
7 Edmund Burke, *Reflections on the Revolution in France*, ed. by Conor Cruise O'Brien (Harmondsworth, 1970), p. 135.
8 Ibid., p. 183.
9 In Butler, *Revolution Controversy*, p. 216.
10 Ibid., p. 219.
11 Ibid., p. 215.
12 In a letter to William Windham of 1803 Cobbett draws up a list of papers for and against the government. In this list he counts himself among the dailies. Reproduced in Lewis Melville, *The Life and Letters of William Cobbett in England and America: Based upon Hitherto Unpublished Family Papers* (London, 1913), p. 200.
13 William Cobbett, *Weekly Political Register*, 27, 14 January 1815, col. 41.
14 David Aers, Jonathan Cook and David Punter, 'Coleridge: Individual, Community and Social Agency', in *Romanticism and Ideology: Studies in English Writing 1765–1830* (London, 1981), pp. 83–4.
15 In Richard Price, *A Discourse on the Love of Our Country* (London, 1790) reproduced in Butler, *Revolution Controversy*.
16 Burke, *Reflections*, p. 194.
17 Jeremy Black, *The English Press in the Eighteenth Century* (London, 1987), p. 46.
18 *The Courier and Evening Gazette*, 5 February 1804.
19 Cobbett, *Political Register*, 3, 4 June 1803, col. 820.
20 Ibid., 1, 15 May 1802, cols. 573–4.
21 Ibid., 1, 27 February 1802, cols. 219–22.
22 *Ecclesiastes*, 3.1.
23 *I Corinthians*, 13.11–12.
24 In a *Political Register* article of 26 February 1814, to be discussed in the next chapter, Cobbett identifies this common usage, cols. 257–9.
25 Burke, *Reflections*, pp. 169–70.
26 Cobbett, *Political Register*, 1, 6 March 1802, cols. 250–5.
27 Ibid., 6, 22 September 1804, col. 448.
28 Ibid., 1, 26 June 1802, cols. 790–8.
29 Burke, *Reflections*, p. 120.
30 Ibid., pp. 169–70.
31 William Cobbett, *The Life and Adventures of Peter Porcupine*, in *The Life and Adventures of Peter Porcupine with other Records of His Early Career in England and America*, ed. by G. D. H. Cole (London, 1927), p. 38.
32 William Cobbett, *Important Considerations for the People of this Kingdom*, reproduced in *Selections from Cobbett's Political Works*, ed. by J. M. and J. P. Cobbett, 6 vols. (London, 1835), I, p. 310.
33 Ian Dyck has recently discussed the battle for popular literature waged

between Cobbett and More in *William Cobbett and Rural Popular Culture*, (Cambridge, 1992), pp. 76–106.
34 In Butler, *Revolution Controversy*, p. 183.
35 William Shakespeare, *As You Like It* (Harmondsworth, 1968), III, ii, 69–73.

3 OPPOSITIONAL STYLES 1804–1816

1 *The Courier and Evening Gazette*, 8 January 1805. This has been attributed to Coleridge and is reproduced in *The Collected Works: Essays on his Times*, ed. by David V. Erdman (London, 1978), III, p. 87.
2 Ian Dyck, 'From "Rabble" to "Chopsticks": the Radicalism of William Cobbett', *Albion* (1989), 56–87, especially 71–2, and *William Cobbett and Rural Popular Culture*, pp. 30–2.
3 Raymond Williams, *Cobbett* (Oxford, 1983), p. 1, quotes Cobbett's much later description of his own behaviour at a political meeting when opponents declared their resolution to eject him from the hall: 'I rose, that they might see the man that they had to put out', as exemplary of Cobbett's autobiographical tactics.
4 William Cobbett, 'Letter I to the Rt Hon William Pitt', *Weekly Political Register*, 6, 29 September 1804, cols. 449–60.
5 Ibid., 6, 15 December 1804, cols. 929–50.
6 Ibid., 29 September 1804, cols. 455–6.
7 Ibid., 5, 7 January 1804, col. 32.
8 William Cobbett, *A History of the Protestant Reformation in England and Ireland*... (London, 1829), I, para. 479.
9 John Carswell, *From Revolution to Revolution: England 1688–1776* (London, 1973), pp. 163–4.
10 The factual matter which follows is taken from Ian McCalman, *Radical Underworld: Prophets, Revolutionaries and Pornographers in London, 1795–1840* (Cambridge, 1988), pp. 75–7. George Spater, *William Cobbett: the Poor Man's Friend*, 2 vols. (Cambridge, 1982), also briefly describes this episode, II, pp. 544–9.
11 McCalman, *Radical Underworld*, p. 76.
12 Ibid., p. 78.
13 McCalman, ibid., tentatively identifies 'A. B.' as a pseudonym for Cannon, p. 254 n. 8.
14 Cobbett, *Political Register*, 24, 20 November 1813, cols. 644–7.
15 Ibid., 24, 4 December 1813, cols. 716–17.
16 Ibid., 25, 26 February 1814, cols. 257–68.
17 According to McCalman, *Radical Underworld*, p. 77.
18 E. P. Thompson, *The Making of the English Working Class* (Harmondsworth, 1968), pp. 40–6.
19 Marilyn Butler (ed.), *Burke, Paine, Godwin and the Revolution Controversy*, (Cambridge, 1984), pp. 23–4.
20 McCalman, *Radical Underworld*, pp. 50–72.
21 Thompson, *English Working Class*, p. 54.

22 David Hall, 'Introduction', in *Understanding Popular Culture: Europe from the Middle Ages to the Nineteenth Century*, ed. by S. L. Kaplan (Berlin, Amsterdam, New York, 1984), p. 15.
23 Olivia Smith, *The Politics of Language 1791–1819* (Oxford, 1984), Chapter 3, especially pp. 128–30 and 171–201.
24 As McCalman points out, in *Radical Underworld*, p. 61. A similar recognition has allowed Jon Mee to relocate Blake's famously obscure apocalyptic writings within a firmly political discursive context, *Dangerous Enthusiasm: William Blake and the Culture of Radicalism in the 1790s* (Oxford, 1992).
25 Richard Price *A Discourse on the Love of Our Country* in Butler, *Revolution Controversy*, pp. 31–2.
26 Quoted in McCalman, *Radical Underworld*, p. 72.
27 Quoted in Thompson, *English Working Class*, p. 422.
28 Cobbett, *Political Register*, 18, 22 December 1810, col. 1249.
29 Ibid., 22, 24 December 1812, col. 513.
30 Ibid., 18, 31 October 1810, col. 769.
31 Ibid., 19, 2 January 1811, cols. 2–11.
32 Ibid., 27, 14 January 1815, cols. 33–54.
33 *Revelation*, 18.19; 16.13.
34 William Hazlitt, 'Character of Cobbett', in *The Complete Works of William Hazlitt*, ed. by P. P. Howe, 21 vols. (London, 1931), VIII, p. 51.
35 Smith, *Politics of Language*, p. 200.
36 Ibid., p. 198.
37 William Hone, *The Three Trials of William Hone, for Publishing Three Parodies* (London, 1818), III, p. 38.
38 Quoted in Spater, *The Poor Man's Friend*, II, p. 479.
39 Cobbett, *Political Register*, 31, 2 November 1816, cols. 545–76.
40 It is interesting to note that Ian Dyck's recent *William Cobbett and Rural Popular Culture* rejects this kind of discursive reading of Cobbett's nostalgia, and instead insists upon its basis in actual memory of better times, Chapter 6. In the discursive context I have traced, however, it seems impossible that Cobbett's nostalgia should be entirely unselfconscious. A discursive reading also most satisfactorily explains his mixed and changing opinions on the matter as rhetorical strategy.
41 The specific medieval dates occur in Letter 4 of *The Poor Man's Friend: or, Essays on the Rights and Duties of the Poor*, in parts, 1826–7 (London, 1829). By *Advice to Young Men and (Incidentally) to Young Women in the Middle and Higher Ranks of Life...*, in parts, 1829–30 (London, n.d.), he has settled on the reign of Edward III as the zenith of English freedoms. Cobbett's parallel valorization of 'the dark ages' of his own childhood is famous, but he is supported by both Dorothy George, *England in Transition: Life and Work in the Eighteenth Century* (Harmondsworth, 1953), pp. 17–18 and James Sambrook, *William Cobbett* (London, 1973), Chapter 1.
42 Christopher Hill, *Puritanism and Revolution: Studies in the Interpretation of the*

Notes to pages 113–23 227

English Revolution of the Seventeenth-Century (Harmondsworth, 1986), Chapter 3.

43 Quoted in J. G. A. Pocock, *The Ancient Constitution and the Feudal Law: A Study of English Historical Thought in the Seventeenth Century. A Reissue with a Retrospect* (Cambridge, 1987), p. 35.

44 Edmund Burke, *Reflections on the Revolution in France*, ed. by Conor Cruise O'Brien (Harmondsworth, 1970), p. 120.

45 In a discussion of Paine's response to Burke, John C. Whale notes that Burke's state is actually inorganically eternal, 'The Limits of Paine's Revolutionary Literalism', in *Revolution in Writing: British Literary Responses to the French Revolution*, ed. by Kelvin Everest (Milton Keynes, 1991).

46 Thomas Paine, *The Rights of Man*, ed. by Eric Foner (Harmondsworth, 1985), pp. 41–2. For recent alternative readings of this debate between Burke and Paine see John C. Whale, see note 45, and Tom Furniss, 'Rhetoric in Revolution: the Role of Language in Paine's Critique of Burke', in *Revolution and English Romanticism: Politics and Rhetoric*, ed. by K. Hanley and R. Selden (Hemel Hempstead, 1990).

47 Daniel Green, *Great Cobbett: the Noblest Agitator* (London, 1983), pp. 35–6.

48 William Cobbett, *Remarks of the Pamphlets*, reproduced in *The Life and Adventures of Peter Porcupine, with Other Records of His Early Career in England and America*, ed. by G. D. H. Cole, (London, 1927), p. 93.

49 William Reitzel (ed.), *The Autobiography of William Cobbett: the Progress of a Ploughboy to a Seat in Parliament* (London, 1947), p. 15.

50 Cobbett, *The Life and Adventures of Peter Porcupine*, in *Life and Adventures*, pp. 35–6.

4 REPRESENTING OLD ENGLAND

1 William Cobbett, *Advice to Young Men and (Incidentally) to Young Women in the Middle and Higher Ranks of Life...*, in parts, 1829–30 (London, n.d.), paras 5–6.

2 Margaret Beetham, 'Open and Closed: the Periodical Press as a Publishing Genre', *Victorian Periodical Review*, 22 (1989), pp. 96–100.

3 G. D. H. Cole, *The Life of William Cobbett* (London, 1947), pp. 25–6.

4 James Sambrook, *William Cobbett* (London, 1973) notes that Old England survives through Cobbett, p. 159.

5 Quoted in Asa Briggs, 'The Language of "Class" in early Nineteenth-Century England', in *The Collected Essays of Asa Briggs, Volume 1: Words, Numbers, Places, People* (Brighton, 1985) p. 5.

6 William Cobbett, *Rural Rides*, from articles in the *Weekly Political Register* 1822–6 (London, 1830) pp. 15–16.

7 William Cobbett, *The Life and Adventures of Peter Porcupine*, reproduced in *Porcupine's Works*, ed. by William Cobbett, 21 vols. (London, 1801), IV, p. 34.

8 William Cobbett, *Remarks of the Pamphlets Lately Published Against Peter Porcupine*, reproduced in *The Life and Adventures of Peter Porcupine, with Other Records of His Early Career in England and America*, p. 105.
9 David Wilson, *Paine and Cobbett: the Transatlantic Connection* (Kingston and Montreal, 1988) makes a similar point, p. 124, though he assumes that this is an unselfconscious process. Moreover, Cobbett at this time is Old England in opposition to Young America, rather than industrial Britain.
10 Cobbett, *Remarks of the Pamphlets*, pp. 35–6.
11 For example, Daniel Green, *Great Cobbett: the Noblest Agitator* (London, 1983), p. 19.
12 Cobbett, *Advice*, para. 288.
13 Cobbett, *Rural Rides*, pp. 17–18.
14 Green, *Great Cobbett*, pp. 19–20.
15 Cobbett, *Rural Rides*, p. 17.
16 Anthony Flew (ed.), *A Dictionary of Philosophy* (London, 1984), p. 152.
17 Jean Perkins, *The Concept of the Self in the French Enlightenment* (Geneva, 1969), p. 93.
18 William Wordsworth, 'Tintern Abbey', ll. 75–83, in *William Wordsworth: the Poems*, ed. by John O. Hayden (London, 1981) pp. 359–60.
19 William Wordsworth, *The Prelude*, ll. 304, 589. 1805 version in *William Wordsworth, The Prelude, A Parallel Text*, ed. by J. C. Maxwell (Harmondsworth, 1971), pp. 50, 66.
20 John Clare, 'Remembrances', ll. 1–10, in *John Clare*, ed. by Eric Robinson and David Powell (Oxford, 1984), pp. 258–61.
21 Ibid., ll. 51–60.
22 Cobbett, *A Journal of a Year's Residence in the United States of America...*, in parts 1818–19 (Gloucester, 1983), para. 6.
23 Green, *Great Cobbett*, pp. 9–10. In 'Cobbett and the French Revolution', *The Yearbook of English Studies*, 19 (1989), James Sambrook conversely argues that Cobbett's autobiography is his major literary achievement and that, in a sense, his political/historical subjects are merely the occasion for the writing of it.
24 Quoted in Green, *Great Cobbett*, p. 189.
25 Quoted in George Spater, *William Cobbett: the Poor Man's Friend*, 2 vols. (Cambridge, 1982), II, p. 393.
26 Hazlitt, 'Character of Cobbett', in *The Complete Works of William Hazlitt*, ed. by P. P. Howe, 21 vols. (London, 1931), VIII, pp. 52–3.

5 DIALOGUE AND DEBATE

1 Lynne Lemrow, 'William Cobbett's Journalism for the Lower Orders', *Victorian Periodical Review*, 15 (1982), 11–20, especially 13–15.
2 William Cobbett, *Weekly Political Register*, 31, 30 November 1816, col. 674.

Notes to pages 136–44

3 Thomas Paine, *The Rights of Man*, ed. by Eric Foner (Harmondsworth, 1985), p. 49.
4 As does the outrageous misrepresentation of his opponent's views – Paine flagrantly misquotes Burke in this passage.
5 Cobbett, *Political Register*, 32, 8 March 1817, cols. 289–90.
6 William Hazlitt, 'Character of Cobbett', in *The Complete Works of William Hazlitt*, ed. by P. P. Howe, 21 vols. (London, 1931), VIII, p. 51.
7 Paine, *The Rights of Man*, p. 51.
8 William Cobbett, *Rural Rides*, from articles in the *Political Register*, 1822–6 (London, 1830), p. 100.
9 Cobbett, *Political Register*, 31, 14 December 1816, cols. 737–8.
10 Daniel Green, *Great Cobbett: the Noblest Agitator* (London, 1983), p. 288. Cobbett, *Political Register*, 9, 14 June 1806, cols. 877–85 describes his common experiences and sense of identification with the farmers.
11 Green, *Great Cobbett*, p. 413.
12 M. M. Bakhtin's *Problems of Dostoevsky's Poetics*, trans. R. W. Rostel (Ann Arbor: MI, 1973) and Lynne Pearce's 'John Clare's *Childe Harold*: a Polyphonic Reading', *Criticism*, 31 (1989) have informed my use of the term and of 'dialogism' in this study.
13 Olivia Smith, *The Politics of Language 1791–1819* (Oxford, 1984), pp. 228–30. Green also notes that some of Cobbett's best writing is in the form of dramatic dialogue, *Great Cobbett*, p. 339, while Lemrow, 'William Cobbett's Journalism', p. 17, points out that Cobbett gives his readers a dramatic voice within the text to question and to argue.
14 Cobbett, *Political Register*, 24 May 1828, quoted in Raymond Williams, *Cobbett* (Oxford, 1983), pp. 54–5.
15 Cobbett, *Political Register*, 15, 21 January 1809, cols. 75–6.
16 Ibid., 1 July 1809, col. 993.
17 Lemrow, 'William Cobbett's Journalism', p. 13; George Spater, *William Cobbett: the Poor Man's Friend*, 2 vols. (Cambridge, 1982), p. 505.
18 G. Himmelfarb, *The Idea of Poverty: England in the Early Industrial Age* (London, 1984), discusses Cobbett as a populist and makes many interesting points. Like other critics, however, she assumes that Cobbett's populist writings are an uncomplicated expression of his own views.
19 See also Ian Dyck, *William Cobbett and Rural Popular Culture* (Cambridge, 1992), pp. 40–4. Like other writers, however, Dyck accounts for this largely as an involuntary 'psychological crutch' necessary to a man who 'could more readily accept innovation in politics than in culture', ibid., pp. 40–2.
20 Edmund Burke, *Reflections on the Revolution in France*, ed. by Conor Cruise O'Brien (Harmondsworth, 1970), p. 135.
21 Ibid., pp. 181–3.
22 Jon Klancher makes the point that Radicals rework rather than reject classical rhetoric, *The Making of English Reading Audiences 1790–1832* (Madison, 1987), p. 28.

23 While Keith Thomas has famously charted the decline of magic in the seventeenth century, in *Religion and the Decline of Magic* (London, 1978) a large popular literature of superstition, charms and fortune-telling survives. Dyck discusses this in relation to Cobbett's practices, *William Cobbett*, pp. 82–4. Clarke Garrett, 'Popular Religion in the American and French Revolutions' in *Religion, Rebellion, Revolution*, ed. by Bruce Lincoln (London, 1985) describes continental superstition. Susan Pederson, 'Hannah More Meets Simple Simon: Tracts, Chapbooks, and Popular Culture in Late Eighteenth Century England', *Journal of British Studies*, 25 (1986), 84–113, addresses the English equivalent, 91. See also Robert D. Storch (ed.), *Popular Culture and Custom in Nineteenth-Century England* (London, 1982).
24 Anonymous, *Mysterious Knockings, Heard in Foleshill Church* (Coventry, n.d., published by E. Bromfield between 1827 and 1830). From the collection held by Coventry City Libraries.
25 Cobbett, *Rural Rides*, p. 500.
26 James Sambrook, *William Cobbett* (London, 1973), p. 112.
27 Ian Dyck discusses Cobbett's relationship with chapbook and ballad culture at length throughout *William Cobbett*. His preoccupations are different from my own, but his discussion is extremely useful for anyone interested in this cultural form.
28 Cobbett, *Political Register*, 15 February 1834, col. 409.
29 *Amusing Prose Chapbooks Chiefly of the Last Century*, ed. by R. H. Cunningham (London, 1889).
30 Ian Dyck, *William Cobbett*. pp. 76–106.
31 *The Comical History of the King and the Cobbler*, in Cunningham, *Amusing Prose Chapbooks*, pp. 13–23.
32 *The Last Dying Speech and Confession of Mary Jones* (Coventry, n.d., first published by Houghton of Bedford, reprinted by W. or B. Hickling between 1830 and 1864). From the collection held by Coventry City Libraries.
33 This figure, plus a reproduction of the broadsheet of 1828, is found in V. E. Neuburg, *Popular Literature: a History and a Guide, from the Beginning of Printing to the year 1897* (Harmondsworth, 1977), p. 138.
34 For example, *A Full and True Account of the Execution of John Dennis, Geo. Crow, Will. Beamis, Thomas South and Isaac Harley* (Birmingham, n.d., published by H. Wadsworth between 1816 and 1818). From the collection held by Coventry City Libraries.
35 For example, Smith, *Politics of Language*, p. 230; Spater, *Poor Man's Friend*, I, pp. 184–5.
36 Cobbett, *Political Register*, 32, 8 March 1817, col. 290.
37 Sambrook, *William Cobbett*, also notes this as an effect of the open-letter form, p. 184.
38 Cobbett, *A Journal of a Year's Residence in the United States of America*..., in parts 1818–19 (Gloucester, 1983), para. 8, p. 17.

39 Ibid., pp. 31–2.
40 Ibid., p. 27.
41 Ibid., pp. 30–1.
42 Ibid., para. 10, p. 18.
43 Ibid., para. 23, p. 62.
44 Ibid., para. 156, p. 106; para. 1015, pp. 303–4.
45 For example, an often-quoted passage from *Rural Rides* remarks that a good religion is one which furnishes its followers with 'plenty to eat and drink and wear', pp. 498–9.
46 James Chandler, 'Settling National Character: the "English Writers on America" (1815–25)', delivered at the British Association for Romantic Studies International Conference on *Romanticism and Nationalism*, University of Strathclyde, 9 July 1993.
47 Cobbett, *Rural Rides*, pp. 288–313.
48 Hazlitt, 'Character of Cobbett', pp. 52–3.
49 My discussion of Cobbett's identification and deployment of his readership in what follows is adjacent to, but different from, Jon Klancher's discussion of the same issues in *English Reading Audiences*.
50 William Cobbett, *Cottage Economy*, in parts, 1821–2, with a Preface by G. K. Chesterton (Oxford, 1979), para. 33.
51 More's *Tales*, in *The Miscellaneous Works of Hannah More*, 2 vols. (London, 1840) will be discussed in more detail in Chapter 7.
52 J. W. Osborne, *William Cobbett: His Thought and His Times* (New Brunswick and New Jersey, 1966), p. 7; E. P. Thompson notes Cobbett's hostility to taxed articles, in *The Making of the English Working Class* (Harmondsworth, 1968), p. 814.
53 W. H. Wickwar, *The Struggle for the Freedom of the Press, 1819–1832* (London, 1928), p. 76. Much fun is had in *The Cap of Liberty* on the subject, 29 December 1819.
54 Cobbett, *Cottage Economy*, para. 22.

6 A RADICAL HISTORY

1 Hereafter referred to as *History*.
2 George Spater, *William Cobbett: the Poor Man's Friend*, 2 vols. (Cambridge, 1982), II, pp. 443–5.
3 J. W. Osborne, *William Cobbett: His Thought and His Times*, (New Brunswick and New Jersey, 1966), p. 79.
4 Raymond Williams, *Cobbett* (Oxford, 1983), p. 25.
5 James Sambrook, *William Cobbett* (London, 1973), p. 136.
6 Cobbett *History*, I, para. 144.
7 Ibid., para. 127.
8 Ibid., II, para. 52.
9 Volume I comprises the history; volume II lists Church lands confiscated by the Protestants.

10 Cobbett, *History*, I, para. 12.
11 Sambrook, *William Cobbett*, describes the narrow meaning of 'the people' in political language of the period, and suggests that Cobbett broadens it, pp. 7, 74. G. K. Chesterton famously describes Cobbett giving a voice to the inarticulate in his Preface to William Cobbett's *Cottage Economy* (Oxford, 1979), p. vii.
12 Cobbett, *History*, I, para. 429.
13 Ibid., para. 127.
14 Ibid., para. 127.
15 Ibid., para. 182.
16 Ibid., para. 149.
17 Ibid., para. 211.
18 Ibid., para. 236.
19 Ibid., para. 456.
20 Ibid., para. 370.
21 Ibid., II, paras. 10, 11, 12.
22 Ibid., para. 5.
23 Ibid., para. 403.
24 Spater discusses Cobbett's attitudes to Jews and rhetorical uses of the term, *Poor Man's Friend*, II, p. 441.
25 Motto for Cobbett's *Weekly Political Register*, 17, 24 March 1810, col. 417.
26 Roy Pascal, *The Dual Voice: Free Indirect Speech and its Functioning in the Nineteenth-Century Novel* (Manchester, 1977), Chapter 1.
27 Linda Colley, *Britons: Forging the Nation 1707–1837* (London, 1992), pp. 11–43.
28 While Linda Colley, ibid., p. 231, stresses the importance of anti-Catholicism to British identity and only briefly mentions Jews, it is instructive to read Cobbett and Scott in the light of Edward Said's *Orientalism* (Harmondsworth, 1985) and its implications about Western identity. Particularly revealing is the brief observation that 'even the most imaginitive writers of an age, men like Flaubert, Nerval, or Scott, were constrained in what they could either experience of or say about the Orient', p. 43. This kind of discursive trap may account for the ambivalence and contradictions evident in the texts I have been citing.
29 Walter Scott, *Ivanhoe* (Edinburgh, 1871) pp. 74–5.
30 Cobbett, *History*, I, para. 457.
31 Ibid., para. 456.
32 Ibid., para. 478.
33 Ibid., para. 144.
34 Ibid., para. 320.
35 Ibid., para. 383.
36 Ibid., para. 386.
37 Ibid., para. 399.
38 William Cobbett, *Political Register*, 30, 10 February 1816, col. 167.
39 Olivia Smith, *The Politics of Language 1791–1819* (Oxford, 1984), p. 27.

Notes to pages 169–79

40 William Cobbett, *Advice to Young Men and (Incidentally) to Young Women in the Middle and Higher Ranks of Life*..., in parts, 1829–30 (London, n.d.), para. 320. These points about the nature of a working-class history and the preference for oral over elite history, are also made by Ian Dyck, *William Cobbett and Rural Popular Culture* (Cambridge, 1992), pp. 126–8.
41 Susan Pederson, 'Hannah More Meets Simple Simon: Tracts, Chapbooks, and Popular Culture in Late Eighteenth Century England', *Journal of British Studies*, 25 (1986), pp. 99–102.
42 Ibid., p. 103.
43 R. H. Cunningham (ed.), *Amusing Prose Chapbooks Chiefly of the Last Century* (London, 1889), pp. 309–23.
44 John Lingard, DD, *A History of England, from the First Invasion by the Romans* (London, 1838), VI, p. 118.
45 Cobbett, *History*, I, para. 6.
46 Ibid., para. 8.
47 Ibid., para. 147.
48 Ibid., para. 64.
49 Ibid., para. 68.
50 Ibid., para. 71.
51 Andrew Marvell, *An Horation Ode upon Cromwel's Return from Ireland*, ll. 28–36, in *The Poems and Letters of Andrew Marvell*, ed. by H. M. Margoliouth, (Oxford, 1927), I, p. 88.
52 Cobbett, *History*, I, para. 117.
53 Ibid., para. 325.
54 Ibid., para. 326.
55 Ibid., para. 338.
56 ll. 16–21, *The Poetical Works of John Milton*, ed. by H. C. Beeching (Oxford, 1900) pp. 40–1.
57 Karl Marx and Friedrich Engels, *Manifesto of the Communist Party*, trans. S. Moore, 2nd edition (Moscow, 1977), p. 38.
58 Cobbett, *History*, I, para. 379.
59 Ibid., para. 380.
60 Ibid., para. 155.
61 Book 1, ll. 174–5, in *George Crabbe, Poems*, ed. by A. W. Ward (Cambridge, 1905) I, p. 124.
62 Walker Gibson, 'Authors, Speakers, Readers and Mock Readers', pp. 3–5; Gerald Prince, 'Introduction to the Study of the Narratee', pp. 9–11; both in *Reader-Response Criticism from Formalism to Post-Structuralism*, ed. by J. P. Tompkins (London, 1980).
63 Daniel Green notes, in *Great Cobbett: the Noblest Agitator* (London, 1983), that Cobbett often addresses 'fictional interlocutors' whose status can vary, p. 296. Lynne Lemrow notes that the wide audience for Cobbett's open letters creates a dual readership – the individual specified, and the general reader, 'William Cobbett's Journalism for the Lower Orders', *Victorian Periodical Review*, 15 (1982), 19.

64 Cobbett, *History*, I, para. 184.
65 Gibson in Tompkins, *Reader-Response Criticism*, suggests that the author can speak to one mock reader over the head of another, pp. 4–5.
66 Smith, *Politics of Language*, p. 175.

7 TRACTS AND TEACHING

1 James Sambrook, *William Cobbett* (London, 1973), p. 140.
2 Ibid., pp. 158–60.
3 John Stevenson, 'Down with Innovation', in *TLS*, 19 December 1983, p. 1380.
4 J. W. Osborne, *William Cobbett: His Thought and His Times* (New Brunswick and New Jersey), pp. 16, 229–30.
5 Olivia Smith, *The Politics of Language 1791–1819* (Oxford, 1984), pp. 95–6. For a historical account of this relationship between Cobbett and More, which I examine in discursive and literary terms, see Ian Dyck, *William Cobbett and Rural Popular Culture*, (Cambridge, 1992), Chapter 4.
6 In Hannah More, *The Miscellaneous Works of Hannah More*, 2 vols. (London, 1840), I, pp. 192–210.
7 William Cobbett, *Advice to Young Men and (Incidentally) to Young Women in the Middle and Higher Ranks of Life* ..., in parts, 1829–30 (London, n.d.), hereafter referred to as *Advice*, paras. 68–74, 296.
8 More, *Miscellaneous Works*, pp. 197–8.
9 Cobbett, *Advice*, para. 89.
10 Ibid., para. 104.
11 More, *Miscellaneous Works*, pp. 201–2.
12 Ibid., p. 217.
13 Cobbett, *Advice*, para. 170.
14 George Spater, *William Cobbett: the Poor Man's Friend*, 2 vols. (Cambridge, 1982), p. 439.
15 For example, Pamela Horn, *The Rise and Fall of the Victorian Servant* (Dublin and New York, 1975), p. 17. Theresa McBride, *The Domestic Revolution: the Modernization of Household Service in England and France 1820–1920* (London, 1976), p. 15.
16 McBride, *Domestic Revolution*, pp. 18–19.
17 E. S. Turner, *What the Butler Saw: Two Hundred and Fifty Years of the Servant Problem* (London, 1962), pp. 138–9.
18 William Cobbett, *Cobbett's Monthly Sermons*, in parts, 1821–2 (London, 1822), p. 30. This description recalls the description of Henry in *A History of the Protestant Reformation in England and Ireland* ... as motivated by 'beastly lust', I, para. 4.
19 Cobbett, *Cobbett's Sermons*, pp. 39–40.
20 William Cobbett, 'God's Vengeance Against Public Robbers', in *Cobbett's Sermons*, pp. 193–4.
21 William Cobbett, 'God's Vengeance on Unjust Judges', ibid., p. 114.

Notes to pages 189–96 235

22 William Cobbett, 'God's Vengeance Against Murderers', ibid., p. 158.
23 William Cobbett, 'The Sin of Drunkenness in Kings, Priests and People', ibid., pp. 33, 48.
24 Eric Hobsbawm, *The Age of Revolution: Europe 1798–1848* (London, 1977), p. 66.
25 Cobbett, *Advice*, paras. 12–19.
26 Ibid., para. 92.
27 Ibid., para. 85.
28 Spater, *The Poor Man's Friend*, p. 552.
29 Cobbett, *Advice*, para. 84.
30 Susan Pederson, 'Hannah More Meets Simple Simon: Tracts, Chapbooks, and Popular Culture in Late Eighteenth Century England,' *Journal of British Studies*, 25 (1986), 94.
31 Harold Smith, *The Society for the Diffusion of Useful Knowledge 1826–1846: a Social and Bibliographical Evaluation* (Halifax, Nova Scotia, 1974), p. 41.
32 E. P. Thompson, *The Making of the English Working Class* (Harmondsworth, 1968), pp. 700–1. He suggests that Cobbett's aversion to organizations was based more on pragmatic fear of government reaction than on principle.
33 Daniel Green describes Cobbett's enjoyment of blood sports, and his clashes with liberals over it, *Great Cobbett: the Noblest Agitator* (London, 1983), pp. 20–2.
34 In More, *Miscellaneous Works*, pp. 2–3.
35 Cobbett, *Advice*, para. 354.
36 More, *Miscellaneous Works*, p. 2.
37 Cobbett, *Advice*, para. 99.
38 Ibid., para. 342.
39 Ibid., para. 341.
40 Ibid., para. 350.
41 Sambrook, *William Cobbett*, p. 156. He notes the price of Cobbett's *The Poor Man's Friend*, p. 140. See note 42.
42 Cobbett, *The Poor Man's Friend; or, Essays on the Rights and Duties of the Poor* (Fairfield, NJ, 1977), para. 69.
43 Ibid., para. 49.
44 Ibid., paras. 113–14.
45 Ibid., para. 109.
46 Ibid., para. 4.
47 Smith, *Society for the Diffusion*, p. 2; though the practical failure of the Society's publications to provide information on relevant topics provoked criticism from all sides, ibid., p. 10.
48 Cobbett states this repeatedly; his comments in *Advice*, para. 41 are a close echo of those in his *Cottage Economy* (Oxford, 1979), para. 11.
49 Raymond Williams, *Cobbett* (Oxford, 1983), notes his hostility to a curriculum out of parental control, pp. 46–7.
50 Cobbett, *A Grammar of the English Language...*, ed. by C. C. Nickerson

and J. W. Osborne (Amsterdam, 1983), pp. 32–3, also noted in the critical introduction, p. 8.
51 Cobbett, *The Poor Man's Friend*, para. 30.
52 Ibid., para. 39.
53 Ibid., para. 97.
54 Ibid., para. 100.
55 Ibid., para. 40.
56 Ibid., para. 83.
57 Spater, *The Poor Man's Friend*, p. 597, n. 28.
58 Cobbett, *The Poor Man's Friend*, para. 112.
59 Ibid., para. 113.
60 Ibid., para. 114.
61 Richard Brothers refers to 'the Caterpillars of Spain', quoted in Thompson, *English Working Class*, p. 128. William Shakespeare, *Richard II* (Harmondsworth, 1969), II, iii, 166.
62 Cobbett, *The Poor Man's Friend*, para. 116.
63 Ibid., para. 121.
64 Ibid.
65 Horace, *The Complete Odes and Epodes with the Centennial Hymn*, ed. by B. Radice (Harmondsworth, 1983), III, 30, 1–5, p. 164.
66 Sambrook, *William Cobbett*, p. 163.
67 Cobbett, *The Poor Man's Friend*, para. 122.
68 Ibid., para. 130.
69 Cobbett, *Advice*, para. 142.
70 Ibid., para. 144.
71 Ibid., para. 145.
72 Green quotes Macauley's comparison of the two men, *Great Cobbett*, p. 434. Cobbett's breakdown and family problems were first identified by Spater, *The Poor Man's Friend*, II, pp. 515–27.
73 Cobbett, *Advice*, para. 44.
74 Ibid., para. 39.
75 Ibid., para. 39.
76 Sambrook, *William Cobbett*, pp. 160–1.

8 CONSTITUTING THE NATION

1 William Cobbett, *Rural Rides*, from articles in the *Political Register*, 1822–6 (London, 1830), pp. 191–3.
2 Daniel Green, *Great Cobbett: the Noblest Agitator*, (London, 1983), pp. 24–5.
3 Cobbett, *Rural Rides*, p. 222.
4 Jonathan Bate, *Romantic Ecology: Wordsworth and the Environmental Tradition* (London, 1991), pp. 87–8.
5 Linda Colley, *Britons: Forging the Nation 1707–1837* (London, 1992), pp. 5–7.

Notes to pages 208–16

6 For example, William Cobbett, *Weekly Political Register*, 9, 15 March 1806.
7 John Williams, *Wordsworth: Romantic Poetry and Revolutionary Politics* (Manchester, 1989), pp. 1–22.
8 Cobbett, *Rural Rides*, p. 522.
9 Ibid., pp. 158–9.
10 Michael Scrivener, *Radical Shelley: the Philosophical Anarchism and Utopian Thought of Percy Bysshe Shelley* (Guildford, 1982), p. 205.
11 Ibid., pp. 201–3.
12 Hone and Cruikshank, 'The Political House that Jack Built', reproduced in Edgell Rickword (ed), *Radical Squibs and Loyal Ripostes: Satirical Pamphlets of the Regency Period, 1819–1821* (Bath, 1971), pp. 35–58.
13 Ian Dyck also discusses Cobbett's changing patriotism, in *William Cobbett and Rural Popular Culture* (Cambridge, 1992), pp. 23–9.
14 Jon Klancher, *The Making of English Reading Audiences 1790–1832* (Madison: NJ, 1987).
15 Linda Colley, 'Whose Nation? Class and National Consciousness in Britain 1750–1830', *Past and Present*, 113 (1986), 103–9.
16 John Lucas, *England and Englishness: Ideas of Nationhood in English Poetry 1688–1900* (London, 1990) Chapters 6 and 7.
17 Richard Cronin, 'Peter Bell, Peterloo, and the Politics of Cockney Poetry' in *Percy Bysshe Shelley*, ed. by Kelvin Everest (Cambridge, 1992). The following extracts from *The Mask of Anarchy* are taken from *Shelley: Selected Poems*, ed. by Timothy Webb (London, 1983), pp. 65–76.
18 David Punter, 'Shelley: Poetry and Politics', in David Aers et al., *Romanticism and Ideology, Studies in English Writing 1765–1830* (London, 1981), p. 164.
19 Timothy Webb, *Shelley: a Voice not Understood* (Manchester, 1977), p. 94.
20 Scrivener, *Radical Shelley*, pp. 205–6.
21 David Punter offers a different reading of this play of language, in Aers et al., *Romanticism and Ideology*, p. 165.
22 For example, Scrivener, *Radical Shelley*, pp. 205–10; Cronin in Everest, *Percy Bysshe Shelley*, pp. 80–4.
23 Scrivener notes this tension between images of violence and non-violence in *Radical Shelley*, p. 209.
24 Jon Klancher makes a similar point, in *English Reading Audiences*, p. 43.
25 Tom Furniss talks about the constitutive nature of political discourse, 'Rhetoric in Revolution: the Role of Language in Paine's Critique of Burke', in *Revolution and English Romanticism*, ed. by K. Hanley and R. Selden (Hemel Hempstead, 1990), pp. 26–30.
26 Colley, 'Whose Nation?', p. 101.

Bibliography

COBBETT'S WRITINGS

COLLECTIONS

Selections from Cobbett's Political Works, ed. by J. M. and J. P. Cobbett, 6 vols., London, 1835
Porcupine's Works, ed. by William Cobbett, 12 vols., London, 1801
The Life and Adventures of Peter Porcupine, with other Records of His Early Career in England and America, ed. by G. D. H. Cole, London, 1927
Letters from William Cobbett to Edward Thornton, written in the years 1797 to 1800, ed. by G. D. H. Cole, London, 1937
The Last Hundred Days of English Freedom, ed. by J. L. Hammond, London, 1921
The Autobiography of William Cobbett: the Progress of a Ploughboy to a Seat in Parliament, ed. by William Reitzel, London, 1947

INDIVIDUAL WORKS

The Soldier's Friend, London, 1792
A Bone to Gnaw for the Democrats; or, Observations on a Pamphlet entitled 'The Political Progress of Britain...,' Philadelphia, 1795
A Kick for a Bite; or, Review upon Review... in a Letter to the Editor, or Editors, of the American Monthly Review, Philadelphia, 1795
Weekly Political Register, 89 vols., London, 1802–35
A Journal of a Year's Residence in the United States of America..., in parts, 1818–19, Gloucester, 1983
A Grammar of the English Language..., 1818, ed. by C. C. Nickerson and J. W. Osborne, Amsterdam, 1983
Cobbett's Monthly Sermons, in parts, 1821–2, London, 1822
Cottage Economy, in parts, 1821–2, with a Preface by G. K. Chesterton, Oxford, 1979
Rural Rides, from articles in the *Political Register* 1822–6, London, 1830
A History of the Protestant Reformation in England and Ireland..., in parts 1824–6, 2 vols., London, 1829

Bibliography

The Poor Man's Friend; or, Essays on the Rights and Duties of the Poor ..., in parts, 1826–7 (reprint London, 1829), Reprints of Economic Classics series, Fairfield, New Jersey, 1977

Advice to Young Men and (Incidentally) to Young Women in the Middle and Higher Ranks of Life ..., in parts, 1829–30, London, n.d.

CONTEMPORARY AND COMPARATIVE SOURCES

COLLECTIONS

Butler, Marilyn (ed.), *Burke, Paine, Godwin and the Revolution Controversy*, Cambridge English Prose Texts series, Cambridge, 1984

Cunningham, R. H. (ed.), *Amusing Prose Chapbooks Chiefly of the Last Century*, London, 1889

Rickword, Edgell (ed.), *Radical Squibs and Loyal Ripostes: Satirical Pamphlets of the Regency Period, 1819–1821*, Bath, 1971

Willis, G. (ed.), *Poetry of the Anti-Jacobin*, London, 1854

INDIVIDUAL WORKS

American Minerva

Aurora or General Advertiser

The Black Dwarf

Burke, Edmund, *Reflections on the Revolution in France*, ed. by Conor Cruise O'Brien, Harmondsworth, 1970

Byron, George Gordon, *Byron's Letters and Journals*, ed. by Leslie A. Marchand, 9 vols., London, 1977

Callender, James, *The Political Progress of Britain: or, an Impartial History of Abuses in the Government of the British Empire*, 3rd edition, Philadelphia, 1795

The Cap of Liberty

Coleridge, S. T., *The Collected Works: Essays on his Times*, ed. by David V. Erdman, London, 1978

Columbian Centinel

The Courier and Evening Gazette

The Craftsman; Being a Critique of the Times by Caleb D'Anvers of Grey's-Inn Esq, 3rd edition, London, 1727

Dickinson, John, *Letters from a Farmer in Pennsylvania to the Inhabitants of the British Colonies*, ed. by R. T. H. Halsey, New York, 1903

A Full and True Account of the Execution of John Dennis, Geo. Crow, Will. Beamis, Thomas South and Isaac Harley, Birmingham, n.d., published by H. Wadsworth between 1816 and 1818

The Gorgon

Hazlitt, William, *The Complete Works of William Hazlitt*, ed. by P. P. Howe, 21 vols., London, 1931

Hone, William, *The Three Trials of William Hone, for Publishing Three Parodies*, London, 1818
Keats, John, *The Letters of John Keats 1814–1821*, ed. by Hyder Edward Rollins, 2 vols., Cambridge, 1958
The Last Dying Speech and Confession of Mary Jones, Coventry, n.d., first published by Houghton of Bedford, reprinted by W. or B. Hickling between 1830 and 1864
Lingard, John, DD, *A History of England, from the First Invasion by the Romans*, VI, London, 1838
Malthus, T. R., *An Essay on the Principle of Population, and A Summary View on the Principle of Population*, ed. and intro. by Anthony Flew, Harmondsworth, 1970
Marx, Karl and Friedrich Engels, *Manifesto of the Communist Party*, trans. S. Moore, 2nd edition, Moscow, 1977
The Medusa
More, Hannah, *The Miscellaneous Works of Hannah More*, 2 vols., London, 1840
The Morning Chronicle
Mysterious Knockings, Heard in Foleshill Church, Coventry, n.d., published by E. Bromfield between 1827 and 1830
The North Briton, 2 vols., London, 1763
Paine, Thomas, *The Rights of Man*, ed. by Eric Foner, Harmondsworth, 1985
Pitt, William, *Orations on the French War, to the Peace of Amiens by William Pitt*, London, n.d.
Quicksilver, James, *The Blue Shop; or, Impartial and Humorous Observations on the Life and Adventures of Peter Porcupine*, Philadelphia, 1796
Shelley, Percy Bysshe, *The Letters of Percy Bysshe Shelley*, ed. by Frederick L. Jones, 2 vols., Oxford, 1964
Tickletoby, Timothy, *The Imposter Detected, or, a Review of Some of the Writings of 'Peter Porcupine'*, Philadelphia, 1796
The Times
Wilkes, John, *The North Briton*, London, 1763

SECONDARY SOURCES

Aers, David, et. al., *Romanticism and Ideology, Studies in English Writing 1765–1830*, London, 1981
Altick, Robert, *The English Common Reader*, London, 1957
Aspinall, A., *Politics and the Press 1780–1850*, Brighton, 1973
Bakhtin, M. M., *Problems of Dostoevsky's Poetics*, trans. R. W. Rotsel, Ann Arbor: Mich., 1973
Bakhtin, M. M., *The Dialogic Imagination: Four Essays by M. M. Bakhtin*, ed. by M. Holquist, trans. C. Emerson and M. Holquist, Austin, 1981
Bate, Jonathan, *Romantic Ecology: Wordsworth and the Environmental Tradition*, London, 1991

Beetham, Margaret, 'Open and Closed: the Periodical Press as a Publishing Genre', *Victorian Periodical Review*, 22 (1989), 96–100
Belchem, J. C., 'Henry Hunt and the Evolution of the Mass Platform', *English Historical Review*, 93 (1978), 739-73
Bertrand, Claude-Jean, *The British Press: an Historical Survey*, Paris, 1969
Birrell, T. A., '*The Political Register*: Cobbett and English literature', *English Studies*, 45 (1964), supp. 214–19
Black, Jeremy, *The English Press in the Eighteenth Century*, London, 1987
Blakemore, Steven, 'Burke and the Fall of Language: the French Revolution as Linguistic Event', *Eighteenth-century Studies*, 17 (1984), 284–307
Blunden, Edmund, *Votive Tablets: Studies Chiefly Appreciative of English Authors and Books*, London, 1931
Boulton, J. T., *The Language of Politics in the Age of Wilkes and Burke*, London, 1963
Briggs, Asa, *The Collected Essays of Asa Briggs, Volume 1: Words, Numbers, Places, People*, Brighton, 1985
Briggs, Asa, *William Cobbett*, London, 1967
Brinton, Crane, *English Political Thought in the Nineteenth Century*, Harper Torchbook Edition, New York, 1962
Brown, P. A., *The French Revolution in English History*, London, 1918
Butler, Marilyn, *Romantics, Rebels and Reactionaries: English Literature and its Background 1760–1830*, Oxford, 1981
Calhoun, Craig, *The Question of Class Struggle: the Social Foundations of Popular Radicalism During the Industrial Revolution*, Oxford, 1982
Canavan, Frances, *Edmund Burke: Prescription and Providence*, Durham: NC, 1987
Carswell, John, *From Revolution to Revolution: England 1688–1776*, London, 1973
Chandler, Alice, *A Dream of Order: the Medieval Ideal in Nineteenth-century English Literature*, London, 1971
Chesterton, G. K., *William Cobbett*, London, 1925
Clark, M. E., *Peter Porcupine in America: the Career of William Cobbett, 1792–1800*, Philadelphia, 1939
Cole, G. D. H., *The Life of William Cobbett*, London, 1947
Colley, Linda, *Britons: Forging the Nation 1707–1837*, London, 1992
Colley, Linda, 'Whose Nation? Class and National Consciousness in Britain 1750–1830', *Past and Present*, 113 (1986), 97–117
Collison, Robert, *The Story of Street Literature: Forerunner of the Popular Press*, London, 1973
Copley, Stephen, and John Whale (eds), *Beyond Romanticism: New Approaches to Texts and Contexts 1780–1832*, London, 1992
Cottom, Daniel, 'Taste and the Civilized Imagination', *The Journal of Aesthetics and Art Criticism*, 39 (1981), 367–80
Cranfield, G. A., *The Press and Society: from Caxton to Northcliffe*, London, 1978

Derry, J. W., *The Radical Tradition: Tom Paine to Lloyd George*, London, 1967
Dickinson, H. T., *Politics and Literature in the Eighteenth Century*, London, 1974
Dinwiddy, J. R., *From Luddism to the First Reform Bill: Reform in England 1810–1832*, Oxford, 1986
Dodd, Philip, 'Literature, Fictiveness and the Dilemma of Nonfiction', *Prose Studies*, 10 (1987), 5–8
Downie, J. A., 'Polemical Strategy and Swift's *The Conduct of the Allies*', *Prose Studies*, 4 (1981), 134–45
Dozier, Robert, *For King, Constitution and Country: the English Loyalists and the French Revolution*, Lexington, 1983
Duff, Gerald, *William Cobbett and the Politics of Earth*, Salzburg Studies in English Literature, Romantic Reassessment Series, Salzburg, 1972
Dyck, Ian (ed.), *Citizen of the World: Essays on Thomas Paine*, London, 1987
Dyck, Ian, 'From "Rabble" to "Chopsticks": the Radicalism of William Cobbett', *Albion* (1989), 56–87
Dyck, Ian, *William Cobbett and Rural Popular Culture*, Cambridge, 1992
Epstein, J. A., 'The Constitutional Idiom: Radical Reasoning, Rhetoric and Action in Early Nineteenth-century England', *Journal of Social History*, 23 (1990), 553–74
Evans, Eric J., *The Forging of the Modern State: Early Industrial Britain 1783–1870*, London, 1983
Everest, Kelvin (ed.), *Revolution in Writing: British Literary Responses to the French Revolution*, Milton Keynes, 1991
Everest, Kelvin (ed.), *Percy Bysshe Shelley*, Cambridge, 1992
Flew, Anthony (ed.), *A Dictionary of Philosophy*, London, 1984
George, Dorothy, *England in Transition: Life and Work in the Eighteenth Century*, Harmondsworth, 1953
Gibbs, F. W., *Joseph Priestley: Adventurer in Science and Champion of Truth*, London, 1965
Gilmartin, Kevin, '"Victims of Argument, Slaves of Fact": Hunt, Hazlitt, Cobbett and the Literature of Opposition', *The Wordsworth Circle* (1990), 90–6
Green, Daniel, *Great Cobbett: the Noblest Agitator*, London, 1983
Green, Daniel, 'The Relevance of William Cobbett', *Cobbett's New Register*, 7 (1985), 3–10
Hanley, K. and R. Selden (eds), *Revolution and English Romanticism: Politics and Rhetoric*, Hemel Hempstead, 1990
Harrison, J. F. C., 'Battling against the Thing', *TLS*, 25 June 1982, 685–6.
Harrison, Stanley, *Poor Men's Guardians: a Record of the Struggles for a Democratic Newspaper Press 1763–1973*, London, 1974
Hendrix, Richard, 'Popular Humour and "The Black Dwarf"', *Journal of British Studies*, 16 (1976), 108–28
Hill, Christopher, *Puritanism and Revolution: Studies in the Interpretation of the English Revolution of the Seventeenth-century*, Harmondsworth, 1986
Himmelfarb, G., *The Idea of Poverty: England in the Early Industrial Age*, London, 1984

The History of the Times: the 'Thunderer' in the Making 1785–1841, anonymous, London, 1935

Hobsbawm, Eric, *The Age of Revolution: Europe 1798–1848*, London, 1977

Horn, Pamela, *The Rise and Fall of the Victorian Servant*, Dublin and New York, 1975

Horn, Pamela, *Life and Labour in Rural England 1760–1850*, Context and Commentary Series, London, 1987

Howkins, Alun and Ian Dyck, '"Time's Alteration": Popular Ballads, Rural Radicalism and William Cobbett', *History Workshop*, 23 (1987), 20–38

Jacob, M. and J. Jacob, *The Origins of Anglo-American Radicalism*, London, 1984

Jack, Ian, *English Literature 1815–1832*, London, 1963

Kaplan, S. L. (ed.), *Understanding Popular Culture: Europe from the Middle Ages to the Nineteenth Century*, Berlin, Amsterdam, New York, 1984

Kelsall, Malcolm, *Byron's Politics*, Brighton, 1987

Kerber, Linda K., *Federalists in Dissent: Imagery and Ideology in Jeffersonian America*, London, 1970

Klancher, Jon, *The Making of English Reading Audiences 1790–1832*, Madison, 1987

Kliger, Samuel, *The Goths in England: a Study in Seventeenth and Eighteenth Century Thought*, Cambridge: Mass., 1952

Lee, Janice, 'Political Antiquarianism Unmasked: the Conservative Attack on the Myth of the Ancient Constitution', *Bulletin of the Institute for Historical Research*, 55 (1982), 166–79.

Lemrow, Lynne, 'William Cobbett's Journalism for the Lower Orders', *Victorian Periodical Review*, 15 (1982), 11–26.

Levinson, Marjorie, *Keats's Life of Allegory: the Origins of a Style*, Oxford, 1988

Lincoln, Bruce (ed.), *Religion, Rebellion, Revolution*, London, 1985

Lindsay, Jack (ed.), *Autobiography of Joseph Priestley*, Bath, 1970

Lorraine de Mont Luzin, Emily, *The Anti-Jacobins 1798–1800: the Early Contributors to the Anti-Jacobin Review*, London, 1988

Loughrey, Bryan (ed.), *The Pastoral Mode*, London, 1984

Love, Walter D., 'Edmund Burke's Idea of the Body Corporate: a Study in Imagery', *Review of Politics*, 27 (1965), 184–97

Lucas, John, *England and Englishness: Ideas of Nationhood in English Poetry 1688–1900*, London, 1990

McBride, Theresa, *The Domestic Revolution: the Modernization of Household Service in England and France 1820–1920*, London, 1976

McCalman, Ian, *Radical Underworld: Prophets, Revolutionaries and Pornographers in London, 1795–1840*, Cambridge, 1988

Massingham, H. J., *The Wisdom of the Fields*, London, 1945

Mee, Jon, *Dangerous Enthusiasm: William Blake and the Culture of Radicalism in the 1790s*, Oxford, 1992

Melville, Lewis, *The Life and Letters of William Cobbett in England and America: Based upon Hitherto Unpublished Family Papers*, London, 1913

Miles, Robert, *Gothic Writing 1750–1820: a Genealogy*, London, 1993
Miller, David, *Philosophy and Ideology in Hume's Political Thought*, Oxford, 1981
Miller, John C., *The Federalist Era 1789–1801*, London, 1960
Morris, K. L., *The Image of the Middle Ages in Romantic and Victorian Literature*, London, 1984
Mott, F. L., *American Journalism: a History 1690–1960*, 3rd edition, New York, 1962
Murphey, Dwight D., *Modern Social and Political Philosophies: Burkean Conservativism and Classical Liberalism*, London, 1982
Murphy, Paul Thomas, '"Imagination Flaps its Sportive Wings": Views of Fiction in British Working-class Periodicals, 1816–1858', *Victorian Studies*, 32 (1989), 339–64
Neuburg, V. E., *Popular Literature: a History and a Guide, from the Beginning of Printing to the Year 1897*, Harmondsworth, 1977
Nurmi, Martin K., *William Blake*, London, 1975
Osborne, J. W., *William Cobbett: His Thought and His Times*, New Brunswick and New Jersey, 1966
Osborne, J. W., *John Cartwright*, London, 1972
O'Sullivan, Noel, *Conservatism*, London, 1976
Parrington, V. L., *Main Currents in American Thought*, New York, 1930
Pascal, Roy, *The Dual Voice: Free Indirect Speech and its Functioning in the Nineteenth-century Novel*, Manchester, 1977
Pearce, Lynne, 'John Clare's *Childe Harold*: a Polyphonic Reading', *Criticism*, 31 (1989), 139–57.
Pederson, Susan, 'Hannah More Meets Simple Simon: Tracts, Chapbooks, and Popular Culture in Late Eighteenth Century England', *Journal of British Studies*, 25 (1986), 84–113.
Perkins, Jean, *The Concept of the Self in the French Enlightenment*, Geneva, 1969
Pocock, J. G. A., 'Burke and the Ancient Constitution: a Problem in the History of Ideas', in *Politics, Language and Time*, London, 1972
Pocock, J. G. A., *The Ancient Constitution and the Feudal Law: a Study of English Historical Thought in the Seventeenth Century. A Reissue with a Retrospect*, Cambridge, 1987
Pykett, Lyn, 'Reading the Periodical Press: Text and Context', *Victorian Periodical Review*, 22 (1989), 100–8.
Rea, Robert R., *The English Press in Politics 1760–1774*, Lincoln NE, 1963
Reid, Christopher, 'Language and Practice in Burke's Political Writing', *Literature and History*, 6 (1977)
Richardson, Lyon N., *A History of Early American Magazines: 1741–1789*, London, 1931
Rickword, Edgell, 'William Cobbett's Tuppenny Trash', in *Rebels and their Causes: Essays in Honour of A. L. Morton*, ed. by Maurice Cornforth, London, 1978
Rogers, Pat, *An Introduction to Pope*, London, 1975

Rogers, Pat, *Literature and Popular Culture in Eighteenth-century England*, Brighton, 1985
Roper, Derek, *Reviewing Before the Edinburgh 1788–1802*, London, 1978
Rose, R. B., 'The Priestley Riots of 1791', *Past and Present*, 18 (1960), 68–88
Royle, E. and J. Walvin, *English Radicals and Reformers 1760–1848*, Brighton, 1982
Rudé, George, *The Face of the Crowd: Studies in Revolution, Ideology and Popular Protest, Selected Essays of George Rudé*, ed. by H. J. Kaye, London, 1988
Said, Edward, *Orientalism*, Harmondsworth, 1985
Sambrook, James, *William Cobbett*, London, 1973
Sambrook, James, 'Cobbett and the French Revolution', *The Yearbook of English Studies*, 19 (1989), ed. by J. R. Watson, 231–42
Schweizer, Karl W. and John W. Osborne, *Cobbett in His Times*, Leicester, 1990
Scrivener, Michael, *Radical Shelley: the Philosophical Anarchism and Utopian Thought of Percy Bysshe Shelley*, Guildford, 1982
Small, Ian, 'Recent Work on Nineteenth-century Prose: "Oeuvre", Genre or Discourse?', *Prose Studies*, 10 (1987), 42–50
Smith, Harold, *The Society for the Diffusion of Useful Knowledge 1826–1846: a Social and Bibliographical Evaluation*, Halifax, Nova Scotia, 1974
Smith, Olivia, *The Politics of Language 1791–1819*, Oxford, 1984
Spater, George, *William Cobbett: the Poor Man's Friend*, 2 vols., Cambridge, 1982
Stafford, William, *Socialism, Radicalism and Nostalgia: Social Criticism in Britain 1775–1830*, Cambridge, 1987
Steadman Jones, Gareth, *Languages of Class: Studies in English Working Class History 1832–1982*, Cambridge, 1983
Stevenson, John, 'Down with Innovation', in *TLS*, 19 December 1983, p. 1380
Storch, Robert D. (ed.), *Popular Culture and Custom in Nineteenth-century England*, London, 1982
Tebbel, John, *The Compact History of the American Newspaper*, New York, 1963
Thomas, Keith, *Religion and the Decline of Magic*, London, 1978
Thompson, E. P., *The Making of the English Working Class*, Harmondsworth, 1968
Tompkins, J. P. (ed.), *Reader-Response Criticism from Formalism to Post-Structuralism*, London, 1980
Turner, E. S., *What the Butler Saw: Two Hundred and Fifty Years of the Servant Problem*, London, 1962
Turner, J., 'Burke, Paine and the Nature of Language', *The Yearbook of English Studies*, 19 (1989), 38–53
Varey, Simon (ed.), *Lord Bolingbroke: Contributions to the Craftsman*, Oxford, 1982
Webb, Timothy, *Shelley: a Voice not Understood*, Manchester, 1977

Whale, John C., 'Hazlitt on Burke: the Ambivalent Position of a Radical Essayist', *Studies in Romanticism*, 25 (1986), 465–81

White, R. J., *Waterloo to Peterloo*, London, 1957

Whitney, Lois, *Primitivism and the Idea of Progress in English Popular Literature of the Eighteenth Century*, Baltimore, 1934

Wickwar, W. H., *The Struggle for the Freedom of the Press, 1819–1832*, London, 1928

Wiener, Joel, 'Book Reviews', *Victorian Periodical Newsletter*, 8 (1975), 135–7

Wiener, Martin, 'The Changing Image of William Cobbett', *Journal of British Studies*, 13 (1974), 135–54

Williams, G. A., *Artisans and Sans-culottes: Popular Movements in France and Britain During the French Revolution*, London, 1968

Williams, John, *Wordsworth: Romantic Poetry and Revolutionary Politics*, Manchester, 1989

Williams, Raymond, *Cobbett*, Oxford, 1983

Williams, Raymond, *The Country and the City*, London, 1985

Wilson, David, *Paine and Cobbett: the Transatlantic Connection*, Kingston and Montreal, 1988

Wrigley, E. A., *Continuity, Chance and Change: the Character of the Industrial Revolution in England*, Cambridge, 1988

Index

Addington, Henry 62
American Minerva 43, 57, 59
American Monthly Review 53
ancient constitution 11, 12, 20ff., 40, 88, 97, 105, 112–32, 144, 150, 159, 209, 214
Anti-Jacobin 64–6, 70, 102, 143, 156
anti-Semitism 9, 10, 12, 164–7
audience 3–4, 9, 12–13, 20–1, 24–5, 26–7, 29–30, 44, 59, 62, 72–4, 82, 90, 108–9, 111–12, 126, 136–8, 147–8, 152–3, 155–6, 172–3, 177, 183ff., 193, 215–16, 218 n.29
autobiography *see also* egoism 57–9, 90–3, 118–32, 139, 145, 147–8, 152, 177–8, 183, 201–4, 228 n.23
Aurora or General Advertiser 37–8, 40–1, 44, 58

Bache, Benjamin Franklin 44
Bentham, Jeremy 27
biblical discourse 17, 27, 73–4, 82–3, 102–8, 114, 176, 178, 198, 214, 226 n.24
bigotry 4, 8–13, 29, 119, 143, 156, 216
Black Dwarf 26, 213–14, 215–16
Blind Beggar of Bethnal Green, The 145
Bolingbroke, Henry St John 22
Bonaparte, Napoleon 26, 62, 73–7, 93–6
Brothers, Richard 103, 107
Burdett, Sir Francis 22, 23, 78
Burke, Edmund 2, 23–4, 27, 30, 37, 40–2, 64, 66, 69, 75, 83–5, 103, 112–18, 136–8, 143, 159, 169
Butler, Marilyn 11, 66, 103
Byron, George Gordon 19, 27

Callender, James 47–50
Cannon, George 98–9, 102
Carlile, Richard 26, 29
cartooning 50, 54, 210–12
Cartwright, Major John 105
Catholic Emancipation 36, 158, 164, 181
Champion The 116

Chartism 12, 24–5
circulation 3, 216
Clare, John 128–9, 213
Cobbett, William
Advice to Young Men 1, 4, 119–21, 125, 156, 169–70, 183–7, 189, 190–3, 195–6, 197, 200, 201–4, 205
A Bone to Gnaw for the Democrats 40, 44, 47–50, 52, 53
Cottage Economy 4, 153–6, 183, 195
A Grammar of the English Language 17, 183, 195–6
A History of the Protestant Reformation in England and Ireland 4, 97, 156, 157–82, 183, 193, 197, 205
Important Considerations for the People of this Kingdom 85–6
A Journal of a Year's Residence in the United States of America 129–30, 144–5, 148–50
'To the Journeymen and Labourers' 30, 108–18, 135, 139, 141, 159, 168, 169, 173, 178, 181, 213
A Kick for a Bite 53–6
A Legacy to Labourers 158
'Letter to Luddites' 111, 135
The Life and Adventures of Peter Porcupine 57–9, 85, 90, 123–4, 127
Monthly Sermons 183, 188–9, 193
Observations on the Emigration of Dr Priestley 44–7, 50–1
The Poor Man's Friend 156, 183, 193–201
Porcupine's Gazette 59–61
Remarks of the Pamphlets Lately Published Against Peter Porcupine 124, 130
Rural Rides 4, 118, 122–3, 125, 126, 138, 144, 148, 150–2, 177, 181, 186, 206–9, 218 n.29, 231 n.45
The Soldier's Friend 28, 33ff., 42, 66, 93
Weekly Political Register 3, 5, 6ff., 15–16, 19, 22, 26, 29, 62, 72–88, 90–118, 120, 135–44, 148, 152, 168, 172, 177, 193,

247

197–8, 200, 213, 216, 218 n.29, 224 n.24
Coke, Sir Edward 23, 112–16, 159, 169
Coleridge, S. T. 68, 89
Columbian Centinel 39–40, 43, 46
Comical History of the King and the Cobbler, The 146, 171, 173–4
Courier 23, 72, 80, 89, 109
Crabbe, George 179
Craftsman 22
Cromwell, Oliver 56–7, 70

deism 97–102, 112
Dickinson, John 58, 141
Dissent 17, 24, 97, 102–8, 112

egoism *see also* autobiography 2, 4, 12–13, 96, 119–32, 199–200
Evans, Thomas 27

Famous History of the Learned Friar Bacon, The 145, 171
Federalists 37ff.
Franklin, Benjamin 46
French Revolution debate 2–3, 14, 26, 28, 36ff., 64

George III 141
Godwin, William 26, 169, 213
Gorgon, The 213

Hazlitt, William 2, 4, 17–18, 20, 34, 107, 131, 152, 159
Hetherington 27, 29
Hobbes, Thomas 69
Holbach 98
Hone, William 16–17, 26, 63, 108, 210–12, 214–15
Horace 199–200
Hume, David 163, 175, 192
Hunt, Henry 5, 27, 139–41, 177–8, 198
Hunt, Leigh 5, 7, 17, 19, 27, 221 n.75

ideology 10, 11, 12–13, 21, 26, 43, 145–6
inconsistency 28ff., 33ff., 51–3, 93
invective 5, 9, 44, 50, 57, 60

Jacobin discourse 24–5, 39–40, 46–7
Jefferson, Thomas 34, 48ff.
Johnson, Samuel 43, 49, 63
Junius 44

Keats, John 19, 221 n.75

Lilburne, John 108

Lingard, John 157, 172

McCalman, Ian 27ff., 98ff., 103
Malthus, Thomas 111, 158ff., 161, 181, 189, 192
Marvell, Andrew 175, 177
Marx, Karl 20, 176
Medusa 213
Milton, John 107, 176–7
mock-reader, *see also* audience 179–82, 183ff., 193ff.
More, Hannah 86–7, 144, 154, 155, 158, 183–7, 189–92, 195, 202–4
Morning Chronicle 22, 71

National Gazette 41–2
national identity *see also* patriotism 35–6, 42, 122ff., 149, 205–16
Norman Yoke 21, 112, 159, 209
North Briton 44
nostalgia 8, 12, 20ff., 119–26, 154, 209, 226 n.40

'Old England' 36, 121ff., 154, 205, 207, 228 n.9
organicism 20, 36, 41, 83, 87, 113, 116, 126–31, 207, 209, 210

Paine, Thomas 2, 3, 4, 8, 16–17, 20–1, 24–5, 29, 37, 63, 66, 68–71, 89–90, 98, 102, 115–17, 132, 136–8, 169, 190–1, 198, 209
pastoral 87–8, 112, 176, 183, 192, 203
patriotism *see also* national identity 34–6, 42, 62, 75–80, 85, 92, 149
Pennsylvania Chronicle and Universal Advertiser 58
persona 12–13, 50–1, 60, 93, 131
Peterloo 209–12
Pitt, William 62, 90–5
Place, Francis 27
Pocock, J. G. A. 23–4
polyphony 132, 141ff., 156, 205, 215
Poor Man's Guardian 27
Pope, Alexander 44, 55
popular literature 26, 29, 57, 132, 144–8, 154, 170ff., 182, 198, 204, 214, 225 n.33
populism 8, 11, 12, 27, 29, 57, 95, 102, 119, 132, 155, 216, 229 n.18
Porcupine, Peter 28, 33–4, 42–61, 136
Price, Richard 24, 37, 68, 103
Priestley, Joseph 44–7, 70–1, 91–2
primitivism 9, 26, 127–8

Quicksilver, James 57

race 10–11, 12, 51–2
Radcliffe, Ann 26
refinement 15ff., 27, 29, 43, 47–8, 49–50, 55–6, 72, 80, 110–11, 117, 120, 135, 158, 164, 173–5, 180–2
Reform 3, 5, 14, 20, 25, 152, 209, 215, 217 n.3
Republicans 37ff.
Rivington, James 56
Robinson Crusoe 144–5, 148
Romanticism 4, 14
Rousseau, Jean-Jacques 127, 130, 131, 202, 203
Rush, Benjamin 60

sarcasm 5, 143
Scott, Walter 166–7
self-consciousness 4, 5, 9, 13, 29, 88, 97–8, 131, 153
Shakespeare, William 87, 198
Shelley, Percy Bysshe 19, 26, 214–15
Smith, Adam 25, 181
Smith, Olivia 14ff., 18, 27, 30, 63–4, 103, 108, 117, 141, 169, 181, 212, 216, 219 n.29
Southcott, Joanna 103, 104

Southey, Robert 65–6, 69
Spence, Thomas 16, 27ff.
style 3, 5–7, 11, 14, 34–5, 43, 45, 54–5, 60–1, 90, 108, 131–2, 135, 141, 157, 160, 218–19 n.29
Sun 72
Sunday Observer, The 3
superstition 29, 143, 144, 146, 156, 198
Swift, Jonathan 15, 43, 51, 81

Thompson, E. P. 5, 8–9, 102–3, 154
Times, The 5, 8, 35, 67–71, 106
True Briton 72

vulgarity 15ff., 27, 29, 50, 57, 110–11, 117, 120, 135, 158, 164, 173–5, 180–2

Wade, John 122
Wedderburn, Robert 27, 104
Wilkes, John 44, 63
William Corder 146–7, 170
Williams, Raymond 8, 21, 141
Windham, William 62, 224 n.12
Wooler, Thomas 26, 29, 213–14, 215–16
Wordsworth, William 128, 131